MW00906202

ENGLISH BLOODS

In the Backwoods of Muskoka, 1878

ENGLISH BLOODS

In the Backwoods of Muskoka, 1878

FREDERICK DE LA FOSSE

NEW AUGMENTED EDITION, EDITED BY
SCOTT D. SHIPMAN

NATURAL HERITAGE BOOKS
TORONTO

Copyright © 2004 by Scott D. Shipman

All rights reserved. No portion of this book, with the exception of brief extracts for the purpose of literary or scholarly review, may be reproduced in any form without the permission of the publisher.

Published by Natural Heritage / Natural History Inc.
P.O. Box 95, Station O, Toronto, On M4A 2M8
www.naturalheritagebooks.com

Cover illustration, Captain Charles Greville Harston's second home on Buck Lake, circa late 1800s. *Courtesy of Fred Hopcraft; back cover,* Frederick de la Fosse as a young man. *Courtesy of the Trent University Archives;* Aemilius Baldwin's home near Ilfracombe. *Courtesy of Martha Preston (Tothill) Woody.*

Design by Blanche Hamill, Norton Hamill Design
Edited by Jane Gibson
Printed and bound in Canada by Hignell Book Printing, Winnipeg, Manitoba

The text in this book was set in a typeface named Adobe Caslon.

Library and Archives Canada Cataloguing in Publication

Delafosse, F. M. (Frederick Montague), 1860–1950

   English bloods : in the backwoods of Muskoka, 1878 / Frederick de la Fosse ; edited by Scott D. Shipman. – New augm. ed.

Includes bibliographical references and index.
ISBN 1-896219-96-9

   1. Delafosse, Frederick Montague, 1860–1950. 2. Frontier and pioneer life – Ontario – Muskoka. 3. Immigrants – Canada – Biography. I. Shipman, Scott D., 1958– II. Title.

PS8507.E382E5 2004   C813'.52   C2004-903574-6

ONTARIO ARTS COUNCIL
CONSEIL DES ARTS DE L'ONTARIO

THE CANADA COUNCIL | LE CONSEIL DES ARTS
FOR THE ARTS | DU CANADA
SINCE 1957 | DEPUIS 1957

Natural Heritage / Natural History Inc. acknowledges the financial support of the Canada Council for the Arts and the Ontario Arts Council for our publishing program. We acknowledge the support of the Government of Ontario through the Ontario Media Development Corporation's Ontario Book Initiative. We also acknowledge the financial support of the Government of Canada through the Book Publishing Industry Development Program (BPIDP) and the Association for the Export of Canadian Books.

This book is dedicated to the memory of Frederick de la Fosse and all the pioneer families who worked the foundations of a settlement dream in the backwoods of the Muskoka District of Ontario, Canada.

Contents

Acknowledgements   IX

Editor's Introduction   X

Introduction by Frederick de la Fosse   3

I   Voyage to the Canadian Backwoods   4

II   From the Canadian Shores   9

III My Trip Into the Interior   16

IV   The Government Road   26

V   The Harston Homestead   32

VI   Harston's Agricultural Farming School   38

VII The Settlers   45

VIII Communities of the District   56

IX   Preparation of the Log Shanty   62

X   Local Dentistry   72

XI   Purchasing Cattle and Sheep   75

XII The First Winter   83

XIII Winter Woodsman   87

XIV The Second Year   94

XV   Emigrants In the Colony   104

XVI Wild Life of the Woods   110

XVII A Permanent Settlement   113

XVIII Our Education   122

XIX Trials and Tribulations   124

XX   Our Third Year   130

CONTENTS

XXI   Moving On to Our Lots   132

XXII   Seeking Employment In Western Canada   137

XXIII   Returning to the Bush   142

Conclusion   149

Editor's Epilogue   155

Appendix A – Research evidence pertaining to *English Bloods*   161

    1.   Letter from C. Greville Harston to the Ontario   161
Agricultural Commission, 1880

    2.   History of the Ilfracombe Mission, 1881   162

    3.   Letter from Frederick de la Fosse to Dr. Talman,   164
dated February 17, 1939

    4.   Notes in the copy of the original *English Bloods*   164
belonging to Mr. and Mrs. Andrew Hickling

    5.   Graphic Publishers Limited of Ottawa, Ontario   166

    6.   Obituary, Frederick de la Fosse – "Librarian   168
Passes Away At Peterboro"

    7.   Newspaper clipping – "Tragic Death at Parry   169
Sound, 1908"

    8.   Excerpt from letter to Mr. John Wilson of   169
Toronto, Ontario, from Frederick de la Fosse,
dated November 24, 1944

Appendix B – Biographic sketch of Frederick Montague   170
de la Fosse

Notes   174

Selected Bibliography   196

Index   200

About the Editor   207

ACKNOWLEDGEMENTS

I WOULD LIKE TO THANK Gail Stupka, for sending me on this amazing voyage, and Freda and Walter De La Fosse for this opportunity to research their family history, Fred Hopcraft and Elsie (Hopcraft) Bennett for the special memories and for providing family photographs. Much appreciation goes to Sheila Petch, Roberta Green and the staff of the Huntsville Public Library, Dr. Fern Rahmel and the Trent University Archives, Freda and Walter de la Fosse, granddaughter and grandson of Frederick de la Fosse, and to the many people too numerous to mention who came to my aid in my burning desire to learn more of the spirit and soul of the pioneer backwoodsman. And, of course my family – I am indebted to my wife Peggy, and to Collin and Carly for their endless support.

While many people, in so many different ways provided research assistance, the responsibility for accuracy is mine. Any errors brought to the attention of the publisher or myself will be corrected in subsequent editions.

Editor's Introduction

Several years ago I chanced to stumble upon a small book titled *English Bloods* written by Roger Vardon.[1] *English Bloods* was a story about a young English boy who had been sent by his guardian from England to Canada in 1878 to learn how to become a backwoods farmer. The book was originally published in 1930 by Graphic Publishers located in Ottawa, Ontario.

The book took three nights' reading and created within me a desire to learn more about the pioneer lifestyles in the backwoods of Muskoka. The story became the focus of many "coffee table" conversations and whenever an opportunity arose, I wasted no time in opening its pages for discussion.

To my disappointment I soon learned that "Roger Vardon" was not the real name of the author, but rather a pseudonym for Frederick Montague de la Fosse,[2] and that, of the names given within the book, many were not the true names of the pioneer settlers of the time. Seemingly this alteration was at the request of the publisher as there was fear of a libel suit from one of the pioneer families being presented in the text. Seemingly, Frederick de la Fosse, as author, also wanted changes to some of the names as it seems that he did not want to embarrass the many friends he had made while being educated at the "Agricultural School" run by Captain Martin[3] in the Muskoka area.

The story was set largely on the Boundary Road, separating the Township of Stisted of Muskoka (to the south) from the Township of McMurrich of Parry Sound (to the north), and along the rugged shores of Buck Lake.[4] The author gave his readers directions into the backwoods on the Muskoka Road, which he travelled on his way to

Gravenhurst,[5] Bracebridge[6] and Utterson.[7] As he lived along the hilly shores of Buck Lake, he also visited places such as Port Vernon[8] and Huntsville.[9]

Despite my disappointment in discovering that the names had been changed, curiosity had taken the better of me. I was determined to learn more. I opened the book once more. De la Fosse[10] wrote that he had been sent by his uncle, Colonel Montague Ricketts[11] to the Harston Farm, at a cost of one hundred pounds sterling per year for a three year term. He was to learn how to farm in the Muskoka area, and upon completion of his education, de la Fosse would be granted one hundred acres in the District of Muskoka. Many came to the conclusion that Captain Charles Greville Harston[12] (the true name) had swindled the students of their money, as it seems that he eventually moved away and was never seen in the area nor heard from again.

I felt saddened by these facts for I believed this to be a great book, a book with a wealth of local history, a true Canadian story of the English pioneers who had lived in the backwoods of Ontario during the 1800s. One can imagine the fears within a young man's mind as he stumbles over the unfamiliar rugged terrain, across rough corduroy roads through dense underbrush and the swampy corridors, in suit and tie, trying to locate his anticipated mentor's cottage in the bush.

I then wondered if anyone had ever considered having this book republished – this neat little book that depicted a true pioneer life story set over one hundred and twenty-five years ago. I learned that *English Bloods* had already found its place in history on a dust-covered shelf in a private collection, recognized as a rare book classic and now fetching prices of several hundred dollars. For me, this recognition was not satisfactory; I could not leave this story alone.

After all those years of benign neglect, *English Bloods* now needed to be brought back into public view. For several months I ventured into the world of local history. I searched for people with knowledge of the story, but to no avail. It was not until one day, with nothing better to do, I found myself at the Huntsville Public Library looking at a microfilm that contained the 1899 *Telephone Directory* of Toronto.[13] Skimming through the pages, curious about the contents, I first located "#465 Greville & Co., Mining Brokers 12 King St." Greville, not Greville Harston – but could it be it, I thought! The excitement of the possibility nearly overwhelmed me. I wanted to jump up and yell "All right!" but this was not the place. There in front of me on page 65 of the directory in the microfilm I found "#4681 Harston, Greville (Mrs.) Residence 11 Wilcox." That was the beginning of an incredible journey that has taken more than eight years of my life to complete.

I decided that I would love to give this book the honour I felt it deserved, and have it published in a new edition. However, at the time the book was still under copyright protection, so I contacted the Copyright Board of Canada to ask for permission to have the contents reprinted. I was told I would have to find the author or a relative to gain permission. Frederick de la Fosse had passed away in 1950. How was I going to find a living relative?

Two years passed. Suddenly, after I had almost given up hope, a notice arrived from the Copyright Board stating that they had located a granddaughter of Frederick de la Fosse, Miss Freda de la Fosse. I contacted her and explained what I had been doing and my hopes of reintroducing her grandfather's book, *English Bloods*, to today's readership. I followed up my conversation with a letter and, after careful consideration of my proposal, Freda de la Fosse and her twin brother Walter de la Fosse gave me permission to seek a publisher for this amazing story.

I should also note that a selection of other works by Frederick Montague de la Fosse have been used to complete this new edition. The original publishing of *English Bloods* did not have an introduction and the headings for Chapters II, VI and VII were missing. In my search for materials to edit and complete this work, I learned that the Trent University Library Archives in Peterborough, Ontario, had a copy of an early transcript annotated in Frederick de la Fosse's own handwriting. The Library Archivist, Bernadine Dodge, was kind enough to send me a copy. There is no date attached to this transcript, but it would seem evident that the work had been written prior to the publication of *English Bloods* in 1930. During this period of my work, another manuscript was brought to my attention. Professor Fern Rahmel of Trent University had been working on a paper titled "Western Reminiscences." I learned that there were two typed copies of an unpublished manuscript titled "Western Reminiscences," one held at the Peterborough Public Library and the other at the Trent University Archives. Although this material had been written by Frederick de la Fosse some years after *English Bloods*, the storyline begins in Muskoka, when he returns to his homestead there. Although not dated, the work tells of Frederick de la Fosse's adventures as he travelled across the Canadian West between the years of 1883 and 1884, the time period immediately following his early farming experiences in Muskoka. After reading this material, I felt compelled to take three chapters from this work and include them in this new book; these are chapters XXI, XXII and XXIII. The work from this previously unpublished material sheds new light on the conclusion in the original story that would otherwise have been unknown. This unpublished work was also acquired from the Trent University Archives.

And now after my many years during which I alternated between hope and despair, feeling that I was being teased and tantalized by a spirit lurking within the pages of *English Bloods*, I now have both a beginning and an ending for this great book. I hope all readers will enjoy this intriguing story, written by Frederick Montague de la Fosse, a saga that began for him as a young man of eighteen in the spring of 1878 when he travelled across the Atlantic Ocean to become a student of the Harston Agricultural School in the Muskoka District. Throughout, the original names of the people have been reinstated as the result of extensive research and communication with many people (see Notes and Appendix A), and the work annotated to allow today's reader greater access to de la Fosse's story.

ENGLISH BLOODS

In the Backwoods of Muskoka, 1878

ENGLISH BLOODS

by

ROGER VARDON

1930

GRAPHIC PUBLISHERS LIMITED

OTTAWA —o— CANADA

INTRODUCTION BY
FREDERICK DE LA FOSSE[1]

I HAVE BEEN MOVED TO write the following account of life in the Muskoka backwoods at the solicitation of various friends who felt that a recital of facts concerning events of half a century ago were bound to be of value from a historical viewpoint, depicting as they do a phase of life that has in many respects wholly passed away. When one has passed the grand climacteric[2] it may well be supposed that bitternesses engendered by disappointed hopes and ambitions has worn away. It certainly has in my case. But the humorous aspect has seized me and come more into prominence. It is from that point of view chiefly that I would wish my readers to peruse these pages. If I shall have succeeded in arousing their interest by depicting that portion of my humble existence that was spent in the abortive attempt to wrest a living from the forest primeval and, if in doing so, I can even slightly lift the veil from the more or less hidden life of the backwoods farmer, my purpose will have been achieved.

FREDERICK DE LA FOSSE
NOT DATED[3]

I

Voyage to the Canadian Backwoods

On the approach of my eighteenth birthday I was invited to spend the Easter holidays with an uncle at the beautiful city of Bath,[1] in England. I looked forward to those holidays with the keenest anticipation, and revelled in rosy visions of cricket and tennis, little conjecturing that they might be the prelude to a long, long severance from English sports and pastimes.

I was taking a walk along Lansdowne Crescent with my uncle, Colonel Montague Ricketts, when the bolt fell.

"Frederick," said he, turning towards me, "how would you like to try your hand at farming in the Canadian backwoods?" It was a glorious evening, but his abrupt question caused a gloom to settle on my soul somewhat comparable to that which was already settling on the valley. I gasped out that such an idea had never entered my head and suggested mildly that the matter might well be deferred to the end of the summer holidays. But my uncle was not to be moved. He pointed out that he was my guardian, that he would soon be returning to India and that it was necessary to have everything arranged in regard to my future prior to his departure.

He produced many cogent reasons, among others that my school life had not been a brilliant one, that I could not pass the Army examinations and that my addiction to sport pointed strongly to my fitness for roughing it in the colonies. "The outlying parts of the Empire are calling for men," he said, "and Canada seems to be the place that offers the most remarkable opportunities at the present time."

When we returned home he produced letters which he had received from a retired army officer who had been resident some years in Canada, in which he offered to take me as a farm pupil at a premium of £100 per annum for three years. The writer expatiated in glowing terms on the wonders of the climate, the magnificent scenery and the blissful and healthful time that a settler enjoyed clearing a farm in the backwoods. It sounded very delightful. My uncle told me he would soon have the business arranged and presented me with various pamphlets dealing with the country.

I discovered that Canada possessed boundless resources, and when I read of its wonderful prairies and magnificent forests, of its splendid lakes and rivers, of the fishing and the hunting, of its glorious summers and bright and cheery winters, the sporting heart within me leapt and I was almost reconciled to the abandoning of my summer's cricketing.

Frederick Montague de la Fosse as a young man. *Courtesy of the Trent University Archives.*

My uncle, Colonel Montague Ricketts, was a man who accomplished things quickly. He had not risen to his high position in the service of the East India Company[2] through incapacity to make up his mind. So I was not surprised that in little over a month I found myself fully equipped, and my passage taken for the historic port of Quebec.

I shall never forget the last days that I spent in England. They constituted a sort of triumphal progress. I never knew how much my relatives loved me till the time came for them to lose me. I received many encomiums on my pluck, and heaps of advice from everyone. At one house a dear old gentleman, a long-retired army colonel, took me aside to bestow a few last words of counsel "Frederick, my dear boy," he said, "I am an old man now, and in all probability I shall never see you again. You have always been very dear to me, and I cannot let you go without giving you some slight token of my regard." Visions of a generous tip floated before my eyes. I was deeply moved. "First of all," he went on, "I beg of you always to remember to say your prayers; you will receive the greatest spiritual strength in doing so." Then he thrust his hand into the capacious pocket of his overcoat and drew forth a small package which he gravely handed to me. "There is nothing I know of," he said, in a voice tense with feeling, "which has proved such a blessing to me as has this wonderful preparation. I never go anywhere without it. I am sure that in the land to which you are bound it will prove a very real boon to you. God bless you, my dear boy, God bless you." He broke down and could say no more. On investigating the package in the seclusion of my room, I nearly broke down also, for I discovered, much to my dismay, that it consisted of three boxes of Cockle's Antibilious Pills.[3]

In the course of fifty years a slightly clearer conception of what sort of country Canada really is has been brought home to the minds of Englishmen. There was certainly a considerable amount of haziness concerning it at the time of which I write. I remember very well being asked to be sure to visit a lady in Winnipeg when I reached Toronto and one or two of my cousins were very insistent that I should let them know when I had caught my wild horse. I was presented with a few somewhat useless gifts. A saddle was one and a pair of expensive riding boots was another. It makes me smile even now to picture myself as a horseman, arrayed in the toggery of the hunting field, chasing my quarry through the Muskoka woods or even riding along those almost impassable highways.

On a certain balmy day in May in the year of grace 1878 I found myself on board the Allan Line steamship *Scandinavian*,[4] en route to my destination. A few of my relatives living near Liverpool had gathered at the dock to wish me god-speed.

It was with mixed feelings that I said my last *adieux*. The spirit of adventure was strong within me and much as I regretted leaving England, I did look forward with a vast amount of ardour to entering life in the wonderful land that lay across the Atlantic.

There were very delightful passengers on board, including two Canadian judges, and three English gentlemen who were journeying to Manitoba to take up land in that newly advertised region. From them I received the first intimation that the venture I had embarked upon was not likely to be a lucrative one. The Canadians on board denounced the deal as a barefaced robbery, and more than one offered to obtain employment for me in something that would show a return for the money

Eugene Haberer, *View of Quebec, from Levis,* August 16, 1873, from the *Canadian Illustrated News, Courtesy of the Library and Archives Canada, Record 3963, C-59291.*

expended. These kindly offers had, of course, to be refused as the agreement had been signed, sealed and delivered, and it only remained for me to put in an appearance in order to fulfill the contract.

The voyage was devoid of special incident. The vessel was not remarkable for its seaworthy qualities as it was one of the slowest of the Line and had a decided tendency to roll, which was not conducive to healthy digestion of one's meals. This was unfortunate as the food was really excellent and the Company spared no pains to make their passengers comfortable.

My cabin mates were two Jews from Montreal and an Englishman of the name of Oldfield.[5] The latter was not a stranger to Canada, having been settled for some years on a farm near Sherbrooke. He and I got a good deal of amusement out of our cabin mates. They were most amiable souls, but their ways were not our ways, and as they proved to be bad sailors, we suffered in consequence. One of them, unfortunately for Oldfield, occupied the berth above him. Mr. Levinsky,[6] the gentleman in question, was of rotund form and very awkward in his movements. He was never able to get into his berth without planting a very dirty foot in poor Oldfield's face. Oldfield was a gentleman, but the constant use of his face as a stepladder caused him at last to lose control of himself, and he poured out language which was most lurid and penetrating. It was an eye-opener to me, who had never heard anything worse than the word "damn" used by one of two prefects at school, but it was not many moons before I acquired a very fair knowledge of the extraordinary inventiveness and fluency in profanity possessed by some of the inhabitants of the district to which I was hastening.

Feelings of exultancy were exhibited by all on shipboard when we entered the Straits of Belle Isle. For me everything was tinged with romance. As we steamed up the majestic St. Lawrence, the wonderful stretch of river, the stupendous cliffs, desolation alternating with grand vistas of farm and woodland, cast a spell over me which was not by any means dissipated when we reached the dock at Point Levis,[7] opposite Quebec. Here I bade farewell to many of my kind friends, including Oldfield, and was generously taken care of by a Chichester Skeffington,[8] who was one of the party bound for Manitoba. He very kindly took me over to Quebec, and we were driven to the various points of interest in that historic and romantic city. We visited the Wolfe and Montcalm Monument,[9] went to the Garrison Club and finally wound up at one of the modest hotels which at that time took care of the tourist trade in the capital of the province. There we had supper and were introduced to the Hon. Mr. Starnes, a member of the Quebec legislature, and also to a famous detective of that day, singularly enough bearing the same name as my kind cicerone.[10] Late in the evening we returned to Point Levis where we had been assigned rooms for the night at a hotel near the railway station.

At this place I received my first reminder that I was now a citizen of the world and called upon to look after myself. Through some error, my place at the *table d'hôte* had been taken by another passenger, and although I had paid my own bill, the landlord called on me to pay for the other man as well. I refused and was nearly arrested. The only thing that saved me was the fact that the passengers who had remained took my part and bore me off to the railway station and put me on the train. Just as it was pulling out the landlord came down to try to make more trouble, but he was too late and the last seen of him he was shaking his fist wildly at three or four men who were saying unpleasant things to him from the windows.

FROM THE CANADIAN SHORES

I HAD MADE ONE LONG passage in my life, from India to England, but it had been at an age when I could not very well appreciate the delights of travel, or rank it in my memory as an event of importance. My only other journey outside England's shores had been made at the age of eleven when, as a special treat, I was taken across the Channel to spend a few weeks in Boulogne. The terrors of that voyage have always been in my mind as I was never so seasick in my life. The Franco-Prussian War² was raging at the time, but although the guns were roaring near Amiens, the utmost placidity and peace seemed to be reigning in Boulogne. People went about their business as usual and there was not the remotest sign of anxiety or disorder.

It may well be imagined, therefore, that the voyage from Liverpool to Quebec proved to be the greatest treats and was the means of enlightening my youthful mind in a variety of ways. I saw nothing of Montreal except from the railway station but found enough enjoyment for the time being in looking at the scenery and listening to the patois of the country people at the various stations where we stopped.

When we reached Toronto, one of my fellow-passengers guided me to the Rossin House,³ which, he informed me, was the best hotel in the province. He also kindly provided me with directions for my further journey to Muskoka and, wishing me good luck, left me to my own devices.

I was seated on one of the lounges in the hotel, feeling rather forlorn, when a well-dressed, dapper-looking young fellow came up to me and introduced himself, stating that he was most anxious to make my acquaintance. He said he had seen my name in the hotel register and was quite sure that he had heard of my family in England. He said, "My name is

Jack Dawkins – aren't you a cousin of my dear old friend, Jim Wordsworth?" I replied that I did not have that honour. "Well, that's strange," he said, "I was quite sure that you must be, as I've often heard Jim speaking most glowing terms of a chap bearing your very name." I assured him again that I knew nothing of such a relationship. "Oh, well," he said airily, "it doesn't much matter, anyhow, come on and let's have a drink." He whisked me off to the bar and took a glass of whisky whilst I took ginger beer. Not content with one, he took another and as soon as he had recovered his breath, remarked that he was always glad to meet an Englishman, there was something so refined and gentlemanly about them. "They are such simple, straight-forward chaps, you know, with their eyes wide open. I always make it a point to endeavour to help a new arrival, and the Englishman is the best settler we have in this country." I felt flattered and thanked him warmly for his friendly sentiments. After a minute or two of conversation he suggested another drink. I told him that I thought a third bottle of ginger beer would be bad for my digestion, to which he answered jovially, "Oh, well, old chap, I'll drink for the two of us." Having refreshed himself thoroughly, he felt in his pocket for some money and after rummaging hurriedly through them turned to me with a concerned face and said, "By Jove, this is a queer go, I must have left all my money at home – would you mind lending me five dollars for a few minutes?" I handed it to him with pleasure and thought nothing of it when a few minutes later he asked to be excused while he went outside to borrow the money from a friend who lived a few doors away.

I waited patiently for about two hours, but my effusive friend never returned and I boarded the train for Gravenhurst, a somewhat saddened individual. On the train I fell into conversation with a dark-skinned creature who poured a woeful tale into my ears about two horses which were suffering from a mysterious complaint called the Epizootic. He said he had only a dollar or two in the world, and would I give him a trifle to buy medicine for the animals. I felt sorry for him and for the horses and handed over five dollars. Evidently he looked upon me as a sympathetic soul, for in a few minutes he began to be confidentially communicative about his wife, whom, he said, he had left at death's door in a Toronto hospital. However, I had expended all the sympathy I possessed on his unfortunate horses; so, when he hinted that a little act of charity for his wife would not be deemed an impertinence, I turned a deaf ear to his

Photograph of the wharf station at Muskoka, circa 1884. James Esson Preston is identified as the photographer and publisher. The *S.S. Nipissing* appears at the right. *Courtesy of the Archives of Ontario, ST 1173.*

pleadings. It was beginning to dawn on me that I was being taken for a "sucker," a new term which I had already added to my vocabulary.

The next acquaintance that I made on the train was destined to have influence on my itinerary. I had noticed a prodigiously fat man eyeing me very curiously ever since I had boarded the train at Toronto. When my garrulous friend with the consumptive wife and "fluey" horses had left the train, he waddled over and sat down in the seat beside me.

"My name's Yearley,"[4] he said, "What might yours be?" I told him. He was so fatherly and so interested in my welfare that he soon won my confidence. He learnt my pedigree to the seventh or eighth generation, my

George Harlow White (1817–1887), *High Road to Gravenhurst, Township of Morrison,* September 1873. The artist arrived in Canada in 1871 and is known for his pencil sketches of the Huntsville area. *Courtesy of the Toronto Public Library (TRL) Special Collections T16492.*

age, my religion, my scholastic acquirements and finally my object in going to Muskoka. He enjoyed the recital hugely. When I enlarged on the fact that I was going to be taught farming in the district, his eyes fairly bulged out of his head. "Well," he ejaculated between puffs and snorts and grunts, "there's nobody on earth like a green young Englishman to make an all-fired fool of himself. I'm an Englishman myself, young man, and I was once just as green as you are. Believe me, you'll have to keep your eyes skinned if you want to get on in this here wooden country."

I hadn't informed him yet that I was paying a premium for my tuition; and when I told him this and added that I intended to clear a farm for myself, he simply looked me over and cried out "My God!" He did it with uncommon vehemence too. "Of all the goldarned swindles I ever heard of," he grunted, "this takes the cake. Look here, my lad, what you need is advice and lots of it. I live three miles out of Bracebridge and you're going to follow me out there and stay a night with me and the missus. I'll be able to tell you a few things. What's more, I'll be able to give you a lift to within five or six miles of where you are going, for I'm starting off to-morrow to settle one of my lads right in your very township." As my money was almost gone, I was glad enough of the invitation and thanked him heartily for his kindness. When the train arrived at

Gravenhurst, Mr. Yearley was met at the station by one of his sons, and they drove off at once to Bracebridge.

I had elected to go by steamer to the same place as I was anxious to get a glimpse of Muskoka Lake, which I had been told was beautiful. I shall never forget that trip from Gravenhurst to Bracebridge. The scenery was glorious, and as we wound our way in and out among the islands and up the sinuous river, I really felt as if earth could not exhibit anything more wonderful. There was not a ripple on the water, the reflections of rock and woodland and sky were perfect. Occasionally a small cottage was to be seen peeping from the dense foliage, but for the most part, on all sides was primeval wilderness. The handiwork of man was hardly to be seen in the way of clearings or buildings. We passed immense booms of logs tied to the shore, the sole guardians of which appeared to be judicial-looking cranes which stood gazing soberly into the water, waiting for a swift peck at some passing fish, or stalked in a solemn manner up and down the logs, like wary sentinels. Now and again a loon would bob up unexpectedly near the boat, give utterance to its weird cry, and dive out of sight, or a flock of gulls would rise in a body from some rock and follow in the wake of the steamer in search of stray fragments

F.B. Schell and J. Hogan, *Muskoka Lake*, circa 1880. The natural beauty of Muskoka was soon to make it a desirable tourist destination. *Courtesy of the Library and Archives Canada, Special Collections C085390.*

of food thrown out from the cook's quarters. The river was as beautiful as the lake, and all along the shores could be seen immense groups of ferns of the stately *Osmunda regalis*[5] variety. The bayous and reaches were filled with lily leaves, and shoots of the strange water plant, the *Sagittaria latifolia,*[6] showed their heads above the water presaging a wealth of colour in the weeks to come.

The trip was all too short but quite long enough to imbue me with the feeling that what my uncle had told me was true and that the land to which I had come was indeed a sportsman's Paradise. Fifty years have created a marvellous change in this part of the country. The Muskoka District is, today, in the 1920s, one of the best-known holiday resorts in the world. Where half a century ago desolation seemed to have marked the region for its own, there are now hundreds of palatial summer homes, catered to by splendid supply boats and commodious steamers. Craft of all sorts, from the humble canoe to the fastest motor boats ply the wonderful chain of lakes, while the telephone, telegraph, and radio render communication with the outside world easy. I often think that if the older generation of Muskoka settlers were to come to life again, they might well imagine themselves on some other planet.

When I reached Bracebridge, I discovered the disagreeable fact that my luggage had been left at Gravenhurst and that there would be no means of releasing it until the checks were presented to the station master. When I searched, I could not find them. Somewhere along the route they had vanished and were irrevocably gone. The upshot of it was that it was fully three months before I got possession of my baggage and then only after strenuous representations to the railway authorities at Toronto.

On leaving the steamer, I went to the British Lion Hotel, then kept by a Mr. and Mrs. Burden[7] who in days gone by had been actors in England. They proved very kind and obliging and told me that they had been apprised of my coming by a message from Captain Harston.

As soon as I had finished my tea, I entered the sitting room of the hotel where I found myself the centre of an inquisitive and loquacious company. At first I felt somewhat flattered by the running fire of questions to which I was subjected, until it began to dawn on me that the attention I was receiving savoured more of amused curiosity than of deference. One gawky individual, with trousers tucked into his boots and wearing a gaudy sash round his waist, put me through a regular catechism.

When I unguardedly betrayed the fact that I had come out to Canada to learn farming, his merriment was intense. "Boys," he said to the assembled company, punctuating his sentences with volleys of tobacco juice at the unlighted stove, "this here beats anything as ever I seed. Most Englishmen as I've know'd I've took to be kinder soft, but blamed if that there geezer has got this here young cuss to pay him for clearing his own farm aint got us all beat. He's a smart one, he is. Blamed if he aint smart enough to be Primeer of Canady – Haw, haw, haw." He was so pleased with his humour that he called all hands to the bar to have a drink to the health of my host in the first glass of whisky that I had ever tasted.

I began to have an uncomfortable feeling that Fate had landed me among a very strange assortment of individuals. They presented such an absolute contrast to those with whom I had been in the habit of associating.

What surprised and disgusted me most was the free and easy salivation indulged in by smokers and chewers who took no pains to remedy the bad shots they sometimes made at the spittoons. With their heels on the stove and their chairs tilted back they looked exactly what they were, horny-handed sons of toil, whose independence of spirit was typified by the remark of one of them that now that he had had his bellyful he wouldn't care to "call the Queen his uncle." My innocent manner and boyish appearance, added to what they were pleased to term my "English accent," proved strong incentives to mirth.

When I ponder the matter now, it does not appear at all strange. It must have seemed in the highest degree ludicrous to those stalwart men to hear a boy whose weight was just one hundred pounds talking glibly of clearing a farm in the woods, but more excruciatingly funny was the fact that he was actually paying out what appeared to most of them a fortune for the privilege of helping a man to clear his farm and attend to his cattle.

III

My Trip Into the Interior

I was so disgusted at the way in which my recital had been received by the company that I determined to leave the hotel forthwith and walk out to Mr. Yearley's place, which he had told me was situated on the main road and would be easy to find. As I had nothing to carry but my cane and overcoat and handbag, it seemed an easy matter to reach his house before he retired for the night. I paid my reckoning at the hotel and, telling the landlord that I was going to put in the night at Mr. Yearley's home, bade him farewell and started on my journey.

Bracebridge has grown a good bit since that day and boasts fine residences, prosperous factories and good streets. At the time of which I write, it was a village of about 1200 inhabitants and was filled with river-men attached to the different [lumber] drives. Situated on a rocky plateau, the village commands a magnificent view of the Muskoka River and Falls,[1] but anything more remotely suggestive of an agricultural centre it would be hard to imagine. Yet, there are now splendid farms throughout the section, eloquent evidence of the pluck and indomitable energy of the early settlers.

It was growing dark when I left the hotel, but I found my way without any trouble and arrived in good time at Mr. Yearley's house. I was rather a miserable-looking specimen of humanity when I arrived as the mosquitoes and blackflies had been holding high revel, and my neck and the back of my head carried big smears of blood. The mud holes, too, were terrible. I had no sooner floundered out of one than I was into another. I was received most kindly by the old gentleman and his wife, the latter of whom I found busily packing up necessaries for the forthcoming trip. "Now that you've come," said the kind old man, "we'll be able to get away to a good early start."

George Harlow White, *Bracebridge from the North Falls*, circa 1872. *Courtesy of the Toronto Public Library (TRL) Special Collections T30527.*

"Missus," he said, turning to his wife, "I guess we can manage to hop off from this here joint at two in the mornin,' eh?" "Yes, Bill, whatever time you say," replied the meek lady. As it was then after ten o'clock I wondered how much sleep would be indulged in by the members of the family.

The household consisted of four persons, Mr. and Mrs. Yearley and two sons, the elder being the one to whom I had already been introduced at Gravenhurst, and the younger, a boy of about twelve or fourteen years of age. The cottage was a neat, unpretentious one, the ground floor consisting of one large room and a kitchen at the further end. What the upstairs portion contained I was not destined to know. The whole family seemed to eat and sleep downstairs. At one end of the room were two beds, one of Brobdingnagian[2] proportions and the other a small truckle [trundle] affair. Both were roughly made of basswood and were evidently home productions. On the walls were a few pictures and bits of ornamental crewel work. One glance at the specimens satisfied me that the term "crewel" should have been spelled in a different way; both designs and handiwork were of a decidedly crude character. But the place was neat and clean in the extreme and showed Mrs. Yearley to be a woman of refinement.

There are certain things that burn themselves indelibly into one's brain. We remember our first proposal and, possibly, our first rejection. We are able to call to mind, as vividly as when it occurred, the first fight in which we engaged at school and the day when we proudly emerged from the chrysalis state of knickerbockers into the transcendent glory of trousers.

Among such prominent incidents in my own career there is another painted in unfading pigments, and that is the memory of the first night that I spent in the Muskoka District.

In order to enjoy immunity from the mosquitoes, the family made a smudge of decayed wood outside the door and around this we sat for the best part of an hour, in order, as the old man expressed it "to get into a good humour for bed." Everything that was required for the trip had been packed on the wagon that evening and, to quote Mr. Yearley again, "all we had to do was to sleep as snug as bugs in rugs and pray for a fine day." I thought him excessively coarse and told him that in England these unpleasant insects were called "B Flats" or "Norfolk Howards" and that, as a matter of fact, they were never mentioned in polite society. The old gentleman took it very affably, remarking that if I had not had a bowing acquaintance with "them critturs" in England I "blamed soon" would in Muskoka, especially if I was going to live in a log house. "Why" he said, "you'll have 'em barkin' at you from the sides of the walls."

A feeling of wonderment had entered my mind as to where I was to sleep, seeing that there were enough in the family already to occupy both beds, without the addition of a stranger. This point was soon cleared up, however, by Mrs. Yearley retiring to the kitchen to ensconce herself by the stove, leaving the small bed for one son whilst Mr. Yearley, his other son and myself were assigned to the other. I had never slept two in a bed in my life, and when it came to having to share one with *two* others my gorge rose and I entered a mild protest. "If you will excuse me," I said, "I would much enjoy sleeping on the floor. I always love a hard bed." But the trouble was that there were no blankets or sheets to spare and Yearley absolutely refused to allow me to use the bare boards as a resting place. The old gentleman did not take much time to disrobe. He merely removed his boots and his coat and rolled into bed. The son went him one better by discarding his trousers. Both of them seemed flabbergasted when I asked if there was a nightshirt that I could borrow, having left mine at the Rossin House. "Sakes alive," exclaimed Mr. Yearley, "I haint gone to bed wearing one of them things side of fifty years – pants and a shirt is good enough for me. You'll learn in time, young man, you'll learn in time."

I crawled resignedly into bed between the old man and his son and soon found I was in for a purgatorial time. The bed, as before remarked, was a huge one, but Mr. Yearley's immense bulk took up most of it, leaving me wedged in and nearly smothered. To make it as uncomfortable as possible, the youth, in order to keep in the bed at all, clung feverishly with one hand to the collar of my shirt and in his convulsive efforts to keep on the mattress, nearly strangled me.

"I snore some," said the old man as he was on the point of turning into bed, "but I quiets down after a time." Then he pointed to his young hopeful. "Johnny,[3] there," he said, "can't sleep a wink when I aint at home, can you, John? I acts on him like a sleeping draught."

"Like hell you do," retorted Johnny who, though young in years, was quite sophisticated in the matter of bad language. To this filial rejoinder the father returned no answer save to remark in a chuckling aside to myself, "That there boy's goin' to make a name for hisself one of these days, he's that quick at takin' yer hup."

It having been arranged that we were to start at 2:00 a.m., the alarm clock was set for 1:30 in order to give Mrs. Yearley an opportunity to get us some breakfast.

"Good-night, boys," said Mr. Yearley as he blew out the light, and darkness fell on the scene. Then with a mighty tug he pulled the blanket off us both and coiled it round himself. "Say, Pop," protested Master John from the outskirts, "what are yer givin' us?" But there was no answer from his parent. He was already in a comatose condition and snoring in a highly stertorous and alarming manner. Before many seconds had passed, the three hundred pounds of flesh was heaving in a terrific fashion. In the course of a somewhat checkered career, I have run across many snorers but never one who could come within miles of the power possessed by that venerable being. After enduring an hour of the most rending torture, I gave a heave which sent Johnny flying to the floor, and followed after him myself. The commotion caused by this sudden action had no effect on the old man. He snored serenely on. Johnny muttered a few imprecations and crawled into bed again, and I thankfully curled up where I had fallen. The mosquitoes had a lovely time with me for the rest of the night, but even they were preferable to the agony that I had been enduring.

Punctually at 1:30 a.m., Mrs. Yearley entered the room. She had wrapped herself in her husband's overcoat and presented a picturesque spectacle, with her hair streaming down her back. She was rather amazed to find my prostrate form stretched out on the floor, but her husband saw humour in the situation. "It takes us old fellers as has led decent, respectable lives," he said "to get a good night's rest. You young fellers as is always runnin' around and gettin' your nerves worked up can't rest nowheres. When I was your age it would have took a cannon right at my ear to have waked me up; so it would." I could quite believe him.

After a hurried breakfast we bade farewell to Mrs. Yearley and started on our journey. Bill Yearley[4] was the teamster and proved a very capable one. He was not in a very good temper, however, and his unfortunate

George Harlow White, *Log Shanty near Gravenhurst*, August, 1875. *Courtesy of the Toronto Public Library (TRL) Special Collections T16495.*

oxen had a hard time of it. But nothing could surpass the good spirits and geniality of the father. He had given his wife a kiss at parting which could have been heard a mile away and, now, ensconced on three or four bags of flour and with his head resting against a side of pork, he seemed prepared to go to the ends of the earth. The old gentleman had apparently a propensity for music and had equipped himself with a horn on which he repeatedly emitted loud blasts. "There's nothing like a little bit of music," he remarked, "to sweeten life." He desired me to notice how the cattle pricked up their ears when they heard the dulcet sounds, and drew a somewhat invidious comparison between these lowly beasts and men of so-called intellect who could not appreciate the power of music. This was levelled at his son Bill, who had been getting very restive under the continual blares from the horn. I was seated with Bill on the front seat and, before we had gone many miles, I obtained a tolerable insight into the depths of profanity to which an ox-driver can descend. His first ebullition occurred when, sent into a frenzy by the continual horn-blowing, he turned round and cried out, "For God's sake, Pa, stop that there damned racket – yer drivin' me clean crazy." Pa stopped his horn-blowing for a time and turned his attention to me and for about two hours served up a diet of stories which made me gape in wonderment. He allowed his imagination to run riot.

"Young man," he said, when he saw me engaged in constant skirmishes with the mosquitoes, "you've come to one of the best countries in God's world for a young gaffer like yourself to keep out of. Why! You complains about these here skitters! Sakes alive! They's only hifants to what they grows as big as butterflies. Why, I've know'd one of em to *kill* a fresh-blooded young feller like yourself *dead* by pizenin' his system. But wait till yer see the Gilliloo birds![5] Some folks makes a livin' around here by trainin' em to catch mice in barns. Gil-lil-oo-like. If they takes a dislike to yer and pecks yer leg they takes a chunk clean out of yer. Then there's the Hodags.[6] There's lots of them around, but they don't attack yer openly. They climbs trees and watches for yer and springs on yer back and *chokes* yer. They jumps forty feet at a lep, they does, and the way they howls is fair devilish. Yer don't need to be afraid of bears and wolves and such mean truck as that, but," he solemnly and impressively concluded, "yer does need to keep yer eyes skinned for them there Hodags."

Notwithstanding sundry doubts that would creep into my mind regarding his veracity, I could not help being impressed by the old man's apparent sincerity. I simply had to believe him and mentally registered a vow that, failing a gun, I would always go armed with a dagger whenever I had to roam the woods alone.

Perhaps some of my readers have experienced the pain or pleasure of journeying on an ox-wagon. Those who have will agree with me that there are swifter and easier modes of locomotion. The country we were traversing was very heavily wooded. There were few clearings to let in the sunlight, and the consequence was that mud was lord of all. We passed over long stretches of rocky upland interspersed with miles upon miles of swamp, and it was a toss-up which was the worse for travelling on; rocks and corduroy roads were equally unpleasant in rendering one's seat uncomfortable and deranging one's interior.

For the benefit of the uninitiated, it may be stated that a corduroy road is made by laying logs horizontally alongside each other at right angles to its direction. This species of road-making is the one primarily adopted for overcoming the difficulties of swamp travel in a wooded district. Our

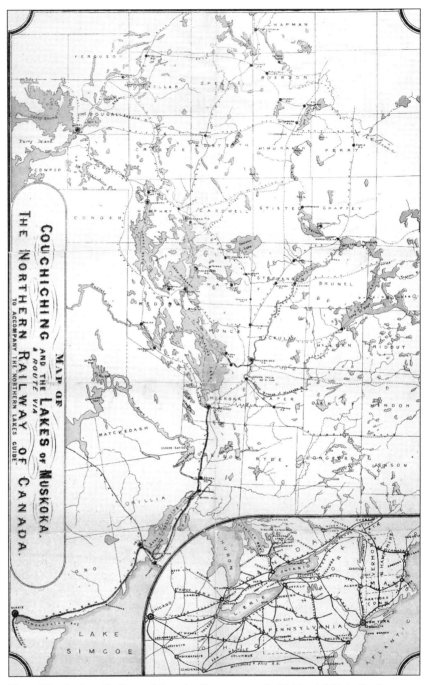

From *The Northern Railway of Canada: direct route to the highlands & lake district.*
Courtesy of the *Archives of Ontario.*

George Harlow White, *Utterson, Muskoka*, August 1875, pencil sketch. This drawing shows the tiny hamlet just a few years before Frederick de la Fosse came into the area. *Courtesy of the Toronto Public Library (TRL) Special Collections T16459.*

rate of progress was exasperatingly slow. The oxen plodded along at a uniform speed of about two miles an hour, and by noon we were still very far from our destination. But the journey was not unexciting, by any means. There were many occasions when the wheels would stick hub-deep in a quagmire, and it was a case of getting out handspikes[7] in the endeavour to extricate the wagon. Needless to say, the splendour of my attire which had been a source of amazement at Bracebridge and in Mr. Yearley's home soon vanished, and a fashionably-dressed young man was transformed into a most disreputable-looking tatter-demalion. It does not take much straining at mud-laden wheels or wading about in swamps to destroy sartorial equipment. My appearance caused great hilarity to my two friends, both of whom kindly remarked that they had never before seen anything quite so funny-looking.

We had passed Utterson, a small hamlet containing a hotel and two or three cottages, before the inhabitants were awake and, at about 8:00 a.m., halted on the outskirts of a small clearing in order to indulge in a second breakfast. There was a shack visible in the clearing, and I volunteered to obtain a pailful of water in order to make some tea. It was a miserable affair with hollowed-out basswood blocks doing duty for a roof and a crazy-looking door with bits of old boots acting as hinges. There was no glass in the window, which had been plastered over with bits of newspaper, some of which had become separated from the casing and were flapping about in the morning breeze. This sordid style of living was somewhat of a surprise, but it was nothing to the shock I received when, in answer to my timid knock, a deep female voice called out fiercely. "What are you wanting?" I replied softly that a gentleman sought to obtain leave to get a pail of water from the well. The door was thrown open suddenly by a middle-aged woman of massive build and menacing aspect. She held an axe in her hand and demanded of me again what was my business.

The formidable weapon that she was holding, combined with her fierce expression, drove all power of speech from me, and I simply stood and gaped at her. The upper part of her clothing consisted of a torn blouse, exhibiting more of her bust than was generally considered essential in society in those days, and the lower half was encased in a ragged pair of trousers. Her dishevelled hair hung partly down her back and partly over her face. In a few moments her features relaxed and she began to smile. This restored my latent powers of speech, and once again I made the request for a pail of water. "Why," she exclaimed, "you're a gentleman, aint you, and I thought it was maybe one of them tramps that's forever trudging up and down this road. Come in and I'll get you a pail with pleasure." Much relieved, I followed her into the shack. She bade me sit down, and while she was at the well I took a mental inventory of the surroundings. The furniture was home-made and meagre in the extreme. It consisted of a table, two chairs, a roughly-made bed, a wash-bench, and a dresser. A few dirty knives and forks were scattered about on the bed. The floor was filthily dirty. My gaze wandered from the furniture to the walls. I noticed several pictures, all cheap chromos, fly-blown, but the main adornment which riveted my attention, was a small and neatly executed device in a dark frame, which bore the pious legend, "God bless our Home."

I had not felt very flattered at being taken for a tramp, but a good deal of *amour-propre* had already been stripped from my mind by the uncomplimentary remarks which Yearley and his son had been firing at me since the commencement of our journey. I had begun to feel that there was a world where I perhaps was not able to shine with as great lustre as in the cricket-field or the fives-court.[8] Before parting with the lady I was given an insight into her history. She told me that her husband who was English, like herself, was working in Bracebridge and came back at the weekends in order to spend Sunday with her. They had only been in the wilds about a year and, never having been used to roughing it, had found it hard to make both ends meet. It was not difficult for me to realize how fierce that battle had been.

When I returned with the pail, Mr. Yearley, who knew the history of the few settlers along the road, substantiated what the woman had told me, stating that they were a very estimable couple; "Much better than lots of others in these here parts," he added, a remark which proved the truth of the old saying that it is never safe to judge from appearances.

IV

The Government Road

THROUGHOUT THE WHOLE DAY MY ears had been assailed, on the one hand, with the blaring of the horn under the able and assiduous blowing of Mr. Yearley, and on the other, by the terrible objurgations delivered to the oxen by his son. The latter had been quite unlike anything that I had ever heard. Armed with a long sapling which he termed a "gad," he kept continually plying it on the backs of the poor beasts, forcefully asseverating that they were the *blankety-blankest* creatures on earth and that if they didn't "whoa back! Or whoa ha!, or whoa gee!" he would *blankety* soon knock their *blankety-blank* blocks off. I ventured to inquire finally why less forcible language would not do as well and was greeted with volleys of laughter by both father and son. "Wait till yer learnin' to drive cattle," remarked Bill. "When yer starts, you'll be sayin' a few strange things yerself. I'm a Sunday school teacher, I am, compared with some. When yer hears a real riproarer at it, it'll surprise yer." Shortly afterwards Bill leaned over towards me and whispered confidentially that "if the old man warn't travelling with us he'd let himself really go some," but that Pa didn't like to hear anything worse than a "hell" or a "damn." The day was not far distant when I heard language that far surpassed even Bill's choicest efforts.

The country which we were traversing was not at all interesting because the heavy timber obstructed one's view. The farther we advanced north the scarcer grew the clearings, until at last we entered on an unbroken stretch of forest that continued for miles.

In many places the going was absolutely hazardous, especially in the swamps. The Government Road[1] on which we were travelling, had only been opened a year or two previously, and the amount of statute labour that had been expended on it had not tended to advance it much toward passability. The spring freshet was then at its highest and, in certain long stretches of swamp, the logs were floating. Sometimes the feet of the oxen slipped between them and it was then that we experienced our worst difficulties. To get the cattle on a firm footing when their legs were jammed between logs in two feet or more of water was a problem that taxed Bill's most ingenious efforts. His father's weight was quite an asset on certain occasions. When he placed his bulk on the end of a hand-spike, something had to go. I did what in me lay to be of use. Whenever it was a case of wading through water, which was fairly often, my serv-ices were brought into requisition. Both father and son showed a certain amount of hesitancy in getting soaked. Their admiration of my aquatic capabilities was great, but this was more than offset by their disgust at my inept use of a handspike. As I had never seen such an implement before, my ignorance was not to be wondered at.

One of the points on which I had asked for enlightenment was the peculiar use they made of the term "rooster" by applying it to the male persuasion in the poultry line. I explained to them as urbanely as I could that, although in the education I had received at school barnyard terms had not formed part of the curriculum, still I knew that the better class of people never alluded to a cock as a rooster. "Why," I said, "every hen and chicken can roost as well as a cock. Why don't you call them all roosters?" Bill had been most uncivil in his reply and had tartly remarked, "Say, you're livin' in Canady now, and when yer wake up yer'll find that when we talks of roosters we means ROOSTERS, – see?" He was so fero-ciously in earnest that I dropped the subject.

At about five o'clock in the afternoon we came to the place where our paths diverged. During the latter part of the journey, Mr. Yearley had been in a state of semi-somnolency and the constant bumps of the wagon and flounderings of the cattle appeared to make no appreciable difference in his condition. Bill said to me, "The old man's that fleshy he can't keep awake nohow." He reached for the horn and placing the instrument close to his father's ear blew a loud blast. It had the desired effect. His parent rose from his recumbent posture and demanded to know what was wrong.

We parted on the best of terms for, notwithstanding the fun they had enjoyed at my expense, they had been excessively kind in other respects and especially in helping me to get so near to my destination. After giving me minute directions as to the route to follow and not to lose sight of the

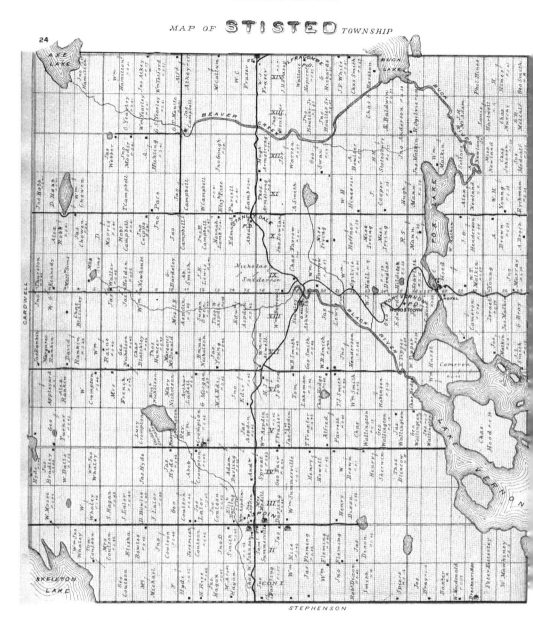

Map of Stisted Township from *The Guide Book and Atlas of Muskoka and Parry Sound*, published in Toronto by H.R. Page in 1879. Maps are by John Rogers. Note the location of Ilfracombe P.O. (top centre) and the southern portion of Buck Lake. *Courtesy of Queen's University, Douglas Library, W.D. Jordan Special Collections.*

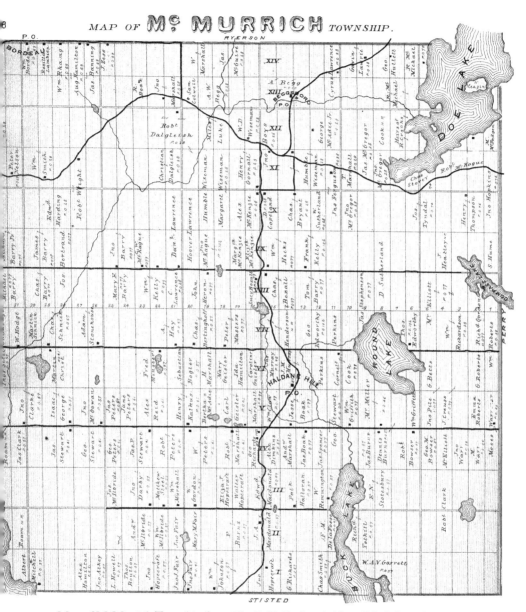

Map of McMurrich Township from *The Guide Book and Atlas of Muskoka and Parry Sound,* 1879. Note the northerly extension of Buck Lake. The property of F.M. de la Fosse is identified immediately to the left of the lake. Directly across the lake is the land belonging to Richard Tothill and, to the south, the property of W.A.V. Garrett. *Courtesy of Queen's University, Douglas Library, W.D. Jordan Special Collections.*

F. Hopkinson Smith, *A Forest Pathway, wood engraving.*
W.J. Dana, engraver. This engraving conveys a strong
sense of the forest's incredible solitude. From *Picturesque
Canada*, published in 1882. *Courtesy of the Library and
Archives Canada, Special Collections C085351.*

"blazed trail" they bade me farewell. I was still six miles from my objective
and the road was as rough as a road could be. For the first time in my life
I was absolutely alone in the wilds and would have given a good deal to
have been in the company of the Yearleys. It may be as well to mention
here that I never saw the old gentleman again although I heard of him
many times. He has been dead these many years, but I hold him in as grateful remembrance as when we parted on the Stisted Road[2] more than fifty
years ago. I venture to express the pious hope that in the land to which he
has gone, no ghosts of Gilliloo birds or Hodags dog his footsteps.

Following the directions given me, I took the road which led to the Harston habitation. Squirrels chattered at me from the branches, and strange, prettily striped little creatures called chipmunks scampered ever and anon across my path. The mosquitoes and blackflies were awful. I thought I would never come to the end of the trail. The least noise in the woods made me wonder if a bear or a Hodag was on my tracks, and I glanced fearfully at every overhanging tree to see if some beast of prey was lying in wait to descend on my shoulders. There was not a sign of a clearing, and I hurried along the well-defined path in order to get to the end of my journey as quickly as possible. Sometimes, on reaching the top of a lofty hill, I would be elated to find easy going in a piece of hardwood bush, and as often my spirits would sink when I found myself descending declivities and forcing my way through mossy swamps and across logs which had been felled to bridge some small gully or stream.

At one time every hair on my head started up and I perspired with horror when a screech owl suddenly gave vent to its diabolical cry about a foot above my head. My teeth chattered and my knees knocked together. Never, in the whole course of my career, have I been so thoroughly frightened as I was at that moment. Half-paralyzed, I looked round fearfully to see what was coming upon me, fully expecting to have a grapple with a Hodag hiding behind a tree. Hearing nothing further I managed at last to gather together my scattered senses and fled like one possessed down the pathway. The further I penetrated into the woods, the worse the footing became until at last I found myself in a veritable slough of despond. Trees had been felled here and there to act as bridges but, as I invariably lost my footing when I attempted to walk across them, I emerged covered with slime from head to foot. Finally, in a state of almost complete exhaustion, I reached the summit of a lofty hill and saw below me, gleaming through the trees, the waters of a lake. Xenophon's troops[3] never welcomed the sight of the sea with greater delight than did I that body of water, for I knew that on its shores I would find rest and refreshment. Summoning up all the strength that I possessed, I pushed on and within a few minutes came to the bars of a rough gateway. From there I could see, at about one hundred yards distance, two small log shanties. There was not a soul visible in the clearing, but a wreath of smoke issuing upwards through a stovepipe on one of the cabin roofs told of life within. I hurried forward and in a few seconds stood knocking at the door of Captain Harston's domicile.

V

The Harston Homestead

IT WAS WITH DISTINCT FEELING of timidity that I waited for the door
to be opened. It was some little time before I heard steps approaching,
and in that period I had been able to take a good survey of the cottage
and its surroundings. When I arrived at the gate, the prospect that met
my eyes had not been very encouraging. To call the place a "clearing" is
somewhat of a misnomer. There *was* a clearing, certainly, of about three
acres, but it was strewn with blackened logs and burnt branches. Where
there were no logs, large boulders were the chief visible features. There
was no arable land at all. South, east and west were forest, while the north
was bounded by the waters of the lake. The dwelling place, which it would
have been a compliment to dignify by the title of cottage, was composed
of two small wooden shacks, each about twelve feet by fifteen in size.
They were made of rough logs and plastered with mud and manure. A
few implements of husbandry in the shape of spades, axes and scythes,
were scattered about outside and, on a wooden block in the narrow veranda,
were a tin basin and a washstand. A somewhat dirty towel was hanging
on a nail above them. I had no time to make further inspection as the
door was at that moment opened, and a lady stood before me. It had not
entered into my calculations that such an abode might harbour a member of the opposite sex although, of course, in the letters that I had read
mention had been made of Mrs. Harston. But the appearance of the place
was so opposed to the likelihood of anyone but a man or men inhabit-
ing it that the reality astounded me.

The look of surprise that came over the lady's face might very well
have been a reflection of my own. It was one of sheer petrifaction. "How
d'ye do," I said timidly, and held out my hand; then I added as a bright

A photograph of a young Charles Greville Harston, circa 1855. It is believe to have been taken at "Stonehouse," Devon. *Courtesy of Mark Grantham, a descendant of Anna Dew Harston, first cousin to C.G. Harston.*

afterthought, "My name's de la Fosse." "Goodness gracious!" ejaculated the lady, "How on earth did you get here, and how *did* you ever get into such a state?" Then, recollecting that she had perhaps not greeted me in quite the orthodox fashion, she added hurriedly, "Oh, pray, come in, I'm very glad to see you." As soon as I entered I found myself being shaken most cordially by the hand by Captain Harston and three other gentlemen. They were seated at the table, having tea, but as soon as Mrs. Harston explained who I was, they rose from their seats and greeted me. It was disturbing, however, to note the same look of astonishment creeping over their features as had been apparent on those of the lady of the house. One glance at the looking glass that hung on the wall was quite enough to explain the cause. My face was streaked with mud and blood and charcoal, the straw hat in which I had taken so much pride was battered and stained, and my clothes soaked and muddied and torn, owing to my endless flounderings in the swamps. An explanation of my condition and the causes that had led to it provided them with a good laugh, but Mrs. Harston was very solicitous concerning me, and insisted on her husband providing me with fresh clothing.

A good clean up made a complete difference in my spirits and appearance, and I was able to do ample justice to the viands which were laid out for me. The party, I found, consisted of Captain and Mrs. Harston, a gentleman named Aemilius Baldwin,[1] and two Englishmen, William Garrett[2] and Richard Tothill,[3] who, I shortly discovered, had come from England in order to learn farming, like myself. Garrett was a Cambridge graduate whereas Tothill and I had come from Public Schools.[4]

They were all most friendly and greatly interested in the account that I gave them of my experiences. In the course of the evening I was informed that the house that Captain Harston had been building for our reception had been accidentally burnt down about a month earlier when they had been engaged in setting fire to some brushwood, and that they had been obliged to raise the two modest structures in which we were housed till such time as a new house could be erected. "I am sorry," said Captain Harston, "that we are not able to make things more comfortable for you, but it will only be a short time before we get to work to build afresh." As events turned out, we were not able to get into new quarters for about fifteen or sixteen months, but the inconvenience which the men suffered paled into insignificance when compared with what the lady of the establishment was subjected to. In looking back at those days, the only sentiment prevailing in my mind is one of sheer admiration for the grit and lightheartedness which she displayed. A short account of the ménage will suffice to show how restricted were her opportunities for enjoying the comforts which, as a woman, she must have sorely needed.

the Start into the woods.

the Foundation of the Shanty

Artist unknown, *Forest Clearing*, (The Clearing 1st Year). From the *Canadian Illustrated News*, December 1879. *Courtesy of the Library and Archives Canada, Special Collections*, CIN C-72615.

The flooring was fashioned of rough-hewn basswood slabs which were a constant source of irritation and developed in us in a short time a sort of goose-step prance whenever we walked about the room. There were three comfortable chairs and a table which had evidently been purchased in a store. It was one of the few things that had been saved from the fire. There were no cupboards visible, but instead there were two or three rough shelves resting on pegs that had been placed in the walls. On these were arrayed the family crockery and bottles containing sundry condiments like vinegar, jam and pickles. One end of the room had been partitioned off to provide sleeping accommodation for Captain and Mrs. Harston and this, on the advent of Garrett who had arrived a few weeks earlier than we had, was again divided to provide a cubicle for him. The main room contained, besides the articles already referred to, the kitchen stove.

The second shanty was the sleeping room of Mr. Baldwin, Tothill and myself. All the beds were homemade productions and the floor was of the same character as the one in the other buildings. This description is not written in any way to make fun of the conditions that prevailed on our arrival. Captain Harston had really done all that was possible to provide a comfortable place for us, and it was only owing to the unfortunate accident of the fire that we were compelled to live as we did.

What struck me as remarkable was the spirit of joviality and abandon in the little circle. They all seemed to feel that it was only a case of waiting for a few months, and they would be on the high road to a dazzling future. Captain Harston was an optimist of the first water, and we were so imbued with his enthusiasm that we believed in all his rosy dreams of coming prosperity. Apart from that, there was the feeling also that, if a lady, bred in a refined atmosphere, was willing to undergo discomfort and exile from society, men, better able to endure hardship, had no right to complain.

On entering the bedroom for the night, I looked round for a washstand and was told that the family had to perform their ablutions at the one basin that had been saved from the fire. This was, of course, a minor trouble. An attempt had been made to make the place look like home. There were a few photographs on the walls, and a picture or two, and these were hung promiscuously among pots and pans and empty demijohns.

I was so worn out that soon after tea was finished I asked leave to retire and went to bed. There were no sheets, but I was too exhausted, body and soul, to mind such a small thing as that; and after borrowing a nightshirt from Mr. Baldwin who stood six feet two in his socks, I curled myself up in a blanket and was soon fast asleep – but not for long. The others would follow and through all the dreary hours the mosquitoes kept up an incessant attack, and first from one bed and then from another imprecations would be wafted out on the air. At last none of us could stand the torment any longer and, by general consent, we got out of bed and sallied forth into the open. It was a beautiful night and the view from our elevated quarters was enchanting. Many a time have I thought of that first moonlit view of the magnificent lake as it lay glistening in all its serenity below us. But it was no time for loitering to gaze at lovely views. The mosquitoes were in full force and necessitated constant movement to gain immunity from their attacks.

I can see the whole incident so clearly now, even after so great a lapse of time. Mr. Baldwin, tall and dignified, leading the way to the lake, his voluminous waterproof floating behind him, Tothill, short and thickset, following him, pipe in mouth, and myself bringing up the rear, with the loose folds of my sleeping apparel wound tightly around me.

Three weird figures we must have looked if there had been anyone to see us. When we reached the shore, we sat down for a short time on a log and cursed the winged terrors of night as volubly as our vocabularies permitted. Then Tothill suggested that we go in for a bathe. It was no sooner suggested than acted upon, and in a trice we were in the water, free for a time at least, from the barbarians of the air. Suddenly there was a sharp yell from Tothill who had stared to wade ashore. "Good Heavens," he cried. "I think a mud turtle or something has got me by the toe." It startled us, and we immediately followed after him to lend a helping hand. On investigation we found that he had wedged his toe in a water-logged piece of wood and that a sharp point had pierced his flesh.

When we reached the shanty, there was no question of sleeping. It was carnival night in mosquito-land. We simply lighted a smudge and sat round it till daylight dawned. Captain Harston and Garrett joined us in short time, and no doubt the scene would have provided an excellent subject for anyone with a talent for depicting it. The streaming moonlight, the smoke slowly curling upwards and five figures, scantily garbed, seated in a circle gazing moodily at the fire, dozing and scratching themselves by turns.

Harston's Agricultural Farming School

––––––––––––

THE SHANTY WAS BUILT ON a rise, with quite a precipitous descent to the water, and there was an almost unobstructed view to the head of the lake. When morning dawned, I felt that I was in Fairyland. Nothing so lovely had ever gladdened my vision before. Before me lay a sheet of water some two miles in length and about a mile wide, glowing in the bright sun and surrounded by unbroken shores of woodland. The air was so still that sky and hovering cloud were perfectly mirrored in the water. Far off, from some hidden clearing, I could hear the call, "Co, bossy, co, bossy," of a housewife calling her cow to the morning's milking. From another quarter came the dull thud of an axe, and from yet another the soft tinkle of distant cowbells or the mysterious cry of a loon calling to its mate. For a wilderness aspect the view was delightful and I feasted my eyes on it for a considerable time, but I had come for the specific purpose of farming, and at last I began to wonder where the farm was.

At breakfast time I ventured to ask Captain Harston, and his answer is worth recording. "Why, my dear chap," he said, "here's the farm. Inside of two years you will see this wilderness flourishing 'like a green bay tree,' the barns will be bursting with grain, and the cattle with fatness. I shall instruct you in every phase of agriculture. You will first start by learning how to chop, then how to log and clear the land. It is the most interesting work that you can imagine. Picture to yourself how intensely comforting it will be to you, one of these days, to stand at the door and gaze at the waving fields. But I think you will find your greatest interest in breeding cattle. It is the most lucrative of all branches of farm life and that is really the department in which I think I am pre-eminently fitted to instruct you. For three years I helped as a farmhand myself in order to thoroughly qualify myself for this business. So you see," he concluded, as if the matter admitted of no further argument, "you are in most excellent hands."

Mr. Yearley had already informed me that he couldn't see how I should find it profitable to pay $500 per annum to learn to chop down trees and milk cows and clean out stables because he felt, looking at it "casual-like," that one could almost learn to do these things oneself. When I began to ponder it over in my mind, it did seem, to my befogged intellect, that there was a certain amount of reason in his remarks. However, there I was, without a relative in Canada to give me the advice that was needed or the authority to apprentice me to something else. It was a clear case of having to carry out the bargain that my guardians, in their ignorance of true conditions, had made in my behalf.

Being the youngest of the party, and apparently regarded as the most willing worker, it fell to my lot to act as choreboy for the establishment. If there was any water to be carried from the lake (a distance of 100 yards or so up a steep incline) I was the one delegated for the duty. I also brought in all the wood for the stove and took messages to the neighbours. When not engaged in these duties, I helped to wash up dishes and do various jobs about the "farm." It was a roundabout way of obtaining a knowledge of agriculture, but Harston assured me that it was only in this way that men could aspire to great heights and become leaders in the world. He cited Abraham Lincoln as a case in point and, in order to further fire my ambition, lent me Smiles' *Self-Help*[2] to read, to hearten me in my work.

It was not many days before I discovered that there was a considerable amount of pleasure to be got out of the life, even if it did entail plenty of hard work. The others were very much of the same mind as myself, and I think the last thing that any of us worried about was the fact that there was not much prospect of learning how to make a living from backwoods farming.

The first real hard work that we went in for, and into which I was initiated two days after my arrival, was "logging up." Now, this is a species of labour which may be bracketed with the most strenuous that falls to the lot of man. For the benefit of my readers, it may be stated that logging is about the third or fourth process in the art of clearing land.

The first is underbrushing, that is, cutting down the small growth in the woods; the second, chopping down the heavy trees; the third, the

A field of stumps referred to as Captain Harston's clearing. The photograph was taken before 1900. *Courtesy of Fred Hopcraft.*

burning off of the fallow in the spring; and the fourth, the task of rolling up the logs into big piles and burning them. As soon as this has been done, the land is ready for the first crop. The reader has to bear in mind that the stumps remain in the ground and that it is only after a period of some seven or eight years that they become sufficiently decayed to allow their being pulled out by oxen or horses.[3] Much depends on the way in which trees are felled and the underbrush cut down. If the work is poorly done and big branches are left on the timber, the fire will not do its work properly and the work is rendered considerably more difficult.

On the piece of land that we were working, the underbrushing had been done very badly. The result was that we had to pile great quantities of brushwood in order to get it burnt off, and cut many large limbs from the fallen trees. Now, when five tyros[4] attempt to clear a piece of land, it may well be believed that the results will prove unsatisfactory. We certainly found it so and, after two or three weeks of abortive effort, Captain Harston gave it up as a bad job and decided to have a "bee."[5] He possessed a splendid team of oxen, and if he had only been able to drive them properly, we might have been able to show some results for our work. But as a matter of fact he knew nothing about it and was only going by what he had seen other men do in the short time that he had been in the bush.

We had a merry time of it with that logging. In the first place, we went out to our work dressed in a manner not at all suitable for such a rigorous undertaking. Stiff collars and patent leather boots are not usually seen in a logging field. Having had the misfortune to leave all my wearing apparel at Gravenhurst, as before related, I was under the sorrowful necessity of borrowing things from my instructor. It is grievous to relate that that day's labour made deep inroads on the future serviceability of those garments. When we returned to the shanty for dinner, Mrs. Harston was appalled to discover that everyone of us had rents in our clothing. Captain Harston had unwisely lent me his best trousers and midday found them reduced to such a condition that the veriest tramp would have turned up his nose at such rags. He felt very badly about it and gave vent to very unnecessary remarks as to the careless way in which I had fallen foul of rocks and snags in my efforts to be of service.

Captain Harston endeavoured to show us, ably seconded by Mr. Baldwin, how to roll the logs into heaps. At one part of the proceedings, when we were engaged in handspiking a large log to the top of a pile, Mr. Baldwin called to me wildly to bring my handspike to his side as his hold was slipping. I rushed out and inserted it under the log by taking a "pry"

Notman and Sandham, *Lumbering in the Backwoods*, photograph. In *Canadian Illustrated News*, January 24, 1880. *Courtesy of the Library and Archives Canada, Special Collections, CIN C-72750.*

between his legs. "Up she goes," shouted Mr. Baldwin, and we all heaved with a will. Unfortunately, my hold slipped in the strenuous effort and the result was that in place of hoisting the log, I hoisted Mr. Baldwin to the top of the pile. I am sure it must have hurt, for the way in which he shook his fist at me and the language he used showed that he was labouring under a very severe strain. I learned that I was a damned young fool and not fit to be out of the nursery, and was asked if I knew the difference between a human crotch and a wooden one. The trouble with Mr. Baldwin was that whenever anything put him out, it was a long time before he got back into an equable frame of mind. Even at night, when he was applying tincture of arnica[6] to the injured part, he couldn't desist from saying a few things derogatory of my intellect.

Captain Harston was essentially a man of action and a splendid organizer of labour. No time was wasted in making arrangements for the logging bee, and Tothill and I were sent forth to ask the inhabitants of the surrounding neighbourhood to come with their teams to help us. We started off with glad hearts. For us a change from that awful work was as good as a rest. But the memories of Mr. Yearley's tales of Hodags and Gilliloo birds were strong in my mind, and I was glad enough to have a companion when walking through the woods. Most of the settlers' homesteads were to be reached only by narrow paths or blazed trails through the bush, as none of them had been in the country long enough to enable them to make proper roads. The Stisted Road was the main highway. Occasionally we came to roughly chopped-out places wide enough to admit of the passage of a wagon and a span of oxen, but these only at infrequent intervals. That day's travel showed us very clearly some of the rigours of bush life.

Our first call was made at the store of a man named Hamilton.[7] It was a small, mean-looking place, situated on the Government Road, about two miles distant from our quarters. We were anxious to meet him as we had been told many tales of his sharp practices and of the tricks that had been played on him by those whom he had victimized. The latest had been worked by a gang of shantymen, who during the progress of a "spree" at his abode, had slipped into the store and turned on the tap of a 40 gallon keg of molasses. It doesn't take much imagination to picture in what state the floor was when Hamilton discovered the deed the following morning. When we sighted the store we came on a curious scene. A small, frenzied female was tugging fiercely at one end of a

side of pork, and a burly, dark-bearded individual was pulling as violently at the other. On a wagon close by were several bags of flour. We
stepped in and took hold of the man and with some difficulty pulled
him away. Then we inquired as to what was the matter. He was very
direct and forcible in his reply. He first told us to get to a warm climate
out of that and then inquired what "in Gehanna" we thought we were.
Mrs. Hamilton, who was a German, was in a highly excited state of mind
and gave us no time to answer. In broken but voluble English, she
informed us that the man was stealing all the stock they had in the store.
Then we turned to the man. He was intelligible enough. By way of pre-
amble he informed us that we were a couple of damned young fools and
that he'd knock the daylights out of us, and then wanted to know once
more why we were butting into his business. To this outburst, both of
us, rendered valiant at the sight of a woman in distress, told him to keep
his tongue quiet and put back the goods in the store. Seeing that we
meant business, the man gave us his version of the story. We learned
that Hamilton was in his debt, and that the only way he could see of
getting even with him was to go to his store when he was absent and
recoup himself for his losses. It did not take long to make him see the
error of his ways, and being, in the main, a good fellow, he put everything back and departed. Mrs. Hamilton, needless to say, was tearfully
grateful for our assistance. This was an exciting commencement to our
day's outing, and we both remarked as we trudged along that one apparently did not need to go to the busy hives of men for excitement; there
seemed plenty of it awaiting us in the woods.

By the end of the day we were more than ever confirmed in this belief.
On the way to our next call we had another startling experience. We
were walking down a narrow pathway in single file, myself leading. A
tree had fallen across the path and, just as we came to it, there was a
deep grunt from the other side of the log, and a bear jumped up and
trotted in an unwieldy manner down the path. The sudden shock made
me bump against Tothill, and we both fell to the ground. Mr. Bruin
never took the trouble to look round but continued on his way.

"Good Lord," said Tothill, "I'm coming to the opinion that this is
rather an awful country."

"Yes," I replied, "it does seem strange that we cannot move without
running into something extraordinary. But do you know, I am not in the
least afraid of a bear. My friend, Mr. Yearley, told me that they are not

dangerous at all, and that the beasts to look out for are the Hodags. He says they are something dreadful. They climb trees and watch for you and jump on your shoulders and strangle you."

Tothill was quite impressed. He said he had never heard of them but that he would look into his Natural History when we got home and read up about them. "You know, Frederick," he said, "I'm afraid there's something lamentably lacking about the education that they dole out to us chaps at home. Now, wouldn't you think that they would teach us something about the fauna and flora of a country like Canada? I think it's nothing short of disgraceful that so little is known concerning a country so close to the old sod as this is. How do you spell it, H-O-D-A-G or H-O-D-A-G-U-E? I should imagine it is a French word."

I told him that I hadn't the faintest idea, but remembering the old man's loose use of the aspirate I though it possible that it might be O-D-A-G.

It was very interesting to meet the settlers. We found that most of those in our vicinity were English people. Our arrival in the district seemed to be widely known and we soon discovered that the epithet applied to us in the countryside was "The English Bloods." In the course of our walk, we met Englishmen and Americans, as well as Canadians, also some Germans and Swedes and one mulatto. Everywhere we were most hospitably received, for if there is one thing more than another that can be said for the pioneer, it is that no matter how poor his resources or how attenuated his means of subsistence, he greets you warmly and gives or lends fully and freely of anything that he possesses.

VII[1]

THE SETTLERS

AMONG THOSE WHOM WE VISITED was a settler named Smith.[2] He and his wife, two highly respectable people, lived with their two sons, in a small clearing a very short distance from ours. Mrs. Smith assisted Mrs. Harston in her laundry work and, generally, in caring for the family.

Although we had seen her so often at our own clearing, she was quite overcome at having us as visitors at her cottage and could not do too much to show her gratification. She was very eloquent as to what she and her husband had gone through in order to get their heads above water. Mr. Smith had been a butcher in a small way in England and, less than two years previously, had migrated to Canada in order to take up land in Muskoka. By dint of hard work and perseverance, he had cleared about five acres and had scraped along with the very small amount of money that he had brought from England. Sometimes they had been so hard put to it that they had lived on lamb's quarter,[3] picked in the burnt patches of the woods, and on whatever Smith had been able to bring down with his rifle. Our coming to the neighborhood, she frankly stated, had proved to be a godsend in enabling her to make a little ready money by helping Mrs. Harston. Mrs. Smith was a splendid specimen of an honest hard-working settler and her husband was a worthy mate for her. It was hard for us to get away as both she and her husband were most anxious that we should stay and have something to eat. But there was too much to be done and we had to leave.

Our next call was on a totally different type of individual, a man by the name of White.[4] We found on arriving at his domicile that his household consisted of himself and his wife. They were also English people. We had witnessed evidences of poverty in various cottages during our tramp, but the only place approaching it in abject wretchedness had been the one at which I had obtained a pail of water when travelling with the Yearleys. Like the former shack, this abode was composed of rough logs, roofed with hollowed-out basswood slabs. The doorway was fashioned of three boards nailed together and swung on pieces of leather. The window was covered as far as was possible with the remains of a calico dress. There was a bed at one end of the room on which was laid an extremely dirty coverlet and a pillow black with grime. A roughly made table, two chairs and a bench comprised the furniture. In a dismal-looking recess was a shabby bonnet, and above it, on a shelf, were arrayed a few pieces of cracked crockery. The further end of the cabin presented extraordinary features. It was apparently used as a manger for a cow, as there were all the accessories in the shape of a feeding-place, a hitching post, and straw on the floor.

The inhabitants of this delectable abode were quite in keeping with the premises. They presented a really fantastic appearance. The man, who was an undersized anaemic-looking creature, with an unkempt beard and drooping moustache, was wearing a tattered shirt. His legs, instead of being encased in orthodox breeches, were covered with flour bags, roughly sewn together. His feet were bare. His wife, even in all her rags and wretchedness, was a handsome woman. She was wearing a blouse and in place of a skirt was sporting the lower part of a man's overalls. Her hair, of which she had a wonderful supply, was tied with a dirty piece of string. At a superficial glance they might have stood as tableau pictures for a couple of cave dwellers. Yet these people had been reared in superior surroundings. We were informed that the man had originally been a nobleman's valet, and his wife a servant in the same establishment. They had elected to try their fortunes in a new country and here they had landed, in a spot the least suited to their ability. We found that they knew little more about backwoods requirements than we did, having only been about eight months in the district. They asked us inside very courteously and invited us to take seats on the bed.

We made our mission known in as few words as possible and, having obtained the man's promise to come to the bee, we arose to take our departure. We were no sooner on our feet than there was a wild uproar under the bed. The dog, a mangy-looking cur, had surreptitiously taken refuge in that quarter and, finding the pig already in possession, had attempted to oust him. The pig, emitting a tremendous squeal, rushed from underneath and tried to find an avenue of escape through my legs.

George Harlow White, *Interior of a Settler's Shanty*, circa mid-1870s. *Courtesy of the Toronto Public Library (TRL) Special Collections T16440.*

He made a bad shot and upset me, causing me to fall in a very undignified manner on the dirty floor. The dog went in full chase after the pig, and a couple of hens which had wandered in for a tour of inspection added to the general hullabaloo by flapping their wings and squawking all over the place.

Our last visit for that day was to an elderly being named Holt.[5] He was a gay old boy not long arrived from England where, he told us, he had been famous as a concert hall singer. "Why," he said in a tone of exalted pride, swelling out his chest, "I've earned as much as two pun ten a night, and to think as I should have come down to this 'ere!" We thought it rather hard luck for him at the time but, after we had heard him perform, we came to the conclusion that "hold Hengland" as he termed his native land was the richer for his departure. We asked him to the logging bee and he accepted promptly and offered to sing a selection of his ditties for the delectation[6] of the gathering when the eventful day arrived. On our return we informed Captain Harston of the find we had made and he was overjoyed, "Just the thing," he said, "Just the thing!"

It took us two or three days to collect enough men and teams for the logging bee. There was a goodly assortment of humanity early on the scene, about twenty men and five teams in all. Many of the wives of those taking part in the logging also came, in order to help lay the tables and attend to the wants of the loggers. There had not been one refusal, it being an unwritten law of the woods that everyone must help his fellow man. It would be impossible otherwise to raise houses and barns or to clear the land for crops.

The day was an ideal one for work. Captain Harston and Mr. Baldwin[7] were known to the majority of those who were present, but the rest of us were not, and the men gaped in wonder when they saw us coming into the logging field, wearing knickerbockers and white shirts. We were certainly attired in outfits which were in marked contrast to those worn by the settlers. For the most part, these consisted of rough flannel shirts, heavy mackinaw trousers tucked into long boots, and cow-feed hats. Many wore gaily-coloured sashes tied round their waists in lieu of belts. That our costume was unsuited to the logging field goes without saying. We hadn't been at work five minutes before we were a very disgruntled set of individuals, and many a laugh went up round the field at the spectacle we presented.

Nobody as yet knew the exact condition under which we had arrived in the district, and the general impression seemed to be that we had either separately or collectively committed some enormity in the Old Country which had necessitated our departure from its shores. I surmised this from the confidential way in which an inquisitive individual leaned over during dinner and whispered raucously in my ear, "Say, sonny, you ain't old enough to have robbed a bank or anything like that, but what in hell did you do to be sent up here?" I replied that I had come there in order to make a living. This was altogether too much for him; like Mr. Yearley, he gave a gasp, invoked the name of the Almighty, and went on with his dinner.

Captain Harston, in order to keep us together, formed a logging party of his own, with himself, of course, as driver. We had a gloriously exciting time of it. The oxen, perplexed by his method of handling them, refused to work and looked stolidly ahead, whilst he frantically begged them to get a move on. He had informed us earlier in the day that he could see no reason on earth why cattle should not be driven in as gentlemanly a manner as horses. "I cannot understand," he said, "why it should be necessary to swear at an ox any more than at a horse. For my own part, I intend never to descend to profanity and I trust that you boys," turning to Tothill and myself, "will also always comport yourselves like gentlemen with all classes of the brute creation."

James Weston, *Logging Bee in Muskoka.* From *Canadian Illustrated News, May 1, 1880. Courtesy of the Library and Archives Canada, Special Collections CIN C72985.*

His politeness to the oxen worked so much on one of the men that he came up to him at last and asked him if he thought cattle understood such baby talk as that. "Why," he said, "give them a damned big biff or two with that gad and tell them to get to hell out of that." Captain Harston's attempts to get out of the realm of baby talk into that of good red-blooded language resulted in the cattle bolting several times with all gangs in hot pursuit. His efforts in the logging field were soon terminated for the day. Unfortunately, when the oxen were being brought into position for placing the chain over a log, the round hook caught in a cuff of his trousers, and in a trice he was being dragged over logs and stumps and snags at a rate that threatened to end his mortal career at any moment. That was one time in his life when poor Captain Harston must have been sorry that he had purchased good old English fustian.[8] The cloth held well and, by the time the cattle had been headed off, he was half dead with cuts and bruises. He was so shaken up with his experience he went off to the shanty and helped the women lay the platters for the evening meal.

I would like to give a picture of the scene that that logging-bee supper presented. We had had a very successful day, and the evening saw the whole clearing of some two or three acres freed of logs and underbrush save where the former had been rolled into massive piles for burning. It was a joyful and tired crowd of men therefore, that filed their way to the shanty to wash themselves clear of grime in preparation for the meal. There were only one or two towels available for the entire gang, but those who were present were quite used to such exigencies as this and, when a towel was not available, rubbed their faces and hands on such parts of their shirts as seemed the least soiled by the day's work. A long table composed of boards placed on roughly made trestles proved excellent for the viands, and pieces of lumber on smaller trestles made first-class benches. They were a merry crew and the way that they made the victuals disappear was marvellous. Some of the jokes dispensed that evening were not of the choicest, but they were as clean as the Psalms of David compared with the productions offered by our new-found songster, Mr. Holt. Garrett who had a beautiful tenor voice sang "The Blue Alsatian Mountains" and "Nancy Lee" to the great joy of the gathering, but Holt had been left as the *pièce de résistance* to wind up the evening. Captain Harston who presided at the table rose and addressed those present. "My dear friends," he said, "we have all enjoyed the selections we have heard this evening, and I am glad to state that we have yet one splendid treat awaiting us. Mr. Holt, I understand, made a great name for himself on the comic stage in England, his specialty being singing. He has very kindly offered to oblige us with a song or two, and I am sure we shall enjoy his selections. Mr. Holt," he said turning courteously to that worthy, "may I ask you to kindly favour us?" Amid loud applause Mr. Holt stood up and sang. The songs were simply terrible. Even the men looked startled, and the women, accustomed as many of them were to the strongest language, turned and fled. To the honour of those rough backwoodsmen it can be recorded that from only one or two quarters came a request for an encore. Holt was never asked to sing at further functions.

The really great find of the evening was a shy young man of the name of Walter Hopcraft.[9] If he had not himself suggested that he would like to warble a bit for the edification of those present, nobody would have thought of him. He told us that the piece he was going to sing had been composed by himself, and that he intended some day to have the words set to music. At present he was under the necessity of borrowing a tune, "and it was one that most of us know'd well, seein' as how we had heard it ever since we was knee-high to grasshoppers and had worn short pants.

The tune is," he announced proudly, "From Greenland's hicy mountains."
The words of the first verse cling to my memory, owing to the fact that
I asked the author for a copy of them, and kept them by me for many
years. They were really very descriptive of the district of that time:

> Our shanty's in Muskoka,
> And you will find us there;
> Some lives in holes what's hunderground,
> Some's hopen to the hair;
> We aint what's called the big-bug class,
> That's plainly for to see:
> But we's here to sow and reap and hoe
> And make a great countree.

The song was received with rapturous applause. As an encore he followed it up with a love ditty which he was modest enough to tell us was
not his own but had been "giv" to him by a lady friend. It was a lengthy
piece and had a decidedly involved legend. The gist of it was that a young
girl fell asleep and dreamt that she was rolling in the arms of her lover
who was "fightin'" with bold Wellington on board of the Victoree." It
was a touching refrain:

> I dreamt I was so happy, just as happy as could be
> A-rollin' in his ararrums on board of the Victoree –

It quite took the fancy of the crowd for whom historic accuracy had
no value, and everyone joined in the chorus.

After logging came the burning of the log piles. This was work that I
really enjoyed. I found that there was quite a lot to learn even in such a
simple duty as this. It will strike most people that the surest way of setting fire to anything is by placing a flame at the bottom. But this method
does not work with a log pile, at least not with a Muskoka log pile. The
very opposite is the only way, and that is by starting a fire at the top. A
few chips and pieces of birchbark or other combustible matter are placed
in crevices between two logs and ignited. It does not take long for the
pile to be set blazing. Maple timber and, in fact, all hardwoods burn very
easily and it is wonderful how quickly the fire will spread through the

whole pile. It is a fine spectacle, on a dark night, to watch a whole field of log heaps blazing. If the burn is a good one, there will be nothing left to do in the morning but a little branding, that is, pushing together the charred pieces that have been left.

In order to keep marauding cattle out of the crop, it was, of course, necessary when the time came to have a fence, and we were set to work, as soon as the crop was in, to cut poles in the woods for this purpose. It was a very peculiar-looking affair when it was finished. Settlers declared that they had never seen anything like it before. Some of us had half a suspicion that they were telling the truth. Part of it was made of poles stretched on crosspieces driven into the ground; another portion of it was what was called a toggle fence, and the remainder was made up of a confused heap of brushwood and stumps. For the benefit of the uninitiated it may be stated that a toggle fence is composed of logs overlapping enough to allow of a block of wood being placed across the ends. These blocks are hacked in deep enough to allow the other logs being rested on them, and thus the fence is raised tier by tier to the requisite height. It was easy enough to roll the bottom logs into place, but when it came to lifting them into the different tiers, it was a pretty heavy undertaking.

It was in overseeing jobs like this that Captain Harston shone. He was never so complacent and happy, never so serenely judicial as when he was "squatulating" on a log or a rock and guiding us in our work. Mr. Baldwin always acted as ox-driver when Captain Harston was engaged

A homestead along Buck Lake. Note the fence in the foreground. *Courtesy of Fred Hopcraft.*

in expounding things to us, and he was the best in the houshould at that particular sort of work. It took a great deal of very hard labour to complete that fence, and when it was finished it was disheartening to find that it would not stand the weight of any one leaning against it. It had such an unhappy faculty of falling down that Captain Harston cautioned us on no account to exert undue pressure against it. But the cattle wanted to scratch themselves more than we did, and they seemed to like nothing better than to tickle their sides against it. When they discovered that the process proved an "Open Sesame," they made a practice of it. The result was that there was never a day during the whole summer that we were not repairing some portion of the wonderful structure.

The first crop that we essayed to sow was Lucerne.[10] It was not a successful one. Not a blade of it appeared above the ground, owing to the fact that on that particular part of the clearing there was no soil fit to grow anything. Whatever earth there may have been originally had been either burnt up when the fallow was set fire or washed into the lake during the heavy rains. The good old granite bobbed up serenely everywhere. But there were bits of vegetation hidden behind boulders, to which the cattle loved to come at night. They preferred also the clear open spaces to the murkiness of the woods, and the constant jangling of their bells used to be irritating beyond measure. Apart from the exasperation caused by the noise, there was the serious question of the crop involved. The beasts could not be allowed to destroy the turnips, of which we had a possible quarter of an acre planted. I use the word "planted" deliberately because we were instructed to plant them. Tothill and I were allotted the task and we took turns in digging holes for seed. We put them into the ground just as if we were putting in potatoes. It took us quite a time planting half a bushel, for turnip seed is small and three or four seeds planted in a hill don't take up much room. Any farmer will tell you that. We would have been planting them for a considerable time longer if we hadn't got disgusted and thrown three or four full pans into the woods.

When the turnips showed above the ground, Harston was tremendously excited. One would have thought that the humble vegetables were rare specimens of orchids, he was so sedulously eager to preserve them. The cattle were excited too. They just loved to peer across the fence and survey the succulent tops. At night they were rendered so uneasy by what they had seen during the day that they leaned up against the logs to scratch themselves for comfort. It would be hard to say how many times, when the familiar jangling was heard outside the door, we rushed forth in our night attire to chase them out of the clearing. It was not plain sailing by any means because as often as not we would go out without anything on our feet, and many a word of a forcible character floated out on the air when we stubbed our toes on a snag or fetched up hard against a piece of rock.

One night the alarm was raised when there was a perfect tempest raging. The lightning was incessant, and the pealing of the thunder was a thing to be remembered. We were young and healthy and, not thinking for a moment of clothing ourselves or even putting on waterproofs, we all rushed out into the night, clad only in our shirts. Captain Harston had been a bit more thoughtful than we had and had brought his umbrella along with him. It was a spectacle for the gods to see him stepping forward into the rain with the umbrella raised over his head. But his dignified bearing was destined to be short-lived. Before he had gone many yards he slipped on a piece of bark and got a lovely wallow in the mud. He said a few words and, relinquishing the chase after the cattle, went on down to the lake and had a bathe in the thunderstorm. Then he went back to the shanty, gave himself a glass of whisky, and went to bed.

When we set to work to harvest our turnips, we made the discovery that they were frozen into the ground. We tried at first to kick them loose with our feet but found it hard on our toes. Captain Harston discountenanced this style of doing things; he said it didn't look workmanlike and that it would be better to dig them up with a pick-axe. But the job we liked least of all was the slicing off of the tops. They were covered with snow and the experience was decidedly unpleasant.

About this time we received a visit from our Dominion Member. He had heard of our settlement and, indeed, had known Captain Harston prior to his coming to Muskoka. Being on a tour of the constituency, he arrived one evening when he was not expected and was put up for the night. He was a very fine man, of distinctly aristocratic appearance and manners, and it was a delight to meet him. We had a most pleasant evening's chat, and he was, or affected to be, quite charmed with our location and with the progress we had made in the backwoods lore. He remarked that it was not often that one found Englishmen of education so adaptable as ourselves and that it bode well for the future of the colony. He talked most effusively of the golden future that was opening out for the people about us and for ourselves. However, our member had apparently never had much experience of life in the rough and grimaced somewhat when he was asked to wipe his face and hands on the family towel which was still hung for convenience sake on a nail under the veranda.

Our bread [baking] had not been a success that week and was in the brick-bat class. Our household had a reputation for its bread. It was a standing joke in the neighbourhood that if one wanted to get "somethin' to puzzle the squirrels with" or to use in place of biscuit or bones for the delectation of the dogs, the best place to apply for it would be at Captain Harston's. It was unkind because it isn't everyone who can bake decent bread even under favourable conditions and, when one is obliged to go to all sorts of shifts to keep the stove at a proper temperature in frosty weather, it is hard for a housewife to make a presentable offering.

There was always abundance to eat at Captain Harston's, so the reader may be assured that our visitor was treated to a wide range of viands. Unfortunately, Mrs. Harston, in an excess of hospitality asked our visitor if he would like to have some maple syrup. It was taken from its place on the wall, and the jug containing it handed to him. The place was overrun with mice and the top of the jar having been broken, a mouse on an exploring excursion had unfortunately tumbled in and been drowned in the syrup. The trouble was discovered when Captain Harston handed the jug with much civility to his guest, and he, short-sighted man that he was, didn't notice what had happened till he proceeded to spread some of the syrup on his bread. Then his appetite suddenly vanished.

VIII

COMMUNITIES OF THE DISTRICT

As soon as the Spring work was finished, Captain Harston had begun to make preparations for the building of his house. It may be as well, at this juncture, to state that our Spring work consisted, in the main, of the logging already mentioned and the fencing of the ground and the sowing and planting of the crop. I use the term "Spring work" because there is something in its ring that sounds really businesslike. But there was a tenderfoot aspect about everything, even though by now we really considered ourselves quite expert woodmen and farmers, to the great and exceeding merriment of settlers round about us.

As it was found impracticable to get the house finished in time for entering into that winter, we passed the whole of that decidedly cold and breezy season in our humble shacks at the top of the hill. Captain Harston was determined to have the best of everything for his dwelling, but the assembling of the logs proved to be a very long and arduous undertaking. He showed perspicacity, however, in cutting down the best trees he could find on lots that didn't belong to him, for, as he wisely remarked, it was just as well to keep what timber he had on his own lot for other purposes.

Occasionally we would long for some variation in the form of a holiday in Toronto or a bit of amusement nearer home. The approach of Dominion Day gave us a grand opportunity. We decided to send a challenge to the Huntsville Cricketers to play a match against them on that auspicious occasion. The challenge was promptly accepted but we were at our wits' end to find enough men for the team. This difficulty was finally surmounted by our obtaining the services of sundry baseballers among the younger element who were only too anxious to seize the chance

56

George Harlow White, *Vernon River, Entrance to Fairy Lake,* 1875. *Courtesy of the Toronto Public Library (TRL) Special Collections T16447.*

of a glorification. I use the term because it seems the most applicable to the occasion.

Having made arrangements with the other members of our side to meet us in Huntsville, we started off to play against our opponents. In order to get to our destination in good time we had to make a very early start, and the mists were hanging heavily on lake and woodland when we entered our canoes for the journey. Our course lay along three or four miles of winding river and down a couple of lakes the larger of which, Lake Vernon,[1] is about eight miles in length. We went in two canoes, Captain Harston being the steersman of one, and Mr. Baldwin of the other. At the outset certain difficulties were experienced owing to the fog, but as we entered the river the mist began to rise. The scenery was positively enthralling. Everything was perfectly still and moisture hung heavily from twig and overhanging branch. We had paddled only a short distance when the pitiful scream of a rabbit fell on our ears. Almost immediately afterwards we saw, right in front of us, a large hawk flying over the river with the poor little wretch in its talons. The cry of a wounded rabbit is enough to send anyone into a frenzy. We were all madly excited but the impossibility of releasing it was so apparent that after a short diatribe against birds of prey in general, and hawks in particular, in which all of us engaged, we passed on our way.

Half a mile farther down we came upon an enchanting bit of scenery, rendered more delightful by the sight of two deer feeding placidly at the water's edge. We saw them as we rounded a bend. They were standing in the water nibbling at the lilies. It was a lovely picture, and we rested motionless on our paddles and watched them. This only lasted for a few moments, however, for a slight stir in one of the canoes caused them to look up, and with one or two startled leaps they were out of the water and rushing through the woods. After a two-mile paddle down Fox Lake[2] we arrived at Port Vernon, and had to shoulder our canoes and make a half-mile portage to Lake Vernon, one of the loveliest sheets of water in Canada.

Port Vernon, when we first knew it, was quite a thriving little village, possessing two or three stores, two churches, a sawmill and about twelve or fourteen houses and a hotel. Captain Charles Hood[3] was the presiding genius of the place, a fine-looking man in the late fifties. He was an eccentric individual, of grim determination and tireless energy. On his arrival in the district he had seen the possibilities presented by the site and promptly purchased a block of land with the object of turning it into village lots.

Rumours of the railway passing through brought others to the place, and soon a small hamlet came into being. But, although the surveyors ran a line through the property, the railway never came. Instead, it passed through Huntsville, and the changed route sounded the death knell of the budding village. Many of the names of its inhabitants come to my mind as I write. Bright, the hotel keeper, and Jock Henderson; Hilditch, the postmaster; Mr. and Mrs. Piper, Mr. and Mrs. Meade,[4] who kept the best stores in the place, and the Hood family, to whom we were indebted for many kindnesses. Today there is absolutely no sign of there ever having been a building in the place. Every vestige has been swept away, and the bridge alone remains to show that at one time there was considerable traffic in the neighbourhood.

It would be hard for any but those who knew the village in those old days to realize that, if the railway authorities had chosen the route through Port Vernon, it would today be an important centre, transcending Huntsville in importance. In the heyday of its prosperity, the name Port Vernon was changed to Hoodstown in honour of Captain Hood.

Down past the wooded islands and through the beautiful reaches of Lake Vernon we took our way and, by the time the sun was well up in the eastern heavens, had reached Huntsville and found our way to Cann's Hotel.[5]

Huntsville was not as big then as it is now, but it had three or four hotels, boasted a doctor and a weekly paper, and had several stores and

George Harlow White, *Huntsville, Muskoka,* 1875, *Courtesy of the Toronto Public Library (TRL) Special Collections T16438.*

dwelling houses. It was a great centre for the lumber trade, and the village was never without its quota of lumberjacks. When we arrived, we found the place full of perspiring and happy humanity. It was a gala day, and the countryside had sent all its youth and beauty in variegated finery to witness or engage in the different events.

As the swimming and running races were not to be held until the evening, Tothill and I elected to go in for them at the close of the cricket match which was to be a one-inning affair. We met the opposing team of cricketers at dinner at the hotel and spent a most pleasant hour together. The other members of our side had been as good as their word and were at the hotel to greet us on our arrival. When we marched out to the cricket field, clad in all the panoply of war, we were disconcerted to find that it was a newly stumped field and that boulders and snags cropped up everywhere. The pitch itself was a dreadful piece of workmanship, but it had been rendered fairly serviceable by the laying down of pieces of coconut-matting at either end.

To chronicle the doings at that never-to-be-forgotten match would take far too long. It bounded in thrills. The first occurred when Tothill was doubled up by a ball in the stomach and had to be carried off the field for a protracted rest. The next thrill was when Mr. Baldwin was sent back ignominiously for a duck's egg for knocking his wicket down, much to the delight of the opposing team and to the grief of our men. Mr. Baldwin was no cricketer and, when I say that, I mean that there were several things that he could do better. His size intimidated the Huntsvillians to such an extent that, when he came stalking to the wickets, the Captain waved wildly to his players to go to the uttermost parts of the field. A lob bowler was put on with the obvious intention of inducing him to hit up a catch.

The device was successful, for he slammed terrifically at the first ball, missed it completely, and turned a perfect *volte-face*, hitting the wicketkeeper in the hinder parts and knocking him into the stumps. The umpire gave him "out," which caused great umbrage to our team, as it was the wicket-keeper and not the batsman who had hit the wickets, but poor Mr. Baldwin had to go. Later Captain Harston who was acting as captain of our side was accused by the captain of the Huntsvillians of touching the stumps with his foot in order to knock the bails[6] off. This led to a wrangle and was only ended by Captain Harston giving his sacred word of honour that he wouldn't be guilty of such a thing and that his boot had slipped accidentally against the wicket. The result of the game was a victory for the Huntsvillians by a small margin of runs. We found it hard to make out what the real score was as the record had been kept by an individual who had offered his services *gratis* and had been accepted on the strength of telling us that his grandfather had been a cricketer.

When Tothill was hit in the breadbasket, it was jotted down as "hit by a foul ball" and against the name of the stately Mr. Baldwin we found in almost illegible script the words: "Baldwin...Messed up the works...o."

The running events were held down the main street, and it was a cheerful and inspiring sight to see the erstwhile sleekly-dressed and fashionable Tothill flying through the village in his socks, with the rest of the contestants well in the rear. Having noticed that the other aspirants for the crown of laurel had removed their shoes, Tothill removed his also, and the result was the "Eclipse was first and the rest nowhere." So far in advance was he that there was nearly a riot owing to some of the contestants making accusations that he was a ringer from Toronto.

The swimming races in the evening were well fought out, and the one for the championship of the district was captured by myself. After these events had been decided, we adjourned to the hotel and finished up the day with a fine repast at which the two captains made glowing speeches in which eternal fealty was sworn to the noble game of cricket and emphasized in a slightly boisterous manner by the singing of that grand old song "The Englishman" in which the whole party joined wholeheartedly. The entire company came down to the wharf to see us off and long after we had rounded the bend in the river we could hear the stentorian voice of Bernard Phillips,[7] their chief vocalist, who had started the song again, leading his friends in the chorus,

> "It's a glorious charter, deny it who can
> That's contained in the words, "I'm an Englishman."
> It's a glorious charter, deny it who can
> That's contained in the words, "I'm an Englishman."

IX

Preparation of the Log Shanty

It was a long paddle home after such a strenuous day, but we were young and full of life and enjoyed every minute of it. The existence we were leading was making us as hard as nails. We had started out in the early morning, paddling fifteen miles, played a cricket match, and engaged in the various sports that were going forward. Now we were finishing up an eventful day with a fifteen-mile paddle home again.

But it took us a good deal longer going back than it did getting to Huntsville for the night was dark and we were not conversant with the windings of the river. It was full of little bays and backwaters, and we must have explored every one of them on that trip home. Daylight was breaking as we reached the shore, and when we arrived at the shanty we found that poor Mrs. Harston had spent the night in tears in the belief that we had all been drowned.

The house that Captain Harston proposed to build was to be quite an imposing structure. It was to be 20 feet by 40 feet and to be built entirely of pine logs. How he obtained those logs has already been alluded to. Preparations for the house raising took us many weeks, and we received help from many quarters.

The hewing of the timbers was placed in the hands of a man named William Rhamey,[1] and the actual building of the house was given to a carpenter of the name of Nicholas Schneider.[2] William Rhamey did his work beautifully. He was a wonderful axeman, and when he had finished, every log looked as if it had been planed. There was no trouble in obtaining carpenters, and builders seemed to be abound. Altogether, we had seven or eight men, including ourselves, engaged on the building. We had grown to be useful in various ways, and it was remarkable

George Harlow White, *Log House near Huntsville, 1875. Courtesy of the Toronto Public Library (TRL) Special Collections T16432.*

how soon we got accustomed to lifting heavy weights. Inside of six months we were all able to shoulder a hundred-weight of flour with ease, and to lift logs which at our first coming we would certainly have looked at askance.

There was lots of action while Nicholas Schneider had the super-intendency of affairs. There was not a lazy bone in his body, and he believed in making everyone work as hard as he did. Being quite a practical joker besides, he instilled variety into what would otherwise have been a monotonous task. We were all at some time or another victims of his playfulness. The chief butt of his jokes, however, was a man of the name of Humble Wiseman[3] and a morose individual called Robey.[4] Wiseman was a half-baked creature of whom everybody made fun. Robey was the mystery man of the countryside. He was apparently a quiet, inoffensive sort of being, always ready to help in whatever was going forward but as uncommunicative about himself as the proverbial oyster.

During the major part of the work Wiseman proved himself as an able assistant to Nicholas Schneider who was quite taken with his industry. But Nicholas Schneider, who was as open-minded as he could be, resented Robey's secretiveness. He used to open out to me on the subject. "That there George is a funny sort of feller," he said one day, "I tell him all about my missus and the kids to sorter draw him out but he'll never let on whether he's married or single, or if he has a father or mother or brother or sister – he kinder gets me rattled. I asked him only yesterday, 'George,' says I, 'has some gal give you the merry hee-haw or what in hell's wrong with you?' and he turns on me with them there sad-looking eyes of his'n and says to me, 'Bill,' says he, 'I ain't got father or mother or brother or sister – let's talk of suthin' else,' says he, and nary another word could I get out of him – he's a hell of a feller, that's what he is!"

Several months afterwards we were helping to frame a barn on the lot of a newcomer named Philip Bell,[5] and Robey was with us. In order to be near our work we took our blankets and cooking utensils, and ate, worked and slept in the open clearing. Robey and I shared a blanket together. With me, as with the others, he was always courteous, always obliging, but he never cracked a joke and never laughed. One morning he mysteriously vanished. We were living in a district where there were many vanishings, and nothing much was thought of the matter till some months later when it was again brought to our notice by a prominent article in one of the Toronto papers, telling of the hanging of a murderer who, after a long pursuit by detectives, had been discovered in Canada and hurried across the border. The description of the man tallied exactly with that of our whilom[6] friend Robey. In after days we learnt that it was indeed he who had expiated his crime on the scaffold.

Humble Wiseman, however, was of a totally different stamp. He was a bit too communicative and confidential. One morning he appeared with his face bandaged up, and William Rhamey asked him what was the matter. Wiseman had the peculiar faculty of making three or four sentences do the duty of one and he replied somewhat in this manner: "Say, William, I'm kinder thinkin' as how there's something wrong with this side of my face. It's all swelled up like, and I guess as how I must be havin' a spell of what folks calls the teethache." William Rhamey was a man of quick decision and few words. "Come over here, Humble," he said, "and let's see what's wrong with you." Wiseman, confiding soul, came at once, and William Rhamey bade him open his mouth to allow him to peer into the cavity. After a moment's examination, he said, "I can fix that for you, Humble, – lie down on the grass there and open your mouth, and keep it open." Wiseman stretched his form on the ground and did as he was told.

William Rhamey then produced a three-inch nail and a hammer. He bent the nail, and, applying it to the tooth at the part nearest the gum, gave it a sharp tap with the hammer. Away flew half the tooth and up jumped Wiseman with an unearthly yell. "Ye've killed me entirely," he cried, and caught up an adze and made after William Rhamey. We ran after him and held him, while the amateur dentist explained from a safe distance what a beautiful job he had nearly made of it. It took a little time for Wiseman's wrath to cool, but he got so far pacified at last as to allow William Rhamey to examine his mouth again. He felt the remains of the tooth and, finding it quite loose, prevailed on Wiseman to let him use a pair of pincers on it. "Hold him, boys," said William Rhamey, "I don't want him to come cavortin' around with that adze again." However, there was no need for restrictive measures. The root came away very easily and Wiseman was correspondingly grateful.

In the summer evenings while the mosquitoes were bad we did a good deal of still-hunting.[7] It was out of season, of course, and if caught we would have been fined, but it was a positive necessity to get a variation from the everlasting diet of fat pork that confronted us every day. We were not able yet to vie with the general run of the settlers, who seemed to look upon Chicago pork, copiously flavoured with molasses, as the greatest of delicacies.

Our still-hunting in summer took the form of paddling round the lake with a light. My first essay at it was with Garrett. He assured me that he knew exactly how to do it, and as he was a few years older than I, he naturally took it upon himself to act the part of guide, philosopher and friend.

In order to be thoroughly up-to-date in the matter of appliances, he had manufactured a rough circlet of birchbark and pinned inside it a piece of cardboard on which to put a candle. In order to throw the light forward, he had left the front of the circlet open. The contrivance worked beautifully. It was a pitch-black night when we started off on our hunt and the mosquitoes were dreadful. There was not a breath of wind. We were both armed to the teeth. Garrett sat in front with the circlet on his head and a belt of fifty cartridges round his waist. He held his rifle in his hands.

I was deputed to do the paddling, but I also had my rifle and a belt of cartridges. As Garrett very wisely remarked, it was just as well to have

James L. Weston, *Deer Hunting in Muskoka, Last Day of the Season*. In *Canadian Illustrated News*, February 1880. *Courtesy of the Library and Archives Canada, Special Collections CIN C-72779.*

too many cartridges rather than too few, for there was no knowing what we might meet on such an occasion. I think, although they are not noted as water animals, we had visions of encountering wild cats and wolves as well as the harmless creatures we were hunting.

With stilettos pushed through our belts and our faces smeared to a horrible hue with a mixture of tar and pork fat to fend off the mosquitoes, we must have looked formidable individuals to meet either in the daylight or the dark. It was an ideal night for the undertaking. Slowly and silently we made our way round the shores, the lantern casting a broad glow of light ahead of the canoe. We had been paddling for fully half an hour past headland and swamp and were beginning to wonder if we were going to have any luck, when all of a sudden there was a rush through the bushes about fifty yards ahead of us, followed by a mighty splash in the water. We were wildly excited. "There's a deer," we both exclaimed together. "Shut your mouth," hissed my companion tersely and firmly. "Shut your own," I replied as affably. "You were talking as much as I was."

Neither of us said any thing further at the time as we realized that talking and deer stalking don't go well together. But we felt sore. Slowly and quietly we crept on, and suddenly the deer loomed up in the light of the lantern. It was a beautiful buck.

Garrett was so excited when he saw it that he incontinently put his gun to his shoulder and fired. The report reverberated in a tremendous fashion round the lonely hills. The deer had been fascinated by the ghostly approach of the light, but there was nothing fascinating about a rifle shot, and with a few leaps through the water he was off into the woods. Garrett turned on me at once and told me in an acidulous tone that it was all my fault that he had missed the deer. "If you had only had the sense to keep the canoe still," he said, "nothing would have been easier than to have killed it." "If you hadn't been so infernally excited" I retorted, "the canoe wouldn't have rocked." We were bad friends for the rest of the night.

More as a forlorn hope than with any prospect of further sport, we made our way to the end of the lake with the idea of completing the circuit of its shores. After the noise of the shot we naturally concluded that every deer for miles around would be alarmed. But the unexpected happened. We had been paddling for a long time in moody silence and were on the verge of turning for home, when we again heard a loud splash in the water, this time much farther ahead of us.

Quietly and slowly we crept along the shore. When at last the light shone on the deer, it showed another beautiful buck standing with just its head and shoulders above the water. Foot by foot we came up to it, but Garrett never moved. We had approached to within twenty feet of it, and I was beginning to wonder when he was going to fire when, to my astonishment, I saw him put down the rifle and draw the dagger from his belt. As we approached, the deer had been wheeling round slowly till now it presented its hindquarters to our view. Its head was thrown back and it was gazing in a stupefied way at the light. Ten feet – five feet – three feet only separated us. I can see Garrett now, leaning forward – his right hand holds the gleaming dagger aloft – with the left he reaches for the tail and then – !!! Everything had happened so quickly that we were in the water before we realized it. Of course, as soon as the deer had felt something of a material character touching it, full consciousness asserted itself, and with a mighty kick it caught Garrett on the side of the head and sent him flying out of the canoe. I naturally followed in quick order, and the canoe capsized. We returned home dejected and deeply humiliated. Our rifles went to the bottom of the lake, and there they remained till the next morning, when we puddled around for them for quite three hours before we located them. Thus ended our first attempt at still-hunting.

Another of our hunting experiences had much the same ending. This was on a strictly legal occasion for it was during the hunting season. Two of us were keeping watch out on the lake when we heard the baying of the hounds, and shortly afterwards a large buck plunged into the water. We did not see it at first, and it was well on its way across the lake when we sighted it. I was in the bow of the canoe. We had two guns with us, double-barrelled breech-loaders.

It did not take us long to catch up to the deer, and then a happy thought struck my partner. "Look here, Frederick," he cried out, "don't shoot it, catch it by the tail and make it draw us home. It's easy enough to guide it." He continued, "I've done it often. All you have to do is to place your paddle first on one side of its head and then on the other and keep it in the straight path." The idea appealed to me as a good one, and I leaned over the end of the canoe and grabbed hold of the animal's tail. Things went beautifully for about ten yards and then, unguardedly, I raised the tail in order to obtain an easier position in the canoe. It never entered my head that if I raised its hind part its head would go under water. We were sent clean out of the canoe, and when we came to the surface, there was our hoped-for venison scurrying might and main down the lake. Our guns went to the bottom in about 200 feet of water and repose there still, in company with logging chains, bricks and various implements of husbandry, which at one time or another we were unfortunate enough to lose in our trips up and down the lake.

The raising bee for the house proved to be quite a large affair. Some of the most expert axemen in the vicinity had been asked to act as cornermen. They were needed to dovetail the logs and make them fit well and truly into each other. In order to make the occasion a really notable one, Captain Harston had ordered five gallons of whisky from Bracebridge. He had been told by an enterprising swain that no bee was really a success without it, and unfortunately he had believed him. Those who have assisted at raising bees do not need to be told that it is quite an undertaking to shove solid pine logs measuring forty feet, up an incline into position and that, as the building gains height, the difficulty in pushing up the logs increases in proportion. There was no lack of help. Almost at daybreak men began to arrive, some in canoes and others on foot, and drivers with teams were early on the scene. By eight a.m. the raising

Artist unknown, *Raising the Shanty,* in *Canadian Illustrated News,*
December 1879. *Courtesy of the Library and Archives Canada,*
Special Collections CIN C-72632.

began, and as the men warmed to the work, the logs went up apace. By
noon more than half the required height had been reached and we saw
with satisfaction our dreams of some day enjoying a comfortable habitation approaching realization.

The midday meal was a great function. There was no stint of victuals
and, it is almost needless to add, there was no appreciable stint on the
part of those who were partaking of them. Gourmandizing is not con-
fined to the rich. "I guess I'm crowded," I heard one worthy remark to
his mate as he rose and commenced to pick his teeth with the pocket
knife with which he had been cutting tobacco. The answering reply of
the other, to the effect that he had "had his bellyful too," showed clearly

that the wants of the inner man had not been neglected by either of them. After a reasonable period of rest the men got to work again and at about 3 p.m., Captain Harston, feeling elated at the way things were going, produced the whisky.

It was a fatal mistake. For, after the men had imbibed two or three times, they didn't care much how the logs went up and tried to outvie each other in shoving their end up quickest. The natural consequence followed. A log ran off a skidway when nearly planted on top and jarred the "bull" holding the other end so badly that it broke it. The huge timber came rushing down the skid, and the men made a wild break for safety, all, that is, save Tothill and myself. We were not well enough versed in the ethics, so to speak, of log-raising, to realize that on such occasions necessity knows no law. In the misguided notion that it was our bounden duty to try to stem the downward progress of the log, we stood our ground and endeavoured to stop it with our hands. The log came hurtling down, and in a moment we were caught by it and sent flying. We had a miraculous escape. Luckily there was a small stump which stood in the way of the log and stopped it when within an ace of pinning our bodies to the ground. I got out of the mess with a jammed thumb, and Tothill with a bruised shoulder. It was rather blighting to our pride to be told by the assembled crowd that we were a pair of blithering fools for not getting out of the way as they had done, and that it was plainly to be seen that God Almighty was tender with idiots. The accident gave Captain Harston so much concern that he promptly removed the keg, saying that he wanted to keep the balance for the dance in the evening.

The dance, which took place on flooring roughly laid down in the newly raised structure, was a corkscrew affair in more ways than one. The whisky boss got drunk and the fiddler got drunk. Mrs. Harston had vanished at the first signs of inebriation and, with her faithful friend Mrs. Smith to keep her company, remained in seclusion in the shanty at the top of the hill. But she had her share of excitement before she fled the scene. A big shantyman, florid of face and clad in resplendent raiment consisting of white cotton shirt open at the throat and breeches tucked into a pair of stockings with scarlet tassels, came up to her and said politely, "Come on, ma'am, let's be havin' a whirl around?" She had her whirl. In about two minutes she was so out of breath that she begged her partner to stop. He did so in the most obliging manner. He led her courteously to a seat and, by way of letting her know that she was not the only one who felt the heat, said, "It do be hot for sure – I'm sweatin' somethin' terrible myself, ma'am."

It was a highly demoralized crowd that wended its way homewards towards the small hours of the morning. Those who had to travel by canoe experienced difficulty in getting their bearings, owing to the mist, and we were surprised about 8 a.m. to hear shouts from somewhere in the enveloping haze on the water. In response to our cries eight or ten overnight wassailers beached their crafts on the shore and come up to the shanty. They had been paddling round in circles all night. They were given breakfast and entertained until such time as the mist cleared. There were several women among them, and cold enough the unfortunates had found the night air.

X

Local Dentistry

GARRETT HAD SPRAINED HIS ANKLE and was determined to go to Huntsville to have it attended to, so the day after the raising-bee Tothill paddled him down to the village. They had lots to tell when they returned. Tothill had been obliged to carry Garrett across the portages and had discovered that the shouldering of some 160 lbs. odd of live weight was a pretty formidable task to tackle.

The doctor or the druggist to whom he applied prescribed a Seidlitz powder[1] for the ankle and advised Garrett to offer up a prayer for a quick recovery. Garrett said he intended to present the Seidlitz powder to some institution of learning as an example of the wonderful progress of medical knowledge in the waning years of the nineteenth century.

A short time afterwards I was under the necessity of having a tooth pulled. The gentleman who operated on me informed me that he did not claim to be a dentist and only "jerked out teeth" to oblige his friends. He added that, if I was willing to take him as I found him, he would be pleased to do what he could to oblige me. As almost anything was preferable to the pain that I was suffering, I told him to go ahead. He thereupon placed me in an easy chair with castors and put an evil-looking pair of forceps in my mouth. "Hold on tight to the chair," he said, and I obeyed. "My word," he cried, as he commenced wheeling me round the room hanging on to my molar, "this is about the worst tooth I ever encountered – it seems to be about two inches long." He was a very powerful man, and it is needless to attempt to describe what I suffered. At last with one mighty jerk he extracted the tooth, and I nearly collapsed with the pain.

This episode must not be taken as a commentary on the capabilities of Muskoka practitioners in general. It is simply an example of what is liable to happen in any community when ways and means are in a primitive condition.

The purchasing of butter and eggs from the settlers was one of my regular duties, and I used to make long journeys through the woods to obtain these necessaries. On one of these periodic expeditions I was the victim of a strange incident. We had been used to getting most of our supplies from the cottage of a certain settler of the name of Sandy Hayes.[2] It was some distance away, but we were always sure of getting from his house a plentiful supply of such commodities as we needed.

The Hayes family consisted of himself and four or five children. The eldest of them, a girl, was perhaps seventeen years of age. I had paid several visits to the cottage and had got to know the family fairly well. It was rather a surprise to me, however, to see Sandy enter our room one Sunday morning for the purpose of paying a visit, for we were not intimate friends. The others had taken advantage of the beautiful morning and had gone to the lake for a bath, but I had preferred to remain in bed, and so Hayes and I had the whole place to ourselves.

The first I knew of his appearance was when the door slowly opened and I caught a glimpse of his frowsy, unkempt head as he leaned forward to see if anyone was in. "Come, in, Sandy," I said, "what's brought you here this morning so early?" But Sandy was a taciturn individual and vouchsafed never a word in reply. He slouched into the room and without more ado sat down on the edge of the bed and began to chew viciously at a straw. He was quite a picturesque specimen of humanity, owing to his general getup and commanding figure. He stood fully six feet high and with his red shirt, his trousers tucked into his boots, and a flaming tuft of carroty hair sticking upright through a hole in his greasy straw hat, he might have posed as a model for one of Garibaldi's warriors. He was evidently in a very serious mood; so I concluded to let him take his time. The minutes flew by, and still Sandy chewed and chewed and said nothing. I was just about on the point of again asking him what had brought him to our abode at that unconscionable hour when he brought his heavy fist down on my leg with a resounding smack and broke the silence by ejaculating "Say!" "Yes," I gasped out; but the poor man was again floored and could get no further. Then he began to whistle and after he had got through two or three bars of "Protestant Boys" started to perambulate round the room. This behaviour was beginning to get on my nerves and I jumped out of bed and started to put on a few things.

"You'll excuse me," I said, "but if you will have what you want to say figured out by the time I come back from my bath, I'll see what I can do to help you." This showed him that time was precious and that he had better unbosom himself. He stopped in his stride and burst out with another stentorian "Say!" "Yes," I again answered.

"Oh, hell," he cried in desperation, "what do you say to gettin' hitched up to our Maggie, hey?"

"What!" I roared.

He repeated the question, adding with quite forceful particularity, "She's a hell of a fine gal is Mag, and she do think a powerful pile of yous, so she do." The whole thing was so preposterous that, if it hadn't been for the earnest look in Sandy's face, I would have laughed. But I saw that the subject was much too serious for laughter.

One of the aphorisms which Mr. Yearley had imparted to me and for which I now inwardly thanked him was to "keep a stiff upper lip." The value of those homely words came home to me then. I informed him in the strongest terms at my command that, however estimable a young woman Maggie might be, it was a sheer impossibility for me to entertain any thought of marrying. At the same time I thanked him for his kindly desire to add me to the family but that he would have to leave it out of the question entirely.

Sandy was a very disappointed man. "Aoin't that too bad!" he murmured. He scratched his head and drew his hand across his nose in a meditative way and, then, with the light of triumph breaking over his gnarled features, he gave me a hearty slap across the shoulders and roared out, "My God, mister, there ain't nuthin' mean about me: take her, and be damned if I don't throw in a caow!!" But I was proof against such blandishments, and poor Sandy departed disconsolately for home. I told Captain and Mrs. Harston of my little experience and the upshot of it was that thereafter I was enjoined to buy no more butter and eggs at the Hayes' homestead.

XI

Purchasing Cattle and Sheep

Mrs. Harston was most punctilious in the matter of making us obey the laws current in polite society. Although we were in the depths of the woods, she always insisted that we should come to our meals properly apparelled. It was a hot day indeed when she relaxed so far as to say that we could doff our coats and eat in our shirt sleeves. I think that we all had cause to bless her for keeping us well-regulated in our habits. If it hadn't been for that, we should soon have grown careless. But it was impossible for us to live amid such surroundings without being infected to a certain extent with some of the virus. Often we had visits from settlers who of course took potluck with us and, as their ways were not our ways, Mrs. Harston received very many jolts in her notions of propriety and deportment. But such occasions were rare, so far as she was concerned, for after a time when the house was built, she was enabled to enjoy her meals in private when certain visitors were expected.

The days of autumn were glorious. There were no flies to pester one and a good night's rest could be enjoyed in full measure. It was late in October when Captain Harston surprised us by stating that he was going to purchase some cattle. He had no barn to put them in, but he said cows were hardy animals and could live comfortably in the woods near the shanty. In due course the animals were purchased, and I was deputed to accompany Garrett to drive them in from Bracebridge. It was a thirty-three mile tramp, and we both had our fill of it by the time we finished. The purchase consisted of five head of cattle and six sheep. There were two cows, two steers and a yearling heifer, five ewes and a ram. We took two days and a half making the journey from Bracebridge, and found that cattle and sheep are feckless creatures to drive. Counting chases through the woods and swamps when the brutes broke loose and raced backward over the road, we must have at least doubled our mileage. At the end of the first day's tramp, we drove the animals into a settler's yard and put up with him for the night. But we got no rest owing to the fact that the lady of the house had hit upon an ingenious method of saving the cost of blankets by sewing paper between the sheets. Garrett and I had to bunk together, and whenever either of us moved, the paper set up a dreadful crackling. Garrett's language was painfully free. He told me that I was the most restless being on earth, and together we made such a commotion that the farmer, evidently a stickler for sober words, roared out to us from the next room that, if he had had any suspicion that we "was two boys so far removed from Heaven," he would have refused to take us in.

When we at last reached home, we were worn out morally, physically and mentally; and it was with thankful hearts that we sat down to the sumptuous repast that had been prepared for us. But on that occasion, Mrs. Harston was the recipient of a bad shock, due to the crude bearing and manners of a visitor who had arrived at the house just as we were going to regale ourselves. The event lingers in my memory, for it was the first time that I had ever sat at table with anyone who came to a meal in his "stockinged feet."

Matters progressed quietly for the major part of the repast, as we were all so hungry that we didn't give ourselves time to talk. But when our hunger had been fairly satisfied, our visitor's tongue found full play. He waxed particularly eloquent on the character of a certain gentleman living a few miles away, who, he remarked smilingly to Mrs. Harston, "is that mean, ma'am, that he'd skin a louse for the hide and the fat." The dear lady was so discomfited at his vulgarity that she sat and stared in stony horror at the perpetrator.

We inquired of our guest if he knew anything of a reverend gentleman who came to us at intervals to hold service, and he said he knew him very well indeed and that he had several young English "gaffers" living with him as pupils. We learnt that he was one of the pioneer clergy of the district and had done strenuous work. Sometimes his methods were startling, for he was decidedly eccentric.

On one occasion he paid a visit to Toronto to preach on behalf of his mission at one of the fashionable churches. He was an eloquent man, and there was a crowded congregation to hear him. He was in the middle of a most edifying discourse when he suddenly stopped and announced that he had forgotten one very important matter – "If any of my dear friends here present," he said, "happens to be the possessor of fine, healthy turkeys, I would esteem it a kindly act if he or she would present me with four. I need two for breeding purposes and two for the spit. Now let us return to the subject of my discourse."

In our hunting experiences we were not so far removed from the arm of the law as to be immune from trouble. On one occasion a man from Port Vernon laid an information against us which resulted in Captain Harston being hauled before a Justice of the Peace in Huntsville and fined.

This incensed us, and we longed for a chance of getting even with the individual who had got us into difficulties. The opportunity came when he appeared at our local store one day for the purpose of making purchases. He was a giant in stature and individually would have been a match for any of us. Captain Harston, Bell and I happened to be at the store when he arrived, and Bell no sooner saw him than he made a rush for him. As they were wrestling in the middle of the floor, Captain Harston and I took a hand and, grabbing him by the arms and legs, we carried him down to the lakeshore and waded out far enough to give him a good sound ducking. It didn't matter much to us if we got wet ourselves. We were used to water. The informer wasn't. Four separate times we hoisted him up and flopped him in again, and then we let him go. He left us, breathing threatenings and slaughter. When we came to think it over in the cool of the evening, we realized that we had done a very foolish and cowardly thing.

Two days afterwards Captain Harston had business to transact at Port Vernon where Issachar,[1] the man referred to, had his habitation, and he deputed me to attend to it. I started off in my canoe courageously enough but didn't feel the least bit exhilarated over the trip. I made a mental resolve that if I saw Issachar anywhere within hail I would not thrust myself in an obtrusive manner on his notice. He was no friend of mine, and I was never one of those fellows who aspire to be in the limelight. I had beached the canoe and was just preparing to make a move to the store when I looked up and saw the bulky form of the enemy, not fifteen yards away, walking towards me. I won't say that I felt dejected at the sight, but I do think I would have been a lot more jubilant if I hadn't encountered him. He saw me at about the same time, and we simply stared at each other. Feeling that I must say something to break the awkwardness of the situation, I managed to stammer out "Good day," as I was passing him, accompanied by as cheerful a grin as I could conjure up. He didn't reply but still stood and stared at me. I said to myself in a hopeless way, "Bright world, farewell! I see my finish." Then I stepped forward, and he jerked me round roughly by the shoulder.

"Say, young feller," he said, "where in hell do yous think you're goin'?" Then I tried to be funny. I replied in a jaunty way that I hadn't brought any compass with me but thought that without any undue strain on my intellect I might be able to make my way to the store. I finished up with a ghastly attempt at a jovial "Ha! Ha!" At this, to my surprise, he started to smile and, once more grabbing me by the shoulder, he cried, "My God! damned if you aint got grit in you. I had half a mind to throw yer into the drink when I seen yer first, but you ain't the one I'm after, that there Harston is the man as I wants to get, and, my God, when I gets him he'll know something's struck him." Then he loosened his hold and walked away. I always had a kind of friendly feeling for that individual after that. When I returned I recounted what had happened, to the great gloom of Captain Harston. But the informer never bothered us, although we often saw him, and he never set foot on our stamping ground again. This was the only time that we had any clash with the authorities.

We were always unalterably opposed to slaughtering for the mere sake of killing. It was no uncommon thing for parties of hunters in those days to kill from twenty to twenty-five deer in a fortnight. This was sheer slaughter. But even this was not as bad as what some fiends were capable of, in hunting them through the winter and leaving them to rot. It is one thing to kill for food and a totally different thing to kill for the lust of killing.

Bell and I, on one of our hunting excursions, arrived at a shanty some seven miles away from home. The first snow had fallen, and the ice was just forming on the lake when we decided to make our first attempt to get a deer on the runways. We were acquainted with the owner of the shack, a very cheerful, rough type of Irishman named Peters.[2] His shanty was composed of one large room which did duty as a sleeping room, a parlour and kitchen.

The family consisted of Peters, his wife, and two boys of perhaps ten and twelve years of age. We had been in the woods all day and had met with no luck, and Peters very kindly invited us to take potluck with the family and wait till morning. We were glad to accept as we were tired out and it was a long walk home.

There were two large beds in the room, standing foot to foot and it was arranged that Peters, his wife, and the youngsters should climb into one, and that Bell and I should occupy the other. A blanket was very thoughtfully slung on a string between the beds so as to give it a respectable appearance and, to make things more seemly, Peters asked us as a special favour to look out of the window whilst his wife undressed. When she had accomplished this, Peters turned the lamp out, and in the darkness Bell and I divested ourselves of our outer garments and turned into the other bed. About the middle of the night there was an outcry from Mrs. Peters. Bell had put his feet through the blanket and had happened to touch Mrs. Peters' foot in a tender part. This incident caused Peters to laugh so heartily that he was treated to a short but highly elevating Caudle lecture[3] by Mrs. Peters. Some very colourful language was used by that good lady. She wanted her husband to understand that she wasn't used to having her feet tickled by other people, let alone a strange man, and that if he saw any fun in it she didn't, etc., etc. The quiet fell again on the scene. In the morning we bade farewell to the Peters family and departed for home.

In order to save four miles of a walk, we elected to try our luck across the narrows of the lake. At that particular spot it was about 150 yards wide. Ice had begun to form two days before, and we were both carrying double-barreled shotguns weighing about ten pounds apiece. Being the lighter of the two I went first, Bell following about five yards behind. We had an exciting time of it. At every step we took, the ice waved ominously, and the further we got from the shore the more distant the opposite bank seemed to be. We were stepping gingerly and slowly, and were just beginning to congratulate ourselves that we would get across safely when there was a crack and a splash. I looked round to see poor Bell with his head and shoulders just showing above the ice. He had managed to balance his gun across his shoulders and was holding himself up by his elbows. I gazed at him of a moment in horror, for at any attempt he made to extricate himself he became more involved. "Hold on," I cried, "don't struggle."

He stopped, and I threw down my gun and crept towards him as well as I could, on my stomach. Coming as close as was possible, I reached out my hand to him, and after two or three ineffectual efforts he managed to get out on to the firm ice. It was freezing hard, and he was almost numb with his immersion. There was nothing for it but to exercise all the caution we could and go on. I had reached for his gun before attempting to help him and had slid it across the ice towards my own. Keeping well in advance, I started off, and the ice seemed to get firmer at every step. Bell followed, his teeth clacking like castanets. "I say, Frederick," he called out to me. "I wouldn't want to test the temperature of that water again for ten thousand pounds." He had no sooner said the words than there was a crack and a splash, and unfortunate chap was in again. The same process had to be gone through once more, luckily with happy results, but as soon as he was landed on firm ice, I took both guns.

By my carrying the extra weight we got safely across, but ere we reached the shore Bell's clothing was as stiff as a board and we started off on a dead run for home. Once there we got him safely in bed, administered hot cloths to his feet and hot drinks to his inside, and were glad to hear from him again in the course of an hour or two that he felt quite himself again.

One of the things that struck us as remarkable was the lack of interest which the average farmer evinced in the affairs of the great world outside. Here and there were to be found men who showed a desire to be in touch with world happenings and went so far as to subscribe to a weekly paper. They were to be seen any Sunday in the summer months reading the news with avidity, seated on their doorsteps, or in the winter, warming their feet under the kitchen stove, trying to decipher the print by the light of the one miserable oil lamp in the room. But such men were few and far between. The majority of the settlers struck us as being hopelessly handicapped for taking any intellectual joy out of life. Their idea of what the world afforded in the way of relaxation consisted of sitting with their pipes in their mouths, gazing out at the landscape or in idly whittling at a stick for hours. There were very few illiterates in the district, but men simply would not lend their minds to such an occupation as reading when the day offered them the chance of sitting down and doing nothing. Sunday observance was fairly rigidly adhered to, a great deal better, in fact, than in many districts nearer to civilization.

It was so hard to get to a regular church service that when the opportunity arose of hearing a clergyman or a minister of any of the denominations, people would travel miles to be present. I have known whole families to turn out for a ten mile drive over execrable roads, and

Christ Church of Ilfracombe, shown circa early 1900s, was built on Aemilius Baldwin's property. The first church was made of logs. *Courtesy of Elsie Bennett.*

men and women to break down, listening to words to which their ears had been strangers for years. When our own clergyman came as a resident minister, people flocked from far and near to hear him, with the exception of the Roman Catholics, who had a regular service from their own priest, and some misguided individuals who preferred to be bawled at by a man who professed to be a descendant of John the Baptist and immersed adherents in a muddy little stream near his dwelling. His knowledge of natural science was so limited that he believed the earth to be flat.

There were two local preachers who aspired to do some spiritual work. Their value to the community, however, was shorn of much value by the fact that one was discovered to be a convicted thief, while the other was living with an affinity who was not his wife.

But of the regularly ordained ministers who laboured in the district in those early days, nothing too complimentary can be said. They visited and preached in true earnestness. Many a strange tale could have been unfolded by them concerning the lives of those among whom they worked. They had their own share of trouble and danger in their constant travels through that wilderness. Chances of infection from the sick was one of them; exposure to the elements was another. I am referring now to clergymen of the Anglican denomination, but the same tale could have been told of members of all the others.

81

I call to mind, in grateful memory, the Rev. William Crompton[4] of Aspdin to whom reference has already been made, the Rev. Lawrence Sinclair, the Rev. William Chowne of Rosseau, the Venerable Archdeacon Gilmour and Canon Llwyd of Huntsville. Of these the Rev. Lawrence Sinclair is today the sole survivor.

As an instance of the dangers the clergy have to face I call to mind one special incident. A clergyman, whose peripatetic propensities were widely known throughout the district, was called to the cottage of a settler whose child was ill with diphtheria. During dinnertime the boy was taken with a fit of coughing. The mother left the table, went to the cot of the little one and, putting a finger down his throat, cleared the passage, and then returned to the table and handed the clergyman a piece of bread with her unwashed hands. The recital of this may be nauseating to the reader but it affords a very good picture of a certain aspect of life in the woods.

The bishops were just as fine men as the ordinary clergy. Bishop Fauquier was a most saintly character. He was not famous for his eloquence in the pulpit, but he was beloved by all for his great-heartedness and honoured for his devotion to his duty.

At his death, Bishop Sullivan was appointed to the See of Algoma and proved to be a man of action. Under his fostering care the diocese did not languish. One of the most eloquent preachers in the Canadian church, he carried his message far and wide and laboured in England as well as in various sections of Canada to obtain help for his diocese. He was a most lovable man whose Irish wit made him acceptable everywhere.

About the living one cannot speak as unreservedly as of the dead, but Archbishop Thorneloe is known and revered throughout the length and breadth of Canada. For many years he laboured unceasingly, and today, although he has now retired, there is no clergyman held in greater love and esteem by his fellowmen.

XII

The First Winter

OUR FIRST WINTER WAS A terrible one. We had revelled in the days of autumn and had watched with delight the leaves turning to the glorious colours of the fall. No one, unless having already witnessed the spectacle, can realize the surpassing beauty of a backwoods autumn, when the forest is reflected in an absolutely placid body of water. The colouring is so gorgeous that no painter could possibly do such a scene justice. Every leaf, every limb is reflected so clearly that one is treated to a double store of enchanting pictures. Poets and prose writers have extolled the scenic beauties of various countries, but I doubt if there is any spectacle so serenely lovely as that presented to the visitor who happens to be in the Muskoka region on a calm October day.

But the autumn had passed and the leaves had been swept from the trees, and biting winds and flurries of snow warned us that we must bestir ourselves to provide for the cold days to come. We had chopped our firewood and piled it in great heaps outside the shanty door and had stuffed up as many crannies as possible in our dwelling place, and nothing remained now but to await their advent.

It would be hard to say, when the winter did come, whether we enjoyed it or abhorred it. There were days when we regarded ourselves as quite on a par with any Arctic explorer who ever lived, for the conditions seemed to us to be fully as severe as any that could be encountered.

We discovered that the shanty, notwithstanding all our efforts, was not built for keeping out the frost for, as soon as the fire went out in the stove, the temperature was bleak enough to suit a polar bear. The water would freeze solidly in the ewers[1] and pails, and butter and meat be frozen so hard that an axe had to be brought into play to cut off such portions as were required. It was quite a common occurrence to have our cheeks and ears and noses frozen, and it was a very ordinary sight to observe one or other of us rubbing his physiognomy with snow in order to take the frost out.

At night when the temperature was low the woods were noisy. There would be a constant repetition of sounds like rifle shots, interspersed with prolonged roars as the frost rent some stout old tree or the imprisoned air made an opening for itself in the fettering ice. Usually when it was very cold there was an absolute stillness of the atmosphere, and on a moonlight night, with the stars shining and the snow-clad trees glittering in their spotless robes, the scene was weirdly fascinating. We learned then the true inwardness of the poet's reference to the "pitiless moon" when we saw it in its cold and merciless serenity lighting up the landscape.

We got a full taste of winter's asperities when it was necessary to go on a journey. With the mercury down to 30 or 40 below zero [Fahrenheit], it was anything but a treat to start off on a heavy sleigh behind a span of oxen. The unfortunate driver either had to snuggle up as best he could under the coverings he had brought or march behind the sleigh in order to keep from freezing. If it happened to be a windy day, the blast would almost petrify one. If thermos bottles had been in existence then, the lot of the settlers would have been materially alleviated. But such comforts were not for us. We had to be content with waiting till we reached a wayside tavern where we could obtain a drink of steaming tea or coffee or any strong liquid that could be obtained.

But however severe we may have found the winter, we were living in clover compared with some of our neighbours. Our troubles were nothing compared with theirs for there were cases of misery which almost passed belief.

On one of the coldest days of that terribly cold winter the wife of a settler named Hanson Quinn[2] gave birth to a child. The couple lived in a wretched, ramshackle dwelling hidden in the woods. Poverty in its most hideous form had settled on them, and there was not a bite to eat in the house. There was hardly any furniture in the place, and the aperture that had been cut in the log walls for a windowsash was simply covered with an old cloth. There was a heavy blizzard raging and the covering had been loosened from the nails, leaving half the opening bare for a clear sweep of the gale into the room. The snow came in heavy gusts and was piled on the floor in little heaps. Under these desperate conditions the little child was ushered into the world by the friendly hands of a settler's wife living close by. Captain Harston had heard of the need of the pair and had sent me with some creature comforts to relieve their immediate necessities, and this was the state of affairs that confronted me on my arrival. But the child lived, and the woman lived, and when I last had the pleasure of seeing them, several years later, the forlorn little boy had grown into a strapping youth, and the mother was a hale, happy woman, for her husband had surmounted his early difficulties and done well for his family.

Strangely enough Captain Harston had not provided a stable for his cattle. Perhaps he believed that they were hardy enough to withstand the rigours of the climate. To do him justice he had not had any prior experiences of a Muskoka winter, but his knowledge of Canada should have been sufficient to teach him that there are very few parts east of the great plains where cattle can be left to roam unsheltered and uncared for. Beyond setting up a small lean-to, open to the south, where the beasts might get some cover from the storms, nothing was done, and no feed was obtained for them. The thermometer went down several times to forty degrees below zero and once or twice to several degrees below that.

Perched on top of the small precipice where the wind had a clean sweep from the North Pole, it can be imagined that we suffered, but our sufferings, severe though they were, were nothing compared with those that the unfortunate beasts must have endured. I think all the sheep died that winter and also three of the cattle. The others emerged so emaciated that they were never fit for anything afterwards. Their feed during the winter months had been hemlock boughs with an occasional sleighload of hay which we were able at rare intervals to obtain at exorbitant rates from one or other of the settlers.

One of my liveliest recollections is of the everlasting tramp, tramp, tramp of the cattle as they perambulated through the livelong nights, around and around the shanty. As for ourselves, we were cold enough, Heaven knows, and many and many a night we crawled into bed with everything on that we had worn during the day, with the addition of greatcoats and comforters round our necks and toques over our heads. Even with such protection as this, Garrett got his nose frozen in bed. He belonged to the cult that affects to find enjoyment in baring one's chest to the breeze, no matter how cold that breeze may be. "Fresh air, my boy, fresh air's the thing," he would often remark. But he found he could get too much of it on occasion. He made a few remarks the following morning on the iniquity of bamboozling people into coming to such a country, which were frank and free, and caused great umbrage to Captain Harston.

XIII

Winter Woodsman

It was mentioned in a former chapter that arrangements had been made that we should take up free grants of land round the lake as soon as we had completed our novitiate. All had agreed that it would be nice to be together and form one colony. Captain Harston, in his grandiloquent way, had told us how pleasant it would be to have a little settlement, with his house as the parent, so to speak, of the others. "The day is surely coming," he cried, "when I shall be proud to boast that I have been the means of forming such a colony in the district." Captain Harston always was an optimist. I think Dr. Coue[1] would have found an ardent supporter in him if he had lived at an earlier day.

As there was nothing to do during the winter but work in the woods, we passed part of the time in chopping on Captain Harston's place and part in chopping on our own. It was easy enough to get to our holdings when the lake was frozen, but it was not so easy to get at the timber to chop it down. Muskoka is a great country for snow. In some years it will lie as deep as four feet on the level. It can be seen, therefore, that the task of scooping out standing places in order to be able to chop trees down was not an easy one. All of us had become more or less versed in the use of an axe; we had had plenty of chances to learn. But to the best of axemen there come times when, however expert he may be, the axe may glance off a knot or a twig and place him out of business for a time. There are many troubles that beset him in felling the timber. The woods could tell many a tragic tale of lives lost in this occupation. We had our fair share of narrow escapes. At one time Tothill was engaged in felling a black birch. He cut it so as to bring down a large snag in its flight, but the snag unfortunately held firm and the birch tree came rushing back

F.B. Schell and J. Hogan, *Lumbermen's Camp.* This picture appeared in *Picturesque Canada*, Vol. I, 1882. *Courtesy of the Library and Archives Canada, Special Collections C-005082*

through the air on him. He had only just time to jump clear when it whizzed past him and buried its butt in the snow. A man was killed on an adjacent clearing by a tree falling on him and, in another case, a poor fellow who was chopping by himself was pinned to the ground by a branch piercing his shirt and nailing him down. He was held prisoner there for the best part of a day and night until a search party found him. Luckily for him the weather had turned warm and he came out of the trouble uninjured and unfrozen.

It was too far for us to walk home to our dinners, so we used to start off to work with small tin pails, filled with a generous amount of pie and meat sandwiches tied up in paper. By dinner time everything had frozen solid and, as we couldn't very well light fires in the snow, we simply ate the victuals as they were and washed down everything with water obtained from a hole cut in the ice. We soon got used to these conditions. What we did not get used to was having to work all day in wet socks and moccasins. It often happened that the days would be warm and the snow would soak us through and through. We infinitely preferred the cold days to the warm ones.

Generally we worked in couples, but it sometimes happened that each one went to his own clearing to chop by himself. On one such occasion I managed to gash my foot pretty badly and, knowing nothing about the principle of the tourniquet, started for home with the blood streaming from the wound. It was a mile's walk down the lake, and at every step a great splash of blood marked my route homewards. I just managed to reach the shanty and fell in a dead faint on the doorstep. Whisky and a bandage soon put me on the road to recovery, and in a few days I was able to get going again.

We used to hold many confabulations concerning our future, for we had come to the conclusion that there were no fortunes to be made in the district. But Garrett declared that he liked the country so much that he was going to build a shanty on his own place as early as possible in the spring, and Mr. Baldwin also announced his determination to do the same thing. They both hoped that the prospect would brighten when the railway came through Hoodstown.[2]

We went to several parties given by the neighbours round about and also made warm friends amongst them. I hold in affectionate remembrance more than one family from whom we received unstinted hospitality and unvarying kindness. Among these were Mr. and Mrs. Malkin[3] who lived on the north shore of Fox Lake and who had a family of six sons. They were English people and had been settled in the district for some years. They were amongst the earliest of those who had come to open up the country. Typically English in all their ways, they were as honest as the day and had brought up their sons to be as honest as themselves. It was a treat to meet such people, and we were often down at their farm. There were settlers living on the shores of Lake Vernon too, who had come out with the Malkins, of the name Tipper,[4] and others of the name Mann, from whom we received the greatest hospitality and kindness. Such families as these gave a distinct tone to the neighbourhood and helped in more ways than one to raise the ideals of the community.

We had other enjoyments also in the way of occasional dances, but after our first season's experience we elected to cut them out from our future pleasures. We felt that we were not well enough up in the *convenances* of society to appreciate them fully. At the first dance we attended there was quite a large gathering. The occasion was a house-warming given by a settler named Overhand[5] who had made some money in river driving and had just been married. There was an air of insouciance about the gentlemen which showed they had all been to many such functions before; as for the ladies, they entered wholeheartedly into every dance that was announced. The fiddler was the same young man who had been overcome at our own dance, but there was no chance of his repeating his eccentricities as there was no whisky on the premises. Our host said he had found that it took him all his time to keep from making a fool of himself when he was sober and his wife said that she quite agreed with him.

The party proved to be gay enough without any whisky and nearly ended in the undoing of poor Tothill as his lack of gallantry towards one of the ladies almost created a riot. We had had a merry time in all the hops and jumps and eccentric movements of the square dances, and things were going with a swing when the announcer called for partners for "Kiss her on the Floor." Tothill and I looked at each other in astonishment. We had heard of "Kiss in the Ring" at country picnics and fairs in England but this was something that mystified us both. We were not left long in doubt, however, as two girls came up to us and told us that they were going to take us for their partners. My young lady was a pretty damsel, and I was quite pleased. Tothill was disconsolate, however, as the lady who had chosen him was easily the ugliest girl in the room. It was a very pleasing dance, and there was an air of Arcadian freshness about it which proved very alluring. It seemed to savour of the days of the Maypole.[6]

The men seated themselves on benches and chairs about the room and the lassies ambled around, two and two, singing a snatch of a rude refrain, at the end of which they delicately spread kerchiefs on the floor for the men to kneel on. Then they knelt down themselves and kissed their partners, not one of your simpering, toying kisses, but a good healthy smack that could be heard everywhere and wasn't ashamed of itself. Afterwards the men took their turn and the same procedure was followed.

Tothill claimed to be absolutely disgusted. He had borne the first chaste salute in silence, hoping that he would have a chance when his turn came of choosing whom he wanted, but it was not to be. He found that each swain had his own lady-love already picked and, when he attempted to force his way to another damsel, he was thrust rudely aside by her admirer with the remark that he had better keep to his own gal if he wanted to escape trouble.

But Tothill was determined not to go through the ordeal again and, when he was at last brought to the presence of his waiting lady, he told her flatly that he didn't want to dance with her. No lady could stand such an affront as that, and she was about to open out on Tothill with some vituperative artillery when a shantyman standing close by who had over-heard the conversation stepped up and tapped him on the shoulder.

"Say, young feller," he said, "where was you brung up? That gal's my sister, and if yer don't fetch around with her for a spell I'll knock some daylight into yer, SEE?" Tothill was not devoid of courage, but he realized that he was in the wrong and, turning from the man with a laugh, he said to the damsel, "Oh well, come along then, let's have the agony over as soon as possible." The young lady evidently did not know what the word implied, and was all smiles in a moment. Talking about it after-wards, Tothill averred that it was about the rottenest evening he had ever spent. Looked at from his point of view it probably was.

Being young, and anxious to see as much of the various phases of life as possible, we took advantage of every opportunity that came our way; so when word was brought to us that there was to be a dance at the house of a German named Geisler,[7] Tothill, notwithstanding his former experience, asked me to go with him. We had been told that it was one of those affairs to which everybody was welcome, and that it was to be in the nature of a surprise party. All we had to do was to bring some provisions along and add them to the general stock for the evening. We made a raid, therefore, on Mrs. Harston's larder and started off equipped with one or two pies and some hard-boiled eggs. On our arrival we found about forty people present and noticed by the antics of some of the gen-tlemen that liquid refreshments had not been forgotten.

Mr. and Mrs. Geisler had three or four daughters, all very fine-look-ing girls, just the kind to be worthy helpmates to industrious farmers. They had taken part in all the hard work of clearing their land and had chopped, logged and fenced it, there being no sons to help in the labour. The results of their toil showed itself in a really fine farm, and they were now enjoying the full benefits of their labours with their father and mother.

There was nothing wrong with the family, and it was not their fault that the party was not a success. But trouble began with a fight between two youths, both of whom were enamoured of one of the daughters. Both wanted the same dance and neither would give way to the other. Mrs. Geisler "cut the Gordian knot"[8] of this difficulty most effectively by seizing hold of a heavy walking stick belonging to her husband and hitting the noisier and more insistent of the youths over the head. It was a sturdy blow. He dropped, half-stunned, on the floor and had to be car-ried out to recover on the grass.

The second trouble, and one which put an end to the evening's festivities, was the sudden collapse of the floor during the progress of a square dance. The eldest daughter was responsible for this. She was a very stout female, and every time she obeyed the order to "balance" she did it with the force of a piledriver. She got so worked up in the excitement of the dance that she jumped about like a two-year-old. The frail joists could not stand the strain and gave way, precipitating several unfortunates into the cellar.

The accident was not as serious as it may sound, for the cellar happened to be a very shallow excavation not more than five feet deep. But a ludicrous spectacle was presented of Miss Mary Geisler and the others standing with only their heads and shoulders above the floor, with most bewildered looks on their faces.

The chief damage, beyond the breaking-in of the flooring, was discovered to have been done to a crock of butter, into which the lady's foot had been inserted in her fall. This mishap appeared to be of far greater importance in the eyes of Mrs. Geisler than any possible injury that might have happened to the guests. She was full of indignation and upbraided her daughter in unmeasured terms for not choosing a better place to plant her feet. We went to no more dances after these experiences.

While visiting the district in after days, I made inquires concerning some of my early friends. I asked how the Geisler family had progressed, and learned, much to my pleasure, that they had done well and that the daughters, excepting one, had married happily. The one that had remained single was still living at the old homestead, with an adopted child as her solace and companion. The father and the mother had long since passed away. Only two or three years later, I read in a Toronto paper that Miss Caroline Geisler and the child whom she had adopted had both been killed by the fall of a tree as they were driving in a buggy along the Government Road.

While on the same trip, I paid a visit to the home of my old friend, Peters. I was greeted very warmly by Mrs. Peters and, on inquiring after her husband was told the sad news of his death.

"Why!" she ejaculated, "John's dead." On my expressing my sorrow, she gave me a full account of his illness and the steps she had taken to doctor him. "He got cancer in the heel," she said. "I did all I could to help him, but it weren't no good. Old Mr. Fraser[9] from the seventh line done his very best for him. He got a bunch of sarsaparill[10] in the woods and boiled it and made him drink it, for he said as how the first thing to do was to put his blood in good order. He knows a powerful sight more than them there city doctors does. 'What's the use of payin' them for comin' miles upon miles and chargin' accordin?' he says. 'When you can git me for a quarter of the price,' he says; and thinks I, he ain't very far astray. 'A penny saved is a penny gained,' he says. But it warnt no good. I guess the pizen had got in his symptoms, as they says, and nuthin' we could do was any good for him. I must ha' used four or five tins of hoof ointment on him makin' poultices for him, but there," she finished with her eyes turned heavenward and resigned look on her features, "Him, as the Lord don't want to stop He fetches away, as the sayin' is."

XIV

The Second Year

The following year brought many changes.

At the earliest opportunity Mr. Baldwin went off to the cottage he had built at the foot of the lake, and Garrett departed to his neat little bungalow on the eastern shore. But we still saw them every day, for whenever there was any need of help we joined forces.

Captain Harston had great projects for that year. First of all there was the house to be finished and rendered fit for habitation. Then there were the barn and stable to be built and a church to be erected. With commendable energy he had entered into negotiations with a St. Augustine's graduate and had secured his services for our new parish. The SPCK[1] with their usual generosity gave us a grant to help towards his salary.

The twelve months had transformed Tothill and myself from inexperienced boys into fairly strong and expert woodmen, but we were as far as possible from knowing anything about farming or raising stock. Yet the glamour of woodland life was still strong upon us, and we exulted in the knowledge that in the course of two years we would be our own masters and under the thumb of no man. We forgot that one essential of being one's own master was to have enough of this world's goods to be able to live independently.

In the course of the summer we were able to bid farewell to the shanties that had housed us so long, and descended to the quite commodious structure in the flat below. There had been many a trip to Huntsville for the necessary furniture, part of which had been brought up by ox team in the winter and part on the rafts of lumber which we had floated down the lakes and rivers.

When the building was ready for occupation there was a housewarming, to which many came, and it was considered so important an occasion that one of the Bracebridge papers whose representative happened to be in the vicinity at the time, published a glowing account of the festivities. A somewhat minute inventory of the furnishings was given. "Lounges, sofa, and a grand-piano, whose thorough bass resounds sweetly with the treble over the placid waters of the lake of a summer's evening." The author of this literary gem was a Mr. Alexander Begg[2] who, when he was not engaged in his gristmill at Beggsborough[3] (now the thriving village of Sprucedale[4]), employed his leisure moments in collecting items of fashionable news for one of the Bracebridge papers. Captain Harston certainly endeavoured to live up to his agreement to provide a comfortable house for his pupils. All the appurtenances were there, but the magician's wand, capable of bringing into material existence fine fields and fat cattle, was lacking.

The rafting of the lumber for the house had proved an interesting but heavy task. Generally it was left to Tothill and myself to attend to this task, but on occasion all hands took part in it. Our mode of procedure was to paddle in the early morning to Huntsville, to the spot where our lumber had been delivered from the mill at a specified place on the riverbank. The making of the raft was an easy matter as it simply consisted in piling the boards crossways till they lay six or seven deep. The suction kept them together as if they had been glued. But it was a very slow process to paddle such an unwieldy bulk up a big lake. The raft had always to be built in a different shape for going up the narrow river, and we had to pull the whole thing apart twice in order to get the lumber across the portages.

It was the wettest sort of work. The boards were drawn across the portages by the oxen by means of a drawboy, a contrivance fashioned out of the crotch of a tree, and with a crosspiece nailed to it to place the ends of the boards on. The logging chain would be drawn round these, and then the cattle pulled them across. It usually took us five or six days getting a raft up from Huntsville, and there was more than one thankful heart when the last load was deposited on the landing at Captain Harston's farm. We used to meet shantymen many a time on these trips and came to be very friendly with them. We found them to be fine fellows and willing to take all the enjoyment they could out of life. Men of wonderful strength and vigour they were, capable of performing marvels on the logs. In trying to emulate their feats in spinning them over and over in the water and in riding them down the rivers we got many a ducking. They

Early photograph of lumbermen on a raft in the Muskoka area. *Courtesy of Fred Hopcraft.*

used to invite us sometimes to take dinner with them on their rafts and regaled us with all sorts of tall stories as to the wonders they could accomplish. One man I remember in particular. He was such a cheerful and unembarrassed liar. We were seated on the cook's raft one day, talking to him and a group of shantymen and enjoying a smoke after dinner, when the conversation turned on the value of a knowledge of swimming.

Nate Thompson,[5] the gentleman referred to, gave it as his firm belief that a knowledge of swimming was of no use to a man whom Providence had blessed with a calm and unclouded mind. "Why, boys," he said turning to us, "I've been river-drivin' going on twenty-five years and I've never know'd the need of it yet. Just to kind of show you now. Tain't two weeks gone since we was fixing a boom in the lake at the end of Menominee Island.[6] I guess it was a matter of a hundred yards from shore. The rest of you boys, don't you mind, was waitin' on the bank watchin' me close the boom? You minds the time, Billy?" he said, turning inquiringly to a lumberjack sitting in the crowd. "You bet yer life," returned Bill with a solemn nod, signifying entire agreement with the statement.

"Well," went on Nate, "I ain't given none to slippin', but one of the caulks in my shoes give out and all on a suddent I goes kerplunk into the drink. Down I goes into fifty feet of water. I shuts my mouth and

96

says to myself, 'Nate', says I, 'keep yer eyes open and yer mouth shut', says I, 'the same as your feyther used to tell yous when yous was a lad.' 'Nate,' he says, 'if yer keeps yer eyes open and yer mouth shut, yer'll never come to no harm,' he says, and boys, that there sayin's just as true in the water as it is on the land.

"Well, I warn't long in reachin' the bottom, you may bet, and the minnies was swimmin' round like anythink, wonderin' I guess, if I was some sort of a blasted big whale a comin' among 'em to eat 'em up. But I warn't thinkin' of no minnies. I was thinkin' of which way the land was a lyin'. I scratches my head for a moment and thinks, and blamed if I didn't figure it out to a dot. Off I starts and, say, boys, there was simply nuthin' to it. It was a fine rocky bottom, and I just hoofed it along as if I was a-walkin' down Yonge Street, and before yer could say knife I was in shaller water and showin' my head above it. The boys warn't worrying any, was you, boys – You know'd Nate? – They seen me, mister," turning to Tothill, "thrown off my balance like, but they know'd me. They says to themselves. 'Nate's all right. Let's bet on where he comes up, boys, and, I didn't fool 'em – no sirree!" – And not a muscle moved on one of those lumberjacks' faces.

Amongst other duties that fell almost entirely to our lot was the job of paddling loads of bricks for the chimneys of the new house. That task nearly ended my days on this planet. Mr. Baldwin, who was the owner of a splendid dugout canoe fully twenty feet in length, had lent it to Captain Harston for the purpose of helping him in ferrying them up. He had it built especially for himself, as, being a big man, he needed something larger than the ordinary-sized craft in which we used to disport ourselves.

On the particular occasion of which I write, Tothill was accompanying me in another craft, a smaller-sized canoe. We had got on beautifully, had conveyed the bricks over the two portages and, having helped Tothill load his lighter canoe, I saw him off and proceeded to load my own. It held two hundred and fifty bricks and each brick weighed close on five pounds, so that it was no light load to paddle. When I reached the mouth of the river, I could see nothing of Tothill, who had been able to get a good start and had paddled out of sight round a point in the lake.

The canoe was loaded to within an inch of the gunwale, but, seeing that there was only a slight ripple on the water, I started off. It was just enough, however, to make the ripples trickle in over the side of the canoe, and the further I paddled the worse the situation became. Suddenly the load went straight down and, encumbered as I was with heavy fustian trousers tucked into long boots and a heavy flannel shirt, I went down with it in the suction created.

Like my friend Nate Thompson I kept my head, although, unlike him I didn't attempt to walk along the bottom but gave one or two strenuous kicks and rose to the top. When I came to the surface the shore looked a very long way off, and there didn't seem to be much chance of my reaching it without help. I started to swim and gave a yell or two occasionally, hoping by doing so to attract attention. Luckily Mr. Baldwin heard one of my calls and, rushing down to the water, pushed out a small craft from the beach and made towards me. I was then about one hundred yards from shore. When he reached me, I was just able to hang on to the end of the canoe whilst he paddled and, in this way, I got to land. Sorrowful to relate, the canoe and the bricks are still reposing at the bottom of that lake in about one hundred feet of water.

The loss of the canoe caused quite a breach in the friendship of Captain Harston and Mr. Baldwin, and not till the former paid for it was the strain removed. It was a great nuisance to go all over the work again and bring up fresh loads of bricks to replace those which had been lost, but we did it and had the great satisfaction at last of seeing the chimneys built and of stretching our legs before a comfortable fireplace.

In addition to paddling the bricks up from Huntsville, we had to carry them on our backs, across the portages, and we were not much used yet to carrying anything harder than flour. In all the succeeding years of roughing it I can bring to mind only one burden which I found more irksome and that was when engaged on a survey in the neighbourhood of Michipicoten.[7] We were required to carry, for a distance of three miles, about one hundred and sixty pounds of copper quartz per man, for the purpose of having it assayed at Port Arthur.[8] We all managed to get it through, but those who know that region will realize what it meant to convey it to the lake shore through the virgin forest with only a blazed trail for guidance.

We had great trouble with the chimneys after they were built. They seemed to possess a singular faculty for collecting soot. Every two weeks, on the average, there would be an alarm of fire, and the services of all hands were brought into requisition for the purpose of extinguishing the blaze. In order to do this one of us would have to be hoisted up on the roof, which was a very steep one, and then buckets of water would be passed up to him by the others. As often as not it was I who was entrusted with the task of quenching the flames, and it was quite a hazardous job to maintain one's footing on such an airy perch.

Once, when Mr. Baldwin remonstrated with Captain Harston for detailing me to climb the giddy eminence, my instructor's reply proved enlightening. "Oh, well," he said, "he's such a damned young fool that it wouldn't matter much if he did break his neck; nobody would miss him." I forgave him, however. He was still smarting under the loss of the canoe and the bricks.

Our next problem was the barn, but when built it was quite an imposing piece of work. It was what was known as a bank barn, the lower portion having been dug out of the side of the hill in order to allow for

Artist unknown, *Preparing to Burn Timber.* In *Canadian Illustrated News.*

a stable being constructed. The roof was very steep, and big boulders and stones lay all around it.

The shingling of that barn nearly cost Captain Harston his life. We had progressed so well in our knowledge of rough carpentering that to save expense he made us help him with the shingling, as well as fit up the mangers and stalls in the stable. The contact for manufacturing the shingles had been given to Nicholas Schneider, and when they were ready we started to roof the barn.

Nicholas Schneider was an expert at making shingles. It was very interesting to watch him at work. Having sawn the pine logs into the necessary blocks he would split them into proper thickness with the aid of a broad, straight-bladed instrument and mallet. The next process was to insert these in a wooden vice which he operated with his foot and slice them into shingles with a drawknife.[9] He worked wonderfully fast, and the shingles that he turned out were splendid.

Mr. Baldwin came over to help us shingle, and things went along finely until we neared the top of the roof. The pitch was a very steep one, and there was a drop of close on forty feet from the top of the barn to the ground.

Captain Harston and I were standing on a cleat at one end of the roof, and Mr. Baldwin and Tothill at the other. My instructor was in a very amiable frame of mind that morning. Everything looked rosy; the sun was shining, the cattle were blinking pleasantly at us from below, seeming to show in their very faces how much they appreciated what we were doing for them. It was a morning on which, as Captain Harston genially remarked to me, "it was good to be alive."

He was so pleasant that he was kind enough to inform me that he was extremely gratified at the way in which I was getting a grasp of the work. "You know, Frederick," he said, "there's nothing like sticking to a thing. At first you were a good deal off colour, but now you appear to me to be the best adapted lad for making a success of this life of any that I have seen. There's a 'goaheadativeness' about you, a desire to get to the bottom of a thing that is bound to raise you to success. You have to bear in mind that the greatest figures in history went ruthlessly ahead. They never counted the cost. Look at Napoleon, look at Julius Caesar, look at Alexander, look at – look at – look at – oh well, look at a hundred others how well they have done." I couldn't quite see why I should be called upon to follow the example of those great and unprincipled warriors, but I drank in his words of wisdom and went on shingling.

Suddenly I felt the cleat we were standing on give a slight slant. I interrupted him in his remarks to inform him of the fact.

"Excuse me for interrupting you," I remarked, "but I am afraid this cleat is loose." "Oh, pooh, pooh," he replied, "the cleat is perfectly safe, I nailed it down myself." His assurance didn't make me much easier in my mind. Captain Harston's ability in the nail-and-hammer business wasn't appreciably better than ours, and we were not yet experts.

I looked down apprehensively at the yawning depths and didn't feel the least bit like following the examples of Napoleon *et al* in their desire to get to the bottom of everything. The top suited me infinitely better. I felt that it would be most unpleasant to find myself suddenly hurtling down that roof, and it gave me a very shuddery feeling when I remembered that there were a lot of ugly-looking boulders immediately below. In my anxiety to make sure for the two of us, it unfortunately never entered my head that if my end of the cleat gave way his would follow suit, and so I caught at the top of the roof with both hands and gave a shove with my foot. My surmise had been correct. The cleat was loose and I had no sooner given the shove than Captain Harston went sliding down at a terrific rate with hammers, nails, shingles and saws clattering down after him. The last I saw of him, his flowing red beard was wagging convulsively as, with a despairing cry, he caught wildly at the eaves and disappeared from sight. In another instant I heard him fall with a dull thud on the ground! It had all happened so quickly that he was out of sight before the others could rightly divine what had occurred.

They had heard the clatter and, seeing me hanging on to the top of the roof, both of them shouted out with one voice. "My God! Where's Harston?"

I was so sick with fright that I was only able to stammer out in a weak voice. "He's d-d-d-d-down below." "Good God!" they exclaimed. We were a pretty apprehensive lot as we worked our way down to the ground, and when we did so my knees were shaking and my teeth chattering. But our joy was intense when we found him with his legs violently kicking in the air and his head buried in a manure pile.

He was too much shaken up at first to say anything, but when he did start he exhausted his English vocabulary and started into foreign languages to illustrate just what sort of a nincompoop, idiot and damnable apology for a mortal I was. It was really a fine display of abusive oratory. And to think that only a few moments before he had been classing me with Julius Caesar and Alexander and Napoleon!

The stable was finished, and Captain Harston was indeed a proud man when he led the mare into her stall and showed us how to hitch the cattle properly at their mangers. Everything was done in proper order. We stowed away our little crop of turnips and potatoes in the root house which we had built, and prepared to settle down for our second winter. It was not an exciting one from a social standpoint. There were the usual little parties and occasionally a dance at our own house but our chief interest lay in looking after the cattle and in imbibing the knowledge that Captain Harston very graciously imparted to us.

By a strange fate he had collected about as wild an aggregation of animals as could be found anywhere. The mare (which was his second venture in the horse line), we very soon discovered had an ungovernable temper and was as free with her teeth as with her heels. The ram was a tremendously dangerous animal and, when he wasn't trying to send us flying, he was endeavouring to come to conclusions with the bull. We all found life burdensome whilst that wretched creature was roaming about the barnyard. He took a special dislike to me. One day, when I was engaged in the highly cultured occupation of carrying swill to the pigs, he managed to rush up from behind and gave me a hoist which landed me deftly in the dirtiest part of the yard. Then he came and stood over me and kept batting at my prostrate form and blatting out "baa" in a very obnoxious manner. I've always hated the sound of a sheep's "baa" since.

Captain Harston, anxious as always to show us the intricacies of farming, assigned us the job of clearing out the stables and performing the other menial duties of the place. We milked the cows, cut holes in the ice for the cattle to get water, and looked after the mare and other quadrupeds. His first venture in the horse line had been a poor decrepit bag of bones for the sum of one dollar and which he had hoped, by dint of careful feeding and attention, to develop into a serviceable beast. But the poor thing lived only three days, and Harston found himself out of pocket.

As the winter dragged along, the feed gave out, and we used to go into the woods and cut hemlock boughs for the animals. Needless to say, they did not thrive on the bill of fare that was provided.

As a fitting windup to the season's misfortune, a cow walked into the barn, the barn of which had been left unguardedly open, and fell half way through the trap door that communicated with the stable. We discovered her, suspended like Mohammed midway between Earth and

Heaven, with her head and front legs out of sight and her hind parts on the barn floor. She had to be slaughtered.

No sooner was the barn built than we set to work to get the church erected – ground was purchased from Smith, and soon a church and parsonage sprang into existence.

It was a great day when our parson appeared on the scene. He came, accompanied by his wife, and entered upon his duties enthusiastically. But both of them were absolutely ignorant of Canadian conditions and of the habits and customs of the people amongst whom they had come to live. They were very much in earnest, however, and were determined to do all the good they could whilst they were members of the community.

The first christening at which Mr. Sweet[10] officiated was a trial to him. The baby was the offspring of Mr. and Mrs. White to whom reference has been made in a former chapter. Mrs. Bowser,[11] a delightful and eccentric old soul, had begged as a special privilege to be allowed to act as godmother and also to name the child. The Whites did not care much who acted as sponsor, having a sort of idea, I imagine, that it carried with it the custodianship of the infant, and they acceded to the request most gladly. Mrs. Bowser, arrayed in her finery and looking for all the world like a magnified Mrs. Gamp, was sharp on time for the ceremony and surveyed with the proudest air imaginable the large congregation which was assembling. It was a great day for her. When Mr. Sweet came to the words, "Name this child," Mrs. Bowser, was, in the expressive vernacular of the district, 'right there with the goods.'

"Please, mister," she said, bowing and scraping at each word, "he's to be called Aquila Collard Norval Legard Lorenzo Howell." It took Mr. Sweet some little time to get the full nomenclature properly memorized, but he got it at last. The little chap was never known by any of his many names. His parents dubbed him Bob and he went through his short life under that designation. Born in penury, dragged up in semi-starvation, and drowned in a water-butt at the age of four or five, poor little Bob was probably happier dead than alive.

In due course our society was enriched by the arrival of more aspirants to a knowledge of agriculture. We learned also to our great joy that, when another pupil was expected to arrive, he would be accompanied by his sister who was coming with him for a short stay in the district. It will be seen that we were getting on, in a social sense at any rate.

XV

Emigrants In The Colony

I HAVE ALREADY GIVEN A sketch of the sayings and doings of some of those amongst whom we found ourselves in our farming days, and in this chapter will give a few more in order to make plainer still what class of people they were. There are doubtless living today in the section of which I write, sons and daughters and grandsons and granddaughters of those early settlers. If they are animated at all by the courageous spirit of those who preceded them, they will be the last to be ashamed of the struggles and trials of their forebears. They have far more reason to be proud of their ancestry than has the so-called blue-blooded individual who through accident of birth or the crookedness of his father or grandfather has been enabled to live in comfort and can produce no record of having accomplished a hard day's work in his life.

A new country always receives its share of the scum of cities and towns, in addition to those who, anxious to make a home for themselves, cast off the shackles of servitude to try the role of independent workers. Many of the latter class were scattered through the district. They were as honest as the day and brought up their children in a God-fearing manner. They were the salt of the earth, through years of toil flinching at no hardship, and showing themselves men and women of truest worth. Amongst these was Johnson,[1] an Englishman who lived within two miles of us. Two years before, he had arrived with just twenty-five cents in his pocket and a pack of groceries on his back.

He had left his wife in Toronto, giving her, before starting on his journey north, enough money to keep her going for six months in comparative comfort. He had tramped all the way in from Gravenhurst with his load

George Harlow White, *Log Shanty near Huntsville,* 1875. *Courtesy of the Toronto Public Library (TRL) Special Collections T16426.*

and, as the reader has already had sufficient evidence, a forty-five mile tramp over such a track was not a trip to be hankered after.

Arrived on the lot he had located, he lost no time setting to work. It was easy enough to make a small shelter with saplings covered with a piece of sailcloth, and in this temporary abode he slept and ate till he had finished his stock of provisions. Then he tramped back to Brace-bridge and laboured there till he had earned enough to keep himself going for another month in the woods. He kept this up till the fall and then started back to Toronto to earn some money during the winter for the upkeep of his better half.

In the following year, he set his face to the north again and by the fall had things so far advanced that he was able to fetch his wife and set up housekeeping in a rough and ready way in the woods. They had a hard time, and the woman, as usually happens, had the harder. But she stood her ground well and not only attended to her domestic duties but helped her husband in the field and in the woods. Such indomitable pluck was bound to succeed, and when I first met Johnson and his wife they were the possessors of a neat little log house, and had about twenty acres cleared and in crop and also owned a cow and pair of oxen.

It would be pleasant to record that they both lived to enjoy the fruit of their hard-earned prosperity, but two years later poor Mrs. Johnson was burnt to death through her dress catching fire at the stove. She was so much respected in the community that people who had learned of her sad death came from far and near to show their sorrow and sympathy.

I was present at the funeral. There is a certain type of person who seems to revel in being miserable and in causing misery to others. It may be meant kindly but it is a queer way to showing one's grief to stay in a house from which a corpse has just been removed and abandon oneself to guzzling and drinking, interspersed with tearful howls, for the space of two full days and nights. It will hardly be credited that some ten or twelve people were guilty of this and acted as if they felt they were acquitting themselves quite admirably. As one old dame remarked to me when I expressed surprise at such goings on, "Ye know, the poor man did need a deal of cheerin' up, and there ain't nuthin' like havin' a lot of folks around to make one forget one's sorrer."

In course of time Johnson married again, and his second wife, as sometimes happens, was not as helpful as his first. The hard work of the past few years had sapped his vitality, and his second marriage certainly sapped his patience. Having heard that he had remarried, I went to see him and found him in the field toiling away as usual, but his old heartiness had deserted him. "Things ain't like what they used to be," he said in answer to my query as to how he was getting on. "The missus ain't much company."

We went into the house, and I was introduced to his wife. She seemed glad to see me and we sat in front of the stove and I started telling her some of the funniest stories that I knew. But it was a terrible setback to my pride to discover, in a few minutes, that she had gone fast asleep. I looked at Johnson in a puzzled way and said, "I am afraid that your wife hasn't enjoyed what I have been telling her."

"Oh, never heed that," replied Johnson, "she ain't heard a word you've said – she's stone deaf – and she sleeps and snorts like hanythink." I felt Johnson had deserved a better fate.

Remington[2] was a different type of individual. He had scarcely three hundred words in his vocabulary and his stock expression for moments of excitement, or deep feeling was either "Be cracky" or "Be gobs." When his child, an infant, died, he merely gave vent to simple a "Be cracky" in a tone which might as easily have been construed into a token of exultation as of deep feeling, so void was it of all expression, and when a horse kicked him and broke his leg, he presented a variation by a loud ejaculation of "Be gobs." He was a simple soul and had more than one good point in his favour. He and his wife and two children were housed in a very humble log shack, consisting of one room. The furniture was no worse than in many of the shanties round about, and the culinary arrangements were no better.

On two occasions it was my fate to be a guest at Remington's home. The most noticeable thing was the dearth of tableware. His hospitality was immense, but on the first visit I was deeply impressed with the fact that there were only three forks to go round among five people. Having been used to the luxury of a whole fork to myself when it was necessary to use one, I was not altogether prepared for the alternative of sharing one with my host. It was uninviting because his mouth and teeth were stained with tobacco juice. He wasn't at all annoyed at my refusing to deprive him of the weapon but handed it to me without more ado. "Keep it, mister," he said, "I guess me and my old knife can do fust class." With that he took his broad clasp-knife from his pocket and utilized it as a fork. He was an expert. The way he shovelled peas and a soft-boiled egg into his mouth with the two knives without spilling the one or the other was a revelation.

The other occasion was when I drove Bishop Sullivan to Remington's dwelling for the purpose of having his baby christened. It was in winter time. After driving to the head of the lake, we had to pass up a steep clearing at the farther end of which Remington lived. The snow lay in deep drifts, and the cutter in which I was conveying the bishop and his chaplain was altogether too small for the three of us. The bishop was a man weighing in the neighborhood of 230 pounds and the chaplain, Mr. Llwyd, was a man of modest proportions, like myself. Halfway up the hill the cutter overturned, and the bishop was hurled into a deep drift with the chaplain astride of him and myself topping them both. The snow was five or six feet deep at that point, and the bishop disappeared entirely from view. With a great deal of difficulty we got him, half-smothered, out of the drift. He took it all very good-humouredly, remarking, as he brushed the snow out of his hair, "Humph! Bad thing this! Clergy and laity both down on the bishop!"

Still another type of settler was to be found in the person of Mrs. Cudmore.[3] Mr. and Mrs. Cudmore lived two miles away from us; in fact, their property was situated on the same sideline as my own. Between their land and mine were lots owned by an Irishman of the name of O'Halleran.[4] The clearing covered about ten acres, and both husband and wife had worked their hardest to get their heads above water. Mrs. Cudmore had helped to log and fence the farm and, in addition, had raised a family of sturdy boys who in after days became hard-working and prosperous farmers. But she laboured under the distinct disadvantage of possessing a bad temper, probably accentuated by the hardships through which she had passed, and had also developed a penchant for practising a kind of religious witchcraft. Her appearance helped a great deal towards establishing a feeling against her in the countryside for she presented all the hallmarks of a witch. Her chin bristled with hairs, and her eyes gleamed in a malevolent-looking way from under fierce eyebrows. The poor woman had few friends in the neighbourhood, and the prejudice against her was extensive.

I chanced upon her one evening when sent on an errand to obtain clover seed from her husband. Not being able to find anyone in the cottage, I went down to the barn where I discovered Mrs. Cudmore kneeling on the floor, engaged in tying an old piece of rope into knots and at the same time muttering all sorts of weird incantations coupled with supplications to the Almighty. I stood dumbfounded and after listening to her for a short time stepped forward. She was startled and jumped to her feet with a snarl. "What on earth are you doing?" I inquired. "None of your business," she replied fiercely. This was an inauspicious beginning, so I changed the subject by asking if she had any clover seed for sale. The chance of making a dollar or two worked a change in her demeanour at once. When the bargain was clinched, she relaxed and began to tell me her troubles. She said that her cows wouldn't give any milk, and she knew that Mrs. O'Halleran had cast the evil eye upon them. "But I've got even with her," she went on, "I ain't goin' to be downed by the likes of her. These here godless wimmen ain't goin' to put anythin' over me, so they ain't. They says as how the devil takes care of his own, but that there O'Halleran woman will find that there's someone as is stronger than the devil." Her eyes glared wildly, and she went on, "I'll teach her to leave my cows alone, so I will. I've a charm as'll fix her, so I have."

I ventured to ask her what the charm was, but for some time she remained silent. Then she opened out. "I s'pose," she cried, "that you're just like all the rest of them round here. They calls me a witch because I ain't ashamed to pray." I hastened to inform her that although far from perfect, I had not yet sunk so low as to scoff at anyone who prayed. She seemed easier in her mind after this avowal and proceeded to show me the exact way she made her supplications for Divine help against the evil machinations of Mrs. O'Halleran.

"I comes every day, once in the day, from the house," she said, "and as I comes I keeps utterin' words of Scriptur' and I never lets up till I gets to the barn. Then I gets my piece of rope and I begins to tie knots in it, and I prays every time as I makes a knot that that there woman may get a knot in her guts and I knows if I prays hard enough and makes knots enough that that crittur will learn that it ain't a good thing to be wor-ryin' other people with her wicked ways. There's nuthin' like religion, mister; I had a good mother and I've prayed all my life."

I departed homewards pondering deeply over the incident and wonder-ing, if, after all, the out-and-out pagan was not in a better position morally than the sad specimen of a so-called Christian whom I had just left. It will be hardly credited that there were one or two others in the vicinity who saw eye to eye with Mrs. Cudmore and engaged in the same practices in order to destroy the supposed power of Mrs. O'Halleran's "evil eye."

XVI

WILD LIFE OF THE WOODS

I AM NOT A NATURALIST, but I will defy anyone not to get interested in the wild life of the woods. If here and there something does not strike one as interesting, that individual is to be pitied, and if a wonderful intelligence in all forms of fauna is not noticed and a sincere love for bird and beast not developed, that person is to be thoroughly despised.

One of the things that struck me with admiration was the motherly love of the partridge and of the sheldrake for their young. One day in a field I came upon a partridge with a brood of little chicks. It was a revelation to me to note the mother partridge's efforts to safeguard her young ones. She gave a peculiar cry, and in a moment the youngsters had disappeared from view under bits of chips and leaves. But not so the old bird. She simply courted death in her efforts to draw me away from the spot. She flew at my legs and pecked at them and, not content with this, flew right at my face and attempted to peck my eyes out. Shooting her was, of course, out of the question, and I was glad enough to hurry away from the place to be safe from her attacks.

I found the same instinct animating a sheldrake. Paddling down the river one day, I glided into a whole flock of young ones before they were aware of my coming. She scurried the young ones into the reeds on both sides of the river and sailed out bravely into the open to draw me after her. There was absolutely no attempt to get away. It was a clear evidence of willing self-sacrifice, to which many of us, superior creatures that we are, are singularly enough, complete strangers.

They call partridges stupid birds. Perhaps they are, but I have seen one wise enough to completely outwit a hawk which was in full flight after it. The partridge took refuge in a balsam tree close to where I stood, and in a few moments a large hawk descended from the hillside in pursuit. I awaited developments.

Looking up through the branches of the tree I noted that the hawk was hopping from twig to twig in quest of its prey, yet I could see absolutely no sign of the partridge. This continued for possibly three minutes, and then the hawk flew disappointedly out of the tree. At first I thought that the partridge must have flown away without my perceiving it, but, much to my surprise, just as I was turning away, I heard a flutter in the branches overhead, and there was my wise bird sailing away as swift as the wind to a fresh cover.

It would be thought impossible, I suppose, for squirrels to set themselves the task of swimming across a broad lake and yet on more than one occasion I have come upon them half a mile or more from shore, swimming away merrily to get to the opposite side of the water. On such occasions I have put out my paddle and lifted them into the canoe and when, after having finished running the length of the canoe and over my head and back again they would sit quietly on the bow with their tails cocked over their heads, presenting a very pretty picture indeed. As soon as the canoe touched shore, they would be off with a leap into the woods.

When we first went to the district one of the chief features of birdlife was the marvellous number of wild pigeons to be seen everywhere. All around the shores of the lakes there were large flocks of them. In a year or two they suddenly vanished and never returned.[1] Many surmises have been made regarding their strange disappearance, but I have never seen a satisfactory solution of the mystery. Today they are almost as extinct as the Great Auk and Dodo.[2]

We used to have a hard time with our dogs when they started hunting porcupines. Experience never seemed to render them wiser. They would come home, time and again, with their nostrils and mouths filled with quills and it was a miserable business getting them out. It generally took two to do the work – one to hold the animal and the other to pull out the quills with a pair of pincers. On rare occasions they would fall foul of a skunk and had to be treated as pariahs for lengthy periods. Skunks did not bother us much, however, as they favour more settled localities where poultry is plentiful. Foxes sometimes had the audacity to enter our poultry runs, but they usually gave us a wide berth.

For a long time I was mystified, on going to my henhouse each morning, to find one or other of the fowls suffering from a wound in the breast. For a long time the cause was inexplicable. One evening, however, I chanced to espy a weasel slipping round the corner of the henhouse. Half the mystery was solved, but the other half, as to how it found means of entry remained hidden. At length, search revealed the fact that there was a knot hole in the boards about eight inches from the ground, and I discovered that it was through this that the vicious little creature had made its burglarious entry. The only fatality to be recorded in this connection is the death of the weasel.

XVII

A PERMANENT SETTLEMENT

IN COURSE OF TIME THREE or four gentlemen from Toronto and the United States came up to take up land. Our little colony was becoming known, and it began to look as if Captain Harston's prognostication was going to be correct and we were indeed to have permanent settlement. But an overpowering factor had not been taken into consideration, and that was that, unless people possessed assured incomes, it was worse than useless for them to enter in the life.

None of us was wealthy, and most of us were dependent on remittances from home. There were plenty more like ourselves scattered throughout Canada at that period. Much as we plumed ourselves on being pioneers, the reality was that we were only such in the sense of living in the district and undergoing many of the discomforts of a settler's existence. We were very far removed indeed from experiencing the true exigencies of pioneer life. We felt the same cold and the same heat, and we entered fairly thoroughly into the settler's work, but we were always assured of three good meals a day and thus escaped the privations and anxieties that were the common lot of those about us.

In a sense we were playing at pioneering because whatever we did never carried us any farther along the road to prosperity. But we did our share in contributing an appreciable amount towards the prosperity of our fellow man and in providing him with a never-failing fund of amusement and hilarity.

It was only when we had been a considerable time in the country that we realized what very ordinary beings we were and how much the grit and the determination of those poorer than ourselves were to be admired. We discovered a great deal that was ludicrous, a great deal that was deplorable, but even in the most flagrant cases of depravity the central factor of unyielding grit was very observable. I often wonder why, when governments and communities erect monuments to heroes, they forget to erect one to the honour of the Pioneer.

This grand and glorious country has been raised to its greatness by his lowly efforts. Where our greatest cities stand, he was first at work, paving the way for posterity. I have stood many a time on a bleak hillside or in a lonely valley looking in silent contemplation at some neglected grave. The clearings of our back districts can show them by the hundred. What tales of endurance and of hardship borne uncomplainingly by the spirits of those whose bodies lie beneath could unfold. Heroes and heroines they were indeed, waging war against an inflexible and devastating fate. They fought their fight and died, and today on many a flourishing farm their descendants are living in comfort.

It is only fair that, in recording the doings and backslidings of others, I should jot down a few of our own. A very prepossessing young lady had come to pay a visit to a family living a few miles distant from us, and both Tothill and I had been introduced to her. We were eager to make her better acquaintance, and the chance occurred when Captain

Captain Charles Greville Harston's second home on Buck Lake. The photograph dates from the late 1800s. It was here that Frederick de la Fosse wrote the manuscript for *English Bloods*. Note the individual, centre foreground. *Courtesy of Fred Hopcraft.*

Harston proposed a trip to Huntsville for the purpose of purchasing groceries and having a good time. Our route lay past the farm where the young lady was staying.

Much to our disappointment, when we suggested to Captain Harston the great joy we should feel in paying our respects to the fair visitor, he peremptorily vetoed it, saying he couldn't stand such nonsense as that. The blunt refusal annoyed us, and we cast about for some plausible excuse of landing at the farm. At last Tothill had a bright idea. "I have it," he called to me from the stern. "Why not upset the canoe and swim ashore and ask for shelter?" The plan was such an excellent one that I at once acquiesced. The night was dark, but it was not far to the landing, and we were good swimmers. Captain Harston was ahead in a larger canoe with a friend from Barrie, and we knew we could easily engineer the upset.

There were a few groceries in the canoe, and I had forty dollars in my pocket; Tothill had a heavy waterproof covering the groceries. We forgot all about the likelihood of the waterproof sinking. As for the groceries, well, they could be purchased again, while the money in my pocket could be dried out. Over went the canoe, and we clambered on to it and then began calling out lustily for help. We knew that Captain Harston would never suspect us of being such fools as deliberately to tip over the craft and certainly never notice the means we had adopted for doing so.

They paddled back in a high state of nervousness, expecting us to be having a terrible time, and we didn't undeceive them. At great trouble they helped us to land and Captain Harston, in a very solicitous manner, told us to run to the house and obtain a change of clothing and get warmed up. They left us and paddled on homewards and we spent a splendid evening, receiving enough sympathy and congratulations on our narrow escape to make us feel ashamed of the deception that we had practised, but we were hardened young ruffians and exulted in what we had done. "What heroes you boys must be," the young lady remarked, and we took the compliment in a very modest way and didn't attempt to disagree with her. The next morning we found our canoe beached in a shady cove near by and paddled home rejoicing. Captain Harston was, naturally, somewhat rueful over the loss of the groceries but Tothill and I, protesting that we could not possibly allow him to bear the loss due to our "carelessness," made up the amount between us.

In the village that had grown up at the foot of the lake we now had a church and a sawmill, and two stores had been erected, and we were promised a post office for the colony at an early date. The Government thought so well of its future that they built a bridge over the river to give access to the village to those who lived on the opposite side. When finally, the post office did materialize, the arrival of our weekly mail used to be a great event in our lives. Those who have never known what it is to live on the outskirts of civilization can hardly realize what it means to be kept waiting a whole week for letters and papers. We always looked forward with eagerness to the arrival of the carrier, and it was seldom indeed that a week passed without our receiving letters and papers from England.

The post office was kept by a settler named Wallace Hopcraft[1] and was distant from us about one-and-a-quarter miles. Wallace Hopcraft was a farmer in a small way and left most of the duties of the post office to his wife. She was a thoughtful soul and, whenever we called for our mail, was always obliging enough to give us a complete resumé of the contents of such postcards as we received.

Wallace Hopcraft was a local preacher. He came of a religious family whose members had drunk at many a fountain of religious thought. His father had originally been an Anglican but having seen the error of his ways, as he informed us, had changed to Methodism. But the clarifying influences of Methodism had not proved sufficient to purify his mind, and he had become a Christadelphian.[2] Christadelphianism did not suit him for long, as he found that even if a man richer than himself might help him there were others who thought themselves entitled to turn to him for relief, and so he became a Mormon.

His central idea was that there were so many more women in the world than men that it was the bounden duty of every man of marriageable age to take as many of the dear creatures under his wing as possible. God had put man and woman into the world. Each had a set line of duty to follow. It was the duty of every man to take his fair share of the burden of life, and it was the duty of the women to see that their liege lords' comforts were properly looked after

The laws of Canada debarred him from engaging in a practical demonstration of his doctrines, but they didn't hinder him from expressing his opinions, and he would expatiate on them by the hour to his own great personal satisfaction. He was a wonderful man, was old Wallace Hopcraft, and knew the Bible better than any man I have ever seen. He could reel off whole chapters, and what he didn't know about the Apocalypse was simply not worth knowing. His exposition of that wonderful

A photograph of Aemilius Baldwin's house on the shore of Buck Lake, near Ilfracombe. It was built about 1880. *Courtesy of Martha Preston (Tothill) Woody, great granddaughter of Richard Tothill.*

and mysterious portion of the Scriptures was peculiarly profound, or perhaps it would be more correct to say, profoundly peculiar.

If as little as possible is said concerning the moral attributes of certain of the settlers, nothing is lost to the cause of clean living or to the interest of this story. It is not to be understood, however, that the morals of the backwoods at that period were, as a whole, any worse than the morals of more populated centres although it would probably be stretching a point to say that they were any better. Environment makes or mars a community just as easily as it does an individual, and laxity of conduct is not an unknown fault in new ones.

In our immediate neighbourhood there lived a family who, under different conditions, would in all likelihood have been law-abiding and respectable members of society. But poverty had rendered them careless and even desperate.

There were six of them, father and mother, two sons and two daughters. The filth of the interior of their domicile was indescribable. One or two of them, through drinking snow water, had contacted goitre[3] and were not very presentable-looking beings. The girls, grown to womanhood, were in a partially demented condition. They had lived such lives of horror that they fled at the approach of a human being and would hide themselves in corners of the fence or flee into the woods or cower in the pigsty. Theirs was not an isolated case. There were others living not far distant, who were in just as abject and deplorable a condition.

Mention was made in a former chapter of the fact that Garrett and Mr. Baldwin had retired to their own abodes. Garrett had had about ten acres cleared on his farm and Mr. Baldwin about five acres on his. We used to visit them constantly, they forming a very welcome variation in social intercourse, and with the arrival of newcomers and frequent visits from Toronto by friends of Captain and Mrs. Harston we began to find life very bearable.

Both Garrett and Mr. Baldwin were very tidy bachelors and formed a distinct contrast to certain others of whom we had knowledge. In fact, compared with a few of the specimens we saw about us, they might almost have been termed supermen. They were scrupulously neat in regard to their kitchen utensils, and the state of their floors might have served as patterns to many housewives.

One family of four brothers kept house together. They lived not very far from Huntsville. Cooking and washing-up were not enjoyed by any of them and, by mutual agreement, they took week about to do the cooking and for half the week ate off one side of their plates and then turned them over and used the backs for the other half. They considered that one washing-up a week was ample.

Another bachelor living on our own lakefront believed in living the simple life. He dug out a hole close to the water's edge and roofed it over and lived in it for months. It was just large enough for him to crawl into and lie down on a bedding of straw and balsam branches. In course of time he built a house and moved into it but he always said that he preferred having "less style" and averred that the place was getting altogether too civilized when a lot of women folk came paddling around.

Bell and I chance upon him one day about dinner time. We had been out partridge shooting and were very hot and tired, and when Catesby[4] invited us in to take potluck with him we thankfully accepted. If we had realized what was in store for us we would have gone on.

"Come on in, boys, come on in," Catesby, cried when he saw us at his porch, "Glad to see you – you're just in time for dinner. I haven't got much to offer you, only some potatoes and bread and syrup, but what there is you're mighty welcome to." We thanked him and entered. Catesby, it could have been seen at a glance, was not a tidy bachelor. But we were not in a position to criticize, seeing that we had accepted his hospitality and had to make the best of things.

Bell asked for a basin of water in order to have a wash, and Catesby was nonplussed. But not for long. "Here you are, old chap," he said, handing him a dirty tin dish full of potato peelings, "it's the only thing I have, so you'll have to be content with it." Bell scraped out the dish and went to the lakeshore and brought it back filled with water. Having given himself a good laving, he turned to Catesby, with his eyes streaming, and asked for a towel. "I say, old chap, you're getting awfully tony," Catesby replied in an aggrieved tone. "Do you think I'm a millionaire? I haven't got a towel in the place; but here," he said as a bright thought seemed to strike him, "take this." Bell looked at it through his dimmed optics and at last made out that it was a tattered old shirt. "Why," he said to Catesby, "my dear chap, this is a shirt." "Oh, yes, I know," Catesby replied in a jaunty manner, "but you won't hurt it, it's quite dirty."

There were two other bachelors living three or four miles away who possessed a small clearing of some fifteen acres. They were fine fellows, well-educated Englishmen, both of them.

Business took me to their quarters one morning. It was a piping hot day, and by the time I got to their place the sun was beating down in a most pitiless fashion. I mounted the small hill that hid their clearing from view and paused for a moment to gaze at the prospect. Then I looked at the clearing and the neat little house rising in its midst, and turned my eyes to the hayfield.

"What in Heaven's name," I said to myself, "can those figures be?" Two objects in long, flowing vestments of white were passing at a rapid pace through the hay. I rubbed my eyes and looked again. There was no doubt in my mind this time. They were certainly human beings.

I watched for a minute or two and suddenly divined that they must be the two brothers. I ran down and greeted them. They were somewhat surprised and asked with a certain amount of trepidation in their voices if I had brought any ladies along.

"You know, we're not exactly prepared to receive visitors," they remarked. I quite agreed with them. The day being warm, they had conceived the happy notion of mowing in the their nightshirts. They averred that it was about the sanest sort of costume, for a warm day's work, that could be hit upon, and that it was a pity that people were so hidebound in regard to observing the conventionalities of life, that they wouldn't use them for such hot and exhausting work as mowing.

Mr. Baldwin used to bake his own bread and was a first-class cook. For a time he had Wallace Hopcraft's son working for him and used to go to all sorts of trouble in order to provide him with tasty meals. But young Hopcraft was a terrible glutton, and at last Mr. Baldwin decided that some drastic method had to be adopted to curb his appetite. He was eating him out of house and home. A happy thought struck him. Every day he placed before him a plentiful supply of rice and raisins and bread and butter and bade him go ahead. For two or three days Hopcraft stood the fare and then his spirit revolted. "Mr. Baldwin," he said one evening, "don't yer think there's a kind of sameness about yer vittles?" "Sameness!" cried Baldwin, "of course there's a sameness. How the devil do you think anyone not as rich as Vanderbilt could afford to feed such a damned glutton as you are?" If you want to bust yourself I prefer that you should do it as cheaply as possible when I have to pay for it." Hopcraft said no more but meekly kept on till the finish of his job, on the same fare.

The woodpeckers used to be a great annoyance to Mr. Baldwin. They favoured the logs of his dwelling above all others, for tapping at and making a noise. Time and again he would rush out, driven half-distracted, and blaze at them with his gun. Another great source of worry was his bread. In summer he made the best bread imaginable, but when the winter days came he found it a very unpleasant undertaking to sit huddled up at his stove all night, in readiness to put fresh logs on the fire when necessary. No matter how carefully he wrapped up his pan, he was always fated to fall asleep long enough to allow the fire to go out and his baking to freeze, and the language in which he clothed his lamentations was not of the Sunday-school variety.

Garrett, on going to his place, had elected to do without a cow. He had a fixed and firm idea that a goat was the best animal to have about the place. "You see," he remarked, "it doesn't roam in the woods, and its milk, according to established authorities, has quite double the strength of cow's milk." One thing he forgot in his decision to purchase one, was that a goat's smell has double the strength as well. There were other contingencies also which had not entered into his calculations.

One of the drawbacks of allowing the cows to roam in the woods in the spring was that for a considerable time the milk would be tainted with the odour of leeks on which they used to feed extensively. This was really the prime factor that induced Garrett to purchase the goat. The animal arrived, and Garrett, with all the persuasiveness of which he was master, endeavoured to make that goat love him. He called it by the most endearing names, but he was a stranger to goat psychology. When the animal tried to butt him, he regarded it at first as sheer sportiveness and used to give her every opportunity of engaging in her favourite pastime. But when she butted him in the stomach and doubled him up, his desire to cultivate her affection evaporated and he went about the place armed with a stout club in preparation for emergencies.

He found out early in his dealings with the animal that it was impossible for one person to milk her. There may be a few goats, perhaps, that it is possible for one person to milk, but Garrett's required three, one to hold her horns, one to shove her up hard against the side of the shed, and the third to attend to the milking process. Even then, she would sometimes get free and it required the agility of an athlete to keep clear of her.

Our usual procedure was to go into the enclosure armed with a piece of rail or a stick and engage the animal in combat in order that one of us might get hold of her horns. But we sometimes missed, and when we did, she did not miss us. Her conduct at last grew so outrageous that Garrett got rid of her, to the exceeding joy of us all.

Since Bell's arrival on the scene things had grown lively. He was not at all enthusiastic over the idea of working in the way we had been working, and told Captain Harston plainly that, if he paid a good round sum for his board, he didn't intend to do any more than he wanted to. This state of affairs did not suit Captain Harston at all and was the cause of frequent unpleasantness in the household. Bell was an enthusiastic hunter and fisherman and he made us more sport-loving than ever. He was never so happy for partridges and deer, and he found us very willing to join him in his jaunts when opportunity offered. He was under no binding agreement, like ourselves, to work or to learn farming, the understanding being that he would lend a hand whenever his services were required and pick up pointers about the life in the way that suited him best. The trouble was that Captain Harston needed his assistance every day, and Bell objected.

Bell liked the country so well that in due course he wrote for two of his sisters to come and keep house for him, and they built a comfortable residence on a farm adjoining mine at the upper end of the lake.

XVIII

Our Education

As the seasons went by we found ourselves able to hold our own in any company when it came to the question of endurance. At first it had been terribly hard, but now, what with our handling of logs and lifting of big stones and carrying heavy weights across portages, we amazed ourselves with the feats that we performed. It was a very proud day for me, I remember, when I found myself capable of carrying a hundred-weight of flour across a three-quarter mile portage without laying it down. There came a time when we used to carry considerably heavier weights than that. It is wonderful what practice and knack will accomplish. We also became adept at the high accomplishments of cleaning out stables and feeding pigs and hunting for cattle in the woods and milking cows and hoeing potatoes and sowing broadcast. We also learned something about the minor diseases of animals and were told how to deal with cases of indigestion and a mysterious ailment termed a "hardened cud."

Tothill and I took care of Garrett's place for a few days while he was on a trip to Toronto and, in his absence, one of his animals developed a "hardened cud," at least our neighbours told us that that was the matter and we took steps accordingly. At great pains we tethered and tied its legs together to prevent its kicking. We then proceeded to massage its throat and critically probe its entire body. We were both at sea as to the exact location of the three stomachs which we had been informed every well-ordered ox and cow possessed; so we pounded and punched with considerable vim at both sides of its carcass. In addition, we prepared all sorts of hot fomentations for it and gave it bran mashes by the pailful. But, notwithstanding our exertions the wretched creature died. When Garrett returned he found a dead animal on his hands.

He took that loss very nicely but was quite annoyed when he found that during his absence we had managed to make away with a gallon pot of his best marmalade. It had been our first essay at keeping bachelor's hall and we had proceeded to enjoy ourselves. Having been given the free run of the place and told to help ourselves to whatever we could find, we did so. A passing trapper had made us a present of the body of a newly-trapped beaver, and on this and bread and marmalade and tea we had lived for a week.

About this time Captain Harston purchased a purebred Shorthorn bull and two or three grade cows and a mare, also some more sheep. He was a very proud man when he got these animals safely to the farm and lost no time in pointing out to us the merits of the various animals. I am not prepared to affirm that Captain Harston did not know, in a theoretical sense, the points that go towards the making of a fine animal, but he certainly did not know enough to understand that the mere possession of a pedigree does not render its owner any more exempt from the need of food than the veriest plebeian that ever lived. Even monarchs have to have their digestive organs tuned up three times a day.

His first year's experience had not benefited him in the least degree and when the winter days approached he had all these creatures on his hands, with little more than a month's provender to put them through till spring.

XIX

TRIALS AND TRIBULATIONS

AT CHRISTMASTIME IT WAS DECIDED that we should have a right merry time of it, and Mrs. Harston requested me to go to the barn and slay a couple of fowls for our Christmas dinner. I hated killing a fowl by the only method that I knew, that of chopping its head off on a handy stump. Anyone who has killed a fowl in this way will know why. The wretched things jump about in such a convulsive and erratic manner. So I asked Bell to help me.

We sallied forth to the barn together and discovered the entire fowl population lining the roof. It was impossible to get at the creatures save at the imminent risk of breaking our necks, for the weather was very cold, the ground very hard and there was a little snow on the roof.

Bell was always ready-witted. He thought of a device immediately. "By George," he said, "here's a lovely chance to get some shooting. Let's go in and get our guns." Back we went to the house, and loading up with two buckshot cartridges apiece, went out to the barn again. Against the evening sky the birds offered a beautiful mark, and I told him to go ahead. He did so and the results were disastrous to the birds and also to the roof of the barn. He cleared off about ten hens and sent a hundred or more shingles flying off into the clearing.

But he was quite elated at what he had done and insisted that I should have a shot as well. On my pointing out that ten or twelve birds seemed ample for our Christmas dinner his answer was that the others looked pretty lonely up there and that it was just as well to shoot them as let them freeze to death. The results of my shot were somewhat on a par with Bell's only I seemed to get fewer birds and more shingles. We completely cleared the roof and went round to the other side of the barn to pick up our bag. We discovered that the buckshot had been detrimental to the insides of the birds, but we went back to the house laden with our spoils. Mrs. Harston wasn't a bit pleased, and Captain Harston indulged in animadversions which were not friendly and would pain me to repeat. It took all hands the whole of the following day to get the birds in proper condition to hang round the eaves of the house.

During that terribly trying winter one of the trusty oxen sickened and died. The neighbours often used to come to the stable in order to discuss his condition. He got so weak at last that we had to sling him from the ceiling of the stable. When he was just about gone there was a lengthy pow-wow held over him. Old Bowser, who claimed to be an expert in bovine matters came up to the animal and tapped him on both horns. "Just what I've been athinkin' all along," he said, "he's got 'oller 'orn.'" " 'Oller 'orn' be damned!" cried his broad-shouldered son, who was standing in the doorway. "He ain't got no more 'oller 'orn' than I 'ave − no, sirree, tain't the 'oller 'orn' he's dyin' of − it's 'oller belly.'" There were good grounds for presuming that the man was right. Poor old Bright, the ox, died, and it was not long before some of the sheep followed. How any of the animals came out alive from the acid test of that winter was a mystery. But the mare survived, as did the ram and the bull.

None of us fancied the job of attending to and curry combing that mare. It required generalship and agility of a very high order. Having been a witness to Tothill receiving a tremendous kick from her when his back was turned, which sent him to the other end of the stable, I determined not to run any chances with her ladyship. If she had to be curry combed, she was going to be curry combed at long range so far as I was concerned. With this purpose in view I tied the curry comb to a sapling about eight feet in length and scraped at her from a safe distance. It was not the generally accepted way of doing things but I didn't much care about that part of it so long as my person was safe. Captain Harston, however, seemed to think my method a silly one. Finding me engaged in the task one morning he berated me most soundly.

"Shall I never get you to do things in the proper way, you senseless fool?" he asked tartly. "Not so long as that beast has heels and teeth," I replied. "What's more," I continued, getting madder every minute, "I want to tell you that I am about tired of being called a senseless fool. Do you think I'm paying you for the pleasure of finding out how hard this brute can kick? Curry comb her yourself, damn it," and I threw the implement down and glared at him.

Captain Harston looked very much astonished at my outburst but wisely said nothing. Just about that moment I was angry enough to have taken on a whole battalion of Harstons. He picked up the sapling from the floor and, untying the curry comb, approached the mare with endearing words. "Whoa, Polly," he mellifluously gurgled, "dear old pet – dear old thing" – but Polly was not to be wooed with endearments. She was in an extra evil mood that morning and stood on no ceremony whatever. By way of acknowledgment of his cajolements, she let fly with her foot and missed him by inches. He managed to get past the danger zone of her legs and proceeded to stroke her down. "Whoa, now, Polly, whoa, now, old darling." Then he proceeded to curry comb her, emitting that strange hissing noise which ostlers appear to look upon as utterly inseparable from the task of grooming a horse. Tothill and I stood and watched. Captain Harston was going so well that he commenced to give us a lecture on the right way of managing a restive steed. All we had to do, he said was to approach an animal in the proper spirit of friendliness, and the rest was easy. Horses were highly intelligent beasts, and could size up those whom they knew to be their masters. He didn't get any further, for at that identical moment Polly turned round like lightning, caught him by the hair of his head and threw him into her manger, where she started to worry him.

I never heard such agonized cries as that poor man let loose, and I never saw a beast in such a villainous temper. She was simply raging mad. Both Tothill and I realized that something had to be done to save Captain Harston's life, so, armed with a pitchfork and a flail we began to belabour the brute with all our might. The flail was an unwieldy weapon, and once or twice Tothill hit himself on the head instead of hitting the mare which caused him to use unparliamentary language. The combined onslaught was too much for Polly. She diverted her attention from Captain Harston long enough to allow him to crawl into the next manger out of her reach and turned to us. Her heels flew out everywhere. It was a long time before she abandoned the fight. She was never so bad afterwards but always evinced a marked dislike for Captain Harston having anything to do with her. She was, as he had remarked, a very intelligent animal.

Having only one ox and the cow and the mare left with which to do his farm work, our mentor decided to try an experiment. He had often expatiated on the great need of initiative in the district. I remember his saying one evening, when we were sitting smoking by the fire, that it was a great pity to see so many intelligent human beings living round about us who were hampered by the lack of education and whose brains were going to waste. He told us that we were sent to the district for a well-ordained purpose. We had the education and the brains to be leaders in the community, and it was our bounden duty to raise the standard of the people about us. "It is up to us to show the way!"

By way of showing us his initiative and inventive power, he told us he had decided to form a team for the farm by hitching up the cow with the mare. He considered that the cow and the mare being both females would understand each other's idiosyncrasies better than if the mare and the ox or the ox and the cow were to be hooked together. But his knowledge of animal psychology was at fault. The mare did not understand the cow and the cow did not understand the mare. Polly was rather fleet on her feet and the cow – well, she was a cow. They presented a highly diverting spectacle when they were hitched up together and a more diverting one still when Polly started to trot and the cow had to follow. Two or three days of this experiment were quite sufficient for us all. Polly nearly kicked the cow into the realms of eternity and smashed in the buckboard, and this experience, together with the jeers of the settlers, ended in Captain Harston abandoning the attempt.

Towards the end of our pupilage, preparations were made for placing us on free grants of land obtained from the Government. A contract was given to a settler to clear off two acres of land for each of us and fence them and make them ready for a crop, at the munificent rate of $16 an acre. It may well be believed that he had earned his money by the time he had finished his contract.

Shortly before our departure to our farms, there was alarm caused by the non-return of one of our number from a hunting excursion, and Bell and I elected to search for him. We came upon him halfway across a portage, followed by three hounds and accompanied by a settler named Bedworth.[1] He was in high spirits when he saw us and cried out, "What's the use of going home? Come on back with us and we'll have a roaring time of it." We were nothing loth and went with him to the shanty where he and Bedworth had been staying. A good deal happened before we arrived there.

Along the shoreline of Buck Lake. Note the people in the three canoes. *Courtesy of Fred Hopcraft.*

It was a moonless, blustery night and there were whitecaps showing as we started to paddle across the water. Bedworth and I had the guns in our canoe, and Bell and Tryall[2] had the dogs in the other. Tryall was a devil-may-care individual and feared nothing. When about the middle of the lake he attempted to sit on the gunwale of the canoe and capsized it. This little accident didn't dampen the spirits of either Bell or Tryall. A weird conglomeration of noises now arose on the night air. The waves were howling, the wind was howling, the hounds were howling, yet above all the din and turmoil could be heard the voices of Bell and Tryall singing "God save the Queen." We had finally to tow them ashore, each of them hanging on to a side of the canoe.

Tryall had borrowed a woollen waistcoat from me before going on the hunt and, thoughtful chap as he was, put it in the frying pan to dry it out whilst we went to look for Bedworth's cow, the missing beast being catalyst for the whole episode. On our return I was surprised by a cry from Tryall, "I say, Frederick, I'm awfully sorry, old chap, but I'm afraid I've slightly spoilt your waistcoat. I can only find eight buttons in the frying-pan! Never mind, old chap," he added by way of an afterthought, "you were the only one amongst us who had one and now we're all even."

Captain Harston was by no means the only man in our district who essayed to make a living by teaching Englishmen the rudiments of farming. I can call to mind at least ten others who were engaged in the same occupation. One gentleman I remember in particular. He advertised his specialty as dairy farming. I happened to be well-acquainted with one of those who had taken the bait and had come to him to be taught. In giving me an account of his experiences, he said that the dairy farm consisted of one cow grazing on about five acres of land, and that the dairy was a root cellar, one end of which was filled with a miscellaneous supply of potatoes, and the other half by one or two shelves for standing the pans of milk on. For this magnificent method of teaching he was asked to pay £100 per annum. He stayed a month and took passage back to England.

It would be hard to say at this late day how many young fellows came to our colony. It must not be inferred that they all came to Captain Harston. He was responsible for about six or seven. The others followed, owing to being friends of those who had come before them. These took up land entirely on their own responsibility.

XX

Our Third Year

By the beginning of the third year we had cleared about fifteen acres on Captain Harston's place and had sown a field of oats and seeded it down. We had also quite a nice plot of potatoes and turnips. When the crop was ripe, he looked upon it as a favourable opportunity to teach us how to cradle[1] the grain and, when it was in the barn, showed us how to thresh it out with a flail.

We grew fairly adept at flailing, but the cradling was not a brilliant success. Captain Harston had informed us that it was one of the most delectable occupations on earth and grew quite poetic in descanting on its charms. "You feel when you start in," he said, "and lay aside swath after swath, that here indeed is joy. The glorious sunlight overhead, the rhythmical swing of the cradle as the back bows to the stroke, etc., etc.," Ah yes, indeed, what more could one wish for than that one didn't have to do it.

For, here is another picture. Again the glorious sunlight, again the back bowing to the sweep of the cradle, but instead of the sweet paeans that one might feel like raising to the goddess Ceres,[2] a string of mixed utterances in which profanity plays a major part. For there is no rhythmical sweep possible in a field where stumps abound and where roots and snags encumber the ground. Never a day passed without a cradle or two being rendered absolutely unserviceable by having all its fingers dismembered or its blade hacked to pieces against rocks or stones. And it was the same with the mowing. Scythes got bent double and snaths[3] got smashed in our daily fight with the enemy. It was an uneven struggle, for the stumps had always the best of it.

Our ploughing was a delight to the countryside. There was never anything seen like it before, and it is doubtful if there has been anything seen

like it since. Ploughing is not usually regarded as a dangerous employment, but it was positively hazardous with a mare like ours and when
attempted on such rocky soil. Given an uneven-tempered mare and a
field where one had to guide the plough over and through such obsta-
cles as stones, sticks, stumps and roots, it can easily be seen that the work
was perilous. Occasionally it happened that the plough nose got under a
root, and one got a celestial hoist under the chin which knocked one out
as cleanly as if a prizefighter had done it. Then the mare would take it
into her head to get nasty if her traces got awry, and it took a good deal
of ingenuity to get her into such a position that any backfire from her
heels would be wasted on the air and not on one's own carcass.

But those were minor evils in a life which seemed to be full of them,
looked at from an agricultural standpoint.

Artist unknown, *Forest Clearing II, View of the Clearance 3rd Year*. In *Canadian Illustrated News*, December 1879. *Courtesy of the Library and Archives Canada, Special
Collections CIN C-72634.*

XXI[1]

Moving On to Our Lots

AFTER THREE YEARS' TUTELAGE UNDER the supervision of Captain Harston, Tothill and I moved on to our respective lots. These were free grants from the Ontario Government and, of course, were given subject to the same provisions regarding improvements on the property as those obtained by all the other settlers. If I remember rightly we were to have fifteen acres cleared and cropped, and a serviceable habitation erected within five years, otherwise the land reverted to the Crown.

The Crown Lands agent of that day, Mr. Handey,[2] with whom our lots were recorded, and whom we had to consult, lived in Emsdale,[3] some fifteen miles away. It was rather onerous work getting to his residence, for there was no railway and the only means of travel was by horse and buckboard, or with oxen and wagon. The Spring freshets had turned every road into a quagmire. Every corduroyed portion was afloat, so it can be easily seen that progress was slow and hazardous. We wisely elected to take oxen, as a horse could never have travelled safely over the floating logs. We were about eight hours accomplishing the trip, but the warmth of the greeting we received from Mr. Handey caused the trouble we had experienced to fade into thin air.

After two or three hours rest at his hospitable abode, we started on the return trip. It proved, of course, just as arduous as the outward journey. On several occasions we had to wade into the icy water and float logs from under the bellies of the cattle, which was not conducive to our comfort or health. However, we survived the ordeal and copious draughts of hot lemonade, followed by thick layers of goose-grease over our chests on going to bed, saved us from possible dangerous complications.

A later photograph of Aemilius Baldwin's home on Buck Lake, taken in the early 1900s. *Courtesy of Elsie Bennett.*

My property consisted of about one hundred and fifty acres, in which there was a generous mixture of rock and swamp, while Tothill's land which was immediately opposite mine, on the other side of the lake, was little better than a precipice. He had chosen the location, he said, on account of the magnificent view to be obtained from the top of the hill when the land was cleared. When he had cleared about five acres he obtained his beautiful view but found he had no soil, as the first heavy rainstorm had washed all of it into the lake.

Our farms were really in the Parry Sound District,[4] in the Township of McMurrich, about a mile over the border between the two districts. But all our business and social interests lay in Muskoka, so we always regarded ourselves as residents of that area. Only at election times were we reminded that we were in Parry Sound.

We said goodbye to Captain and Mrs. Harston in quite a friendly manner. There were no tears shed at parting as our farms were almost adjoining and we knew we should see them often. Looking back at those years through the gathering mists of time, I see things not quite in the same prospective as I did then, for the views of advanced years are apt to be much mellower than those youth or middle age. The passing of time brings experience in its train and during that journey I have discovered that there are very many worse tribulations than the loss of money.

Far greater than this is the waste of time. I can forgive anyone who deliberately steals my money. He is certainly a jackal, but he is not so much to be despised as the man who deliberately steals your time and, in doing so, strips you of chances for progress and the opportunities for gaining useful knowledge.

Had our time been wasted? In a sense, yes, and in a sense, no. We had lost golden opportunities of trying to make good in more lucrative surroundings, but we gained in health and strength, at least those of us did who took moderate care of ourselves, so when all is said and done we were perhaps the "gainers." I will leave the question there as I am not willing to assert that we were lured to the backwoods by any such philanthropic motives on the part of our whilom pedagogue.

Philip Bell had already moved on to his land, which was just north of mine, and was most comfortably housed, as he had prevailed on one of his sisters to leave Scotland and make her home with him. Garrett also, as has been already mentioned, had settled down in a most commodious bachelor residence at the southern end of the lake, as also had Mr. Baldwin and one or two others. We were really far from being in a pitiable condition socially.

It was a proud day for me, when, just twenty-one years of age, I took possession of the log cabin that had been erected for me, and found myself the owner of a fine yoke of oxen, which I was told by the gentleman from whom they were purchased I must always address as Buck and Bright, "As they doesn't know no other name whatsomedever."

My land had been cleared and fenced for the munificent sum of $16.00 an acre. I forget, at this distance of time, how much my log house cost but as the walls and rafters were placed in position in one day by means of a raising bee, a few days help from a seasoned settler was all that was needed to make the habitation fit for occupancy.

It would not be going beyond the bounds of strict truth to say that we were the wealthiest circle of settlers to be found in that part of the district, for our little company was surrounded by incomers who had brought little besides stout hearts and strong hands with which to wrest a living from the wilderness. We, on our side, were never in want of the necessaries of life, for we were amply provided with food, money and lodging. Our dwellings were well-furnished, pictures and ornaments sent by kind relatives in England covered our walls, and one or two of us even boasted the possession of pianos, banjos and other musical instruments.

The only apology we had for calling ourselves pioneers lay in the fact that we endured the same heat and cold and attempted to clear the land in the same way as our less fortunate neighbours. We shared their labours, helped at their raising and logging bees and entered occasionally into their social festivities, but we were never subjected to any grimmer privations caused by lack of money.

All of us were imbued with the idea of being "gentlemen farmers," so most of us engaged the services of young sons of settlers to perform our chores and help us in our housekeeping. We felt that we could not possibly get along without someone to order about. Thus it passed that I hired the services of a young man named George to be my *factotum*. George was the son of a poor man who dwelt in a miserable shack by the side of Stisted Road, about three miles from my land. Well do I remember journeying to his abode, to find that he and his wife and two sons were housed in a log cabin about eight by twelve feet in size, with a roof formed by hollowed basswood slabs. The interior of the hut held nothing but a tumbled-down stove and one or two chairs, and a table as rickety as the stove. There were two or three dirty knives and forks on the table and a cup or two. The whole family must have slept on the floor, for there was no sign of a bed. One miserably dirty coverlet thrown into a corner seemed to comprise the bedding.

George, who was a youth of about eighteen years of age, was overjoyed at being hired, as also were his parents. He arrived the following morning in scant attire and I found him a thoroughly willing boy, but with somewhat queer ideas regarding certain social amenities. "Before you do anything around the house," I said, "go down and have a good wash." The grime of years must have been engrained in his countenance, for when he returned from his ablutions he was hardly recognizable as the same individual. I kept him for some months but had to part with him at last, owing to circumstances that left no other alternative. He fell foul of a skunk one day, with such dire results to himself that it was impossible to let him into the house and, as he dragged the malodorous creature right to my back door, people who visited me always made hurried departures, making me feel like a pariah myself. It was months before I was reinstated on the lake's visiting list.

Tothill had engaged a young and chubby scion of one of the Scotch clans as his assistant. He was built very much on the lines of the fat boy in *Pickwick*[5] and went to sleep at every available opportunity. Tothill found that the lonely only way in which he could utilize Bobby's services to advantage was in ox-driving, and he also discovered that this youth of tender years when engaged in this occupation was the possessor of a vocabulary of such red-hot profanity as even the devil's myrmidons[6] must have envied.

As we were bachelors, we were not bothered with many of the problems with which housewives are faced. We were able to dress as we liked, eat when we liked and go to bed when we liked. We did our own cooking, which needless to say, was of a somewhat primitive type, but only one or two of us attempted to master the intricacies of baking or roasting. Pork and beans formed our staple diet and the fact that we did nothing else but fry and fry and fry seemed to have no marked effect on our digestive organs. For puddings we would make flapjacks in the frying pan, on which we used to spread marmalade or syrup.

XXII[1]

Seeking Employment In Western Canada

During our three years' novitiate there had floated in from various parts of the Empire, friends who had been tempted by the tales of freedom from social restraints and of the shooting and hunting that we sent them. Bell's brother left his coffee-planting in Ceylon to become a member of our colony, while the eldest son of Bishop Fauquier, the first Bishop of Algoma, purchased a large tract of land close by. Also, one or two residents of the United States who had heard of our venture decided to sample the inwardness of a woodland existence. Memory recalls the fact that inside of four years from the date of our arrival there were no less than seventeen young men in our colony engaged in the task of endeavouring to clear land around the lake. Perhaps it would be a misnomer to apply the term "endeavour" to our life. Some did not endeavour much. Their idea of work consisted, for the most part, in hunting, usually in season. But sometimes out of it, and in taking trips to Toronto when occasion seemed to call for them, and these were fairly frequent. Our usual resort was Gus Thomas' Chop House[2] on King Street, which was situated in what was afterwards the Manning Arcade, and later still became the headquarters of the *Toronto Daily Star*.

It may easily be seen that we formed what we considered was quite a select society. As mentioned before, one or two of the residents had brought in pianos, and Garrett aided greatly in the musical portions of our entertainments by playing on the violoncello. He was the possessor also of a very fine tenor voice.

I have already expatiated on the beautiful scenery of the surrounding country and the fine expanse of water around whose shores we had located. Sufficient stress has already been laid on the fact that the late Fall and

Winter seasons were never of the mild variety. It may be that the dense woods attracted rain and snowstorms to a greater extent than in the more cleared portions of the province but, whatever the cause, we certainly experienced many blizzards and tempests at these seasons. In contradistinction to these were the glorious days of Summer and the absolutely calm days in Winter when the air was sharp as a knife and one could travel through the still woods and hear the trees cracking with sounds like pistol shots, and the ice-bound lake groaning in its binding chains. It was good to be alive then and the exhilaration created in one's breast when travelling behind a pair of willing horses was not the least of the pleasures that we derived from our sojourn in the northern wilderness.

How well I call to mind those winter nights. Furnaces were, of course, unknown to us. All we had to depend on for warmth were stoves, and wood was the only fuel. We had no such things as double windows, but despite these small drawbacks, we managed to keep cheerful and jocund. There were times when things went awry as when the fires went out on piercing nights and attempts at bread-making proved a dismal failure, or when stovepipes caught fire and set the roof ablaze. There were no fire engines at hand and we had to be our own firemen. How so many buildings escaped destruction passes comprehension. Given a shingle roof with a stovepipe stuck through about a foot at the top and with only small sheet of zinc about four feet in length bent over the ridge to catch the sparks that fell, it is easy to see that Providence alone preserved many of the structures from fire. Heavy snowfalls, however, helped a great deal as a shield in winter, and in summer most of the cooking was done in sheds outside.

We had to act as barbers for each other and learned in time to produce quite elegant specimens of our skill. We were also our own patchers and boot menders and did some of our own laundry work. The heavier articles such as shirts and underwear were taken to wives of neighbouring settlers for treatment.

The days immediately following our emancipation were halcyon days. We held logging bees on each other's properties, and chopping and raising bees, and the spirit of gaiety was always amongst us. I know that Garrett, Tothill and I worked like galley slaves. Many a day in winter we used to get up at daylight, in the biting cold, and after breakfast hie forth with our axes on our shoulders, and with slabs of thick pork sandwiched between slices of bread in our pockets, to engage in the task of chopping. Often the temperature would be below zero and we would

Eugene Haberer, *Making Maple Sugar in Canada.* In *Canadian Illustrated News,* March 1875. *Courtesy of the Library and Archives Canada, Special Collections CIN C-62613.*

plunge from tree to tree through two or three feet of snow to continue our job of felling. We revelled in the work, but when the noon hour came and we were confronted with the fact that our food was frozen solid and that to make ourselves any tea we had to scoop out holes in the snow to light a fire, we did occasionally feel that a comfortable seat before a warm stove at home would have been preferable.

But no discontented thoughts entered our minds. We were at an age when we were ready for any venture and looked upon money-making as one of the things in life only fitted for fools. If we had been compelled to sally forth and earn our own subsistence we would have viewed things differently. However, there we were, working on more or less aimlessly but with absolutely no idea of how to form a fixed plan of living. And so we went on, through gladsome days and nights until it began to dawn upon some of us that we were not making much progress. It dawned upon me more quickly than upon the others because I had less money and realized the necessity of breaking away from a life where there seemed to be no possibility of improvement.

Before this painful thought entered my mind, I had been working for over eighteen months on my lot. During that period I had come to the conclusion that in order to be more comfortable I would get my sister to come out and keep house for me. I felt that there would be no hardship entailed upon her in this as she would have several ladies to keep her company.

In order to make her more suited to her future surroundings my uncle decided to send her for six months course in domestic science at Wiesbaden, in Germany. Things went very well for a time after her arrival, but unfortunately she was unable to stand the strain of the climate and after a short stay of a year returned home to England.

This sad ending to my menage determined me in giving up for a time all thoughts of continuing on the farm. The wanderlust was strong upon me and as there was great talk at the time about Manitoba and the wonders of the great North-West Territories through which the Canadian Pacific Railway company was starting a rail line, I made up my mind to try to get on a Government survey and see something of that much discussed country.

Looking about for some means of getting there I was successful in obtaining a place with a surveyor who had a contract for surveying townships north of Medicine Hat. I parted from my friends at Buck Lake in the early Spring, hoping to return to them again in the late Fall, but it was nearly two years before I saw them again. I had tried hard to get one or two friends to apply for positions on the same survey but failed to arouse any enthusiasm. They were content to carry on in the way they were doing.

Prior to my departure I lent my place to a brother Englishman named Price,[3] on the stipulation that he should keep the clearing and the house in good order. I was sorry to say goodbye to those with whom I had been so closely associated. It is only in constant companionship with people that one gets to know the real worth of individual character and I can testify from my inmost soul that one could never wish to meet higher-minded, more generous, more genuinely bred gentlemen than formed our little coterie, in the Muskoka backwoods. And the very same, with regard to their sex, could be said for the ladies. They were true blue in every respect.

Price, in whose integrity I had implicit confidence, knew nothing whatever about farming, having just arrived from India where he had been working for years as a civil engineer. A severe sunstroke had compelled him to leave the country and he had found his way by some means or another to Muskoka, having heard that it was a fine country for invalids, and was a panacea for all ills – from tuberculosis to sunstroke.

XXIII[1]

Returning to the Bush

Upon my return from my western experiences,[2] it caused me some little astonishment to find my old companions were still dyed-in-the-wool Englishmen with all their convictions of the superiority of their countrymen in brawn, brain and bravery wholly undisturbed. This was, of course, owing to the fact that they had kept themselves sealed up in a remote corner of the world where they had been unable to mix with other men.

Many changes had taken place in the sprouting village of Ilfracombe[3] while I had been away. The "decent church that topped the neighbouring hill" had been abandoned for a more pretentious structure opposite Mr. Baldwin's abode, close to the entrance of Buck River,[4] and all the residents round the lake had contributed toward the cost of its construction. Among many improvements a sawmill had been built, two or three stores had opened up and the village had been promoted to the status of a post office so that in place of having to travel to Haldane Hill,[5] a distance of three or four miles, we had the mail brought almost to our doors, two or three times a week from Huntsville.

Some of the owners of farms had gone to England and brought back wives with them and one or two were contemplating doing the same thing. I found Price had been looking after things for me in a satisfactory manner, which, by the way, should not have been difficult, for I had handed the property over to him sans rent, sans taxes, sans expense of any sort, so that all that he and his wife had had to do was to make themselves as comfortable as possible. As soon as I arrived I made my way to my staunch friend Charles Smith[6] and asked him to accept me as a boarder for a few weeks till Price had had time to vacate the premises, and I was on the eve of taking possession of the place when my house was burnt down. I shall never forget how the information was conveyed to me. I had just returned from visiting a farmer in the neighbourhood and was washing my face at the tin bowl on the stoop in the early morning outside Smith's dwelling. Smith was standing beside me and remarked quite casually "That was a tough thing that happened last night." "What was that?" I enquired. "Come on, you're just kiddin', aren't you?" returned Smith. "I don't know what on earth you're talking about," I replied. "Well, you always was a bit of a joker," said Smith, "but I wouldn't take it quite as easily if I was in your shoes." "For Heaven's sake, man," I growled out, "what on earth are you talking about?" Then Smith began to laugh. "I ain't seen nothing like the way you looks at things," he gasped out between spasms of merriment. "I've seen yer almost in tears when your pup was hurt and here you are not carin' a tinker's dam when your house is burnt down!" "What!" I cried. My astonished exclamation convinced Smith that I had known nothing of the occurrence, and he then told me the circumstances.

It was the old story of the stovepipe stuck through the roof. I rushed as fast as I could through the woods to view the ruins and came on Price and his wife hunting assiduously among the still smoking debris for a gold watch that had been lost together with their other belongings. "I'm very sorry," he cried out as he saw me coming, "these flimsy structures do burn terribly fast, don't they?" It sounded to me like a somewhat peculiar morning welcome, but when he went on to say that he was sorry that he had lost his watch without any further reference to the greater loss that I had sustained my gorge did begin to rise. That house had meant a great deal to me. There were many pleasant memories connected with it, but the most poignant feeling that possessed me was that as I was looking forward to getting married in a short time it would mean an upset of my arrangements. When I looked at the orchard I had planted, almost every tree of which had been scorched, and at the outbuildings that had shared in the general conflagration there was a moment or two when I really felt downhearted. But the barn, which was some distance away had escaped and my good spirits soon returned. My cogitations went back to the time when I had proudly taken up ownership of the house. What a fine housewarming we had had, all the people for miles around had come to it. How drunk the fiddler had got! He had offered to keep guard over the keg and in order to do so had sat on top of it and on that coign of vantage[7] had played till he became so incapacitated by the rhythmic strains of music and the fumes of the whisky that he imbibed that he had had to be carried away to a quiet corner, "far from the madding crowd's ignoble strife"[8] where he slept till daylight dawned.

I remembered also the time when I came home one evening and found my sister and the maid huddled up at the entrance to the clearing shaking with terror. They told me that they didn't dare to enter the house for they had seen a bear walking in at the front door and had hurried away fast as they could. I didn't think it at all likely that a bear would walk in such a friendly, neighbourly way as that so I walked in through the wide open door and investigated.

Sure enough, there was a big black creature crouched in a corner of the room. It was getting dusk but a closer scrutiny showed me that what had appeared to the distorted imagination of the two to be a bear, was, in reality, one of the largest specimens of a porcupine that I had ever seen, huddled up in a distant corner of one of the rooms. It didn't take long to eject him with the aid of a long pole but my dog who was not imbued with the same kindly instinct that I possessed immediately flew at him and came off second best with his mouth filled with quills. It was an arduous undertaking to remove them and called forth howls of anguish from the victim.

It is a strange thing that such an intelligent animal as a dog never seems to profit by experiences with porcupines. I have never known one that didn't exhibit eagerness to try conclusions with any that came within fighting distance, The result has always been the same.

There were many other memories stored up in my mind and, when I gazed mournfully at the holocaust and watched my late tenant nonchalantly poking away with his stick among the ruins, I realized that there might be some truth in the contention of foreigners that the true Englishman is the most insouciant being on earth and that it takes nothing less than a downright insult to disturb his equanimity. Plain ruin won't do it.

There was nothing for it but to have my marriage deferred till a new building could be erected. Meanwhile Price found new quarters and I hired a man to help me build a small shack in which to reside until I had obtained funds to start on a new residence. My house had not been insured owing to its possessing no brick chimney, so everything was a complete loss – house, contents and tools in the sheds.

Cooper,[9] the man whom I had hired to help me on the clearing was a good, honest industrious labourer and we managed to get along very amicably together, in the small space left after putting in a stove and cooking utensils in the shack. He slept in the kitchen part and I in a boarded-off room next to it. The weather was February weather and a February in Muskoka is not at all reminiscent of February in the West Indies. The building had a slanting roof and was covered in with ordinary inch boards with battens to hide the crevices. While the stove was alight the cold was endurable, but when the blizzards raged and the snow swept by in cloudy gusts we generally had to sweep bushels of it off the beds and the floor. Sometimes it would rain and suddenly turn cold and we would find our hair frozen to our respective pillows as the rain was no greater respecter of our persons than was the snow. But as Cooper very genially remarked, we had lots to be thankful for, we had "a door that we could close any-how and two windies that was tight." We had not been able to bank up around the foundations with anything more permanent than snow, and as the weather was decidedly changeable, there were days when it had to be replenished to cover up holes caused by the milder atmosphere. How-ever, it was all fresh experience and I enjoyed it even if Cooper didn't. Here I would like to say something about my companion.

There seems to be a sort of impression prevailing everywhere that most of the honesty of purpose and godly living is necessarily to be met with in the ranks of the well-to-do. I cannot conscientiously assert from my own experience that such a state of things is true and I very much doubt if it is true in any country. I have found that good and bad instincts are fairly evenly divided and that there is as much good to be found among the poor as among the rich, the only difference being that when bad instincts prevail the rich are able to cut a wider swath than the poor owing to the greater advantages they possess in dealing in affairs of magnitude.

I found Cooper, a poor man quite unassailable when any chance of doing a bad action came his way. He was as poor as he could be but he was the very soul of rectitude. I used to go away for two or three days at a time to Huntsville and other places and always left large sums of money in an old tin box under my bed. It had no lock and the only "Open, Sesame" to its contents was the simple plan of lifting the lid. On one occasion I left $250 in the box and Cooper held watch and ward over it as if it had been his own. This is a simple tribute to the memory of an honest man to whom the possession of even one hundred dollars would have been wealth almost beyond the dreams of avarice.

Cooper did not stay long with me and, after leaving, went to Toronto and entered the service of the city in one of its many municipal departments. Shortly after his departure I began drawing lumber for my new house for which I had chosen a site close to the lakeshore and immediately opposite my friend Tothill's farm across the Narrows. The lake at this point was about three hundred yards wide and it was easy for us to hail each other across the water on a calm evening.

Tothill had been married about a year and was the proud possessor of a sturdy infant of about one month. Shortly after I had taken up quarters in a part of my new abode my ears were assailed on a calm evening by a piercing cry of distress from Tothill's cottage. It was a woman's voice and I rushed out to find out the cause of the outcry. I discerned Mrs. Tothill waving her arms wildly on the shore and calling at the top of her voice for help. She had a good strong voice and my hearing was extremely good at that time of my life. I could hear her distinctly. "Oh," she cried, "do please come over at once, my baby has got convulsions, and I'm afraid he's dying." I rushed to the canoe, jumped in and paddled quickly across. I found that Tothill was away on some errand and that the baby was in a really serious condition. Mrs. Tothill proved a capable mother. She besought me to rush to the lake and get a boiler-full of water and put it on the stove. We soon had a red hot fire going and when the boiler was sizzling we took the baby and dropped the poor little mite into the steaming liquid. I am glad to say that the effect was magical. The child was soon set to rights but I do not think I ever saw a lobster quite as red in hue as that baby was when we took her from that bath.

In a few months I got married myself [10] and the following two or three years formed a period of really solid hard work. This is not written in any spirit of self-glorification but to show how hard a lot is that of the backwoodsman engaged in carving out a farm for himself. In saying this I would not dream of comparing the trails I had to go through with those of the settler who arrived in the country without means and struggled sometimes frantically, to eke out an existence for himself and family. I am quite sure I worked as hard as any of them but always with the knowledge that there were three good meals ahead of me every day. I was up often before daylight snatching a hasty snack to keep me going till breakfast time and yoking my team of oxen preparatory to engaging in the task of stumping or other work.

For the uninitiated it may be explained that stumping consists of pulling the stumps out of the ground by means of a heavy chain and piling them up in heaps preparatory to burning. As the field in which I was working was swampy, the stumps drawn out were twice as heavy as ordinary ones taken from dry ground. The consequence was that I was not only wet from morning to night but the clay and black muck with which I was covered when making a pile for burning made me generally indescribably filthy. The damage to one's personal appearance mattered little as the lake was handy for a swim but the damage to one's clothing was immense. But I really absolutely revelled in the work. At first I had no extra help but as the days lengthened and the summer began to merge into autumn I began to feel the need of assistance. Fences had to be put in good repair, outhouses had to be properly roofed, a stable had to be built and various other matters to be attended to, so for a short time I hired the services of a young farmhand again.

The man I hired [Billy] had what the Scotch call a "canty conceit" of himself, and possessed the unhappy faculty of using words, many of which are not found in any dictionary whether it be the unabridged Oxford or a pocket Nuttall. At logging bees he shone with wonderful brilliance. He was a wonderful worker and kept everybody from idling. As soon as a logheap was piled up, we would sit on a log for a minute or two's rest but soon be aroused from our seats by an urgent command from the driver, "Com' on boys, com' on," he said on one occasion, "I never seen such a darned bunch of lazy adversaries in my life!" I pondered for a while after hearing this obfuscation and making nothing of it asked him in a favourable interlude what sort of a cuss word "adversaries" was. He turned and looked at me in surprise. "Ain't you never heard that word? Why Dad always used that word. I asked him one day and he says to me 'Billy, my boy, "adversaries" means them as talks a hell of a lot and does nothin.'" I said "Thanks very much. You've taught me a lot." Billy replied complacently, "You'd orter knowed my dad. He was a hell of a clever man."

Billy's personality looms up again in my mind when I remember an incident that occurred the following winter. My brother-in-law, [Philip] Bell, and Billy and I were working in the woods when we heard a hound in full cry after a deer. There was a glare ice on the lake and apparently the deer was heading through the woods straight for it. Nearer and nearer came the continuous baying of the hound and in about half a minute the deer was in full view on the lake with the hound a few yards behind it. Then the comedy commenced. The ice was so slippery that the deer, a yearling fawn, couldn't keep its feet. Neither could the hound. The sight of so much fresh meat so close at hand was more than we could stand, and we immediately left our axes and made off after the deer and the hound. The lake was about three-quarters of a mile wide at that part. As soon as we got onto the slippery surface, we began to tumble head over heels ourselves. Billy got so impatient at last that he pulled off his boots and took up the chase in his socks. About midway on the lake we caught up to our quarry and simultaneously the hound landed on the back of the deer also. Bell put his arms round its neck and Billy and I landed on other parts of its body. We narrowly escaped having our brains kicked out by its feet, which were flailing with lightning speed round our heads. It was a terrific struggle while it lasted but finally we managed to exhaust the poor beast, and Billy gave it the *coup de grâce* with his pocket knife. We pulled the body along the ice to the shore where we loaded it on to the sled we had been using for taking timber out of the woods, and carried it home in triumph. This happened over 55 years ago[7] so I hope the statute of limitations is on my side.

As I have stated before, we were to get many visitors in the summertime, some drawn by curiosity to see our settlement and a few on purely tourist jaunts. A married couple reached my clearing one day, having taken the wrong road and, intent on being courteous to them, we gave them refreshments. Afterwards I took them round to show them my belongings. In our stroll we came to the field where I was taking charge of a bull for a short time for a friend of mine. We went up to the fence and looked over the bars at the animal. The lady was standing next to me and I remarked genially to her "that beast looks very bellicose this morning." She looked at me in surprise and began edging over towards her husband. "Charlie" I heard her say to him, "what a very vulgar man that is!" I have often wondered what she meant or what she thought I meant.

Conclusion

The Muskoka region, as everyone knows, is noted for its sylvan beauty and for the wildness and rugged grandeur of its hills and dales. Anyone will tell you that it is a glorious haunt for the tourist who, weary of the enervating grind of town or city, thirsts for a retreat where he can bask amid balmy breezes and woo the goddess of quietude. But nobody in his senses would be bold enough to assert that it is an ideal agricultural region, although there are many fertile pieces of land to be found scattered throughout the district.

Its grazing qualities are superb. Cattle let loose in the woods in the spring will come out in the autumn as sleek and fat as any cattle could possibly be. Of course, there are drawbacks to set against the luxuriance of its fodder. The prevalence of leeks in the spring has a very bad effect on the flavour of the milk, for one thing, and the tendency of the cattle to roam far afield, is another. Many and many a time have we spent hours upon hours hunting for our beasts in the woods and failed to find them. Then, suddenly, innocent and lamb-like, they would appear at our gates when we had about given up hope of finding them. In all probability they had been sedately squatting within a few yards of the clearing and had wisely kept their bells from tinkling.

When we left Captain Harston to enter upon our own lots as farmers, we were about as well-equipped for practising husbandry as when we first came to the country. In this we were on a par with the other residents round the lake. It would be altogether too much to affirm that he was imbued with dishonest motives in advertising for pupils. At that period it was a common enough occurrence for Englishmen who had settled in the country to endeavour to eke out a livelihood by training young men in husbandry. The marked difference was that many of these individuals had real farms, and others, like our friend, had not.

That he really did his best with the materials at his command is not to be denied, and that we received very much kindness at his hands is not to be denied either. But notwithstanding this, the fact remains that there was no farm and that, if we had worked with him for fifty years, there was not enough good land on his lots to have enabled him or anyone else to practise the art of husbandry.

Another fact has to be noted, and that is that in three or four years, as soon as he had got a few of us planted, he left the district and, I believe, never visited it again. He may have imagined, in the peculiar constitution of his mind, that he had done all he said that he would do. He had laid the foundations of a settlement and had located us on free-grant lands, all according to specifications. But he would never have induced any of us to come to the country if he had not dangled the bait of agricultural plenty before our eyes and expatiated on the glorious possibilities of the district.

That the experience spoilt the careers of most of us goes without saying. We spent nine or ten years of the most valuable period of our lives in wrestling with the timber and undergoing many of the drawbacks inseparable from a settler's existence in a new country. The experience taught us one thing, and that was the magnitude of the difficulties that confront the pioneer. Of this I have already spoken, but it cannot be too strongly emphasized that the lot of the backwoodsman is a hard one. His surroundings make him often uncouth, often worse than uncouth but, like the soldier in the front trenches, he is fighting in the van, and the man who fights in the van is the man to be admired.

Many events I have purposely omitted to chronicle in these recollections. They were of too poignant a character, and no purpose would have been served by mentioning them. My endeavour has been, in the main, to give the humorous aspect of the settler's life so far as we came in contact with it during our farm pupil days or as it applied to ourselves. There were sorrows, many of them. There were happenings of a sort that could only occur in a place remote from the hand of the law. Some of our nearest and dearest friends passed away under the saddest of conditions. One by one, the remainder left the district.

Today, there is a great change to be seen in what was once a fairly thriving settlement. On a recent motor trip I paid another visit to our old haunts and talked to a few of the old settlers who were left in the neighbourhood. It was a depressing pilgrimage. Where once had stood a snug little hamlet, comprising a mill, two stores, a blacksmith shop and three or four dwellings, there was nothing to be seen but a small schoolhouse and a private dwelling. The little stone church that had taken the place of the old wooden structure on the hill was still there, and it made one's heart sad to stand inside and note the various memorial windows with which it was adorned. Most of them had been given by tourists, and only in two instances were names to be seen commemorating those who had been among the earliest of its founders.

Clearings which had once borne more or less of a crop were grown up again, and their wildness was as the wildness of the forest primeval. Ferns luxuriated, and silver birches and balsams and maples raised their heads above the dense undergrowth. By roadsides and in deserted clearings I noted many desolate graves and, in the little cemetery on the way to the village, four or five headstones showed above the all-pervading bracken. A woodchuck, seated on a tomb, gave a grotesque feature to the scene, and formed about as queer an adornment for a headstone as could well be conceived. Yet it presented so clear an illustration of the state of abandonment into which the settlement had fallen.

The eight miles of road leading from the railway station to the lake were rockier and wilder than ever, although here and there detours had been made round one or two of the worst hills. The drive was not a trip to be repeated; most of the clearings one passed were as wretched-looking as ever. Sheep browsed along the roadside, and children clad in next to nothing pattered with bare feet in the mud puddles. Occasionally one met a man clad in nondescript garments trudging along the road, carrying a pack on his back. It was essentially a byway of civilization, where daintily-garbed creatures might hardly be expected and where man would seem safe in assuming any sort of clothing he chose to wear.

When I arrived at the bridge which spanned the well-remembered river, a flood of memories rushed through my brain. I could see the little church and on the opposite side of the road the abode which had once housed my friend of the old times, Mr. Baldwin. I had been at the raising of that little cottage, some forty-five odd years before, and remembered the pride with which he entered into his domain. There was the stone chimney still standing and the little grove of birch trees on the lakeshore in which he had always taken so much pleasure and pride.

The house was not as quiet as in Mr. Baldwin's days, for on entering the enclosure to make inquiries I found the place occupied by a large family. I had known the father and mother in days gone by, and they did not seem to have prospered to any great extent in the interval that had elapsed. There was an all-pervading odour of fox around the place, proceeding from the presence of two small dog foxes which the owner had dug out in the spring and imprisoned within a small wire network.

Passing on over the hill and down to the hollow beyond, another memory flashed into my mind. Well did I remember that stretch of low-lying land, for on it had happened one of the strangest incidents in my life.

A young friend of mine, a settler, had died, and the funeral was to be held at the church. As the ice had vanished from the lake only two of three days previously, the water was very high and had, in fact, flooded the road to varying depths for a distance of about two hundred yards. In some places it was eight or ten inches deep, and in others as much as two or three feet. The funeral *cortège*, in order to get to the church, was compelled to pass over the spot, but it was an impossibility to get the wagon across.

Knowing that the mourners would be unaware of the state of affairs, I took my small skiff across and awaited their coming. Long before the wagon came into sight it could be heard creaking and bumping over the rocks and along the corduroy road. So rough was the route that had to be followed that the mourners had been compelled to sit on the shell holding the coffin in order to prevent it from bumping off the wagon. When the party came to where I was waiting, they gladly accepted my offer to ferry the remains across the submerged potion of the road. The skiff was a very small one and, when the shell was placed in it, there was only room for me to stand at one end and paddle or pole it across. In many places it would strand on projecting roots or stumps and the greatest care had to be exercised to prevent its being tipped into the water.

By dint of great exertion and sundry descents into the icy pools to ease off the craft, I managed to get it safely to the other side and then the problem of unloading it presented itself. There was only one man, a shantyman, waiting to help me and there was nothing for it but to do our best under the circumstances.

Standing with one foot on shore and the other in the skiff, we bent our backs to lift and, as soon as we did so, the boat began to move away from the shore. The language of the shantyman when he felt what was happening cannot be repeated. It was on a par with his size and certainly not suited to the occasion. The inevitable result was that we were both precipitated into the water while the boat floated away with its burden. I had to swim after it and fetch it back to shore where with the help of another man who had appeared on the scene we at last safely deposited the coffin.

It was not a very inspiring sight for the mourners, who were viewing the proceedings from the other side of the flood, and they were naturally somewhat incensed at what had occurred. But in the teeth of an icy blast and soaked to the skin, we helped to carry the remains of our poor friend to the cemetery which was situated about half a mile farther along the road, and left him to his long rest.

My last visit in this trip was to the erstwhile abode of Captain Harston. It would be impossible to give a really adequate description of the condition of the farm. There were about five acres of the original clearing in a state of cultivation. The remainder was just a wilderness of rocks and trees and shrubbery. Standing on the brink of the well-remembered precipice, I saw the magnificent lake, and immediately below me the spot where once had stood the house which we had taken such infinite trouble to build. There was not a sign of a log or a board, and bracken and second-growth birch and balsam had taken over complete possession. It was as if the hand of man had never attempted to reclaim it. The barn, scene of so many untoward happenings, had also passed out of existence. Only a hole remained to mark its site.

But the lake is not entirely deserted. Summer visitors have for years found it an ideal spot for an outing and there are three or four of the old houses still standing, purchased by families who enjoy a holiday in a location far removed from the bustling activities of the larger lakes.

Perhaps in years to come a brighter era will dawn for the settlement. There are signs that the advent of the telephone and the motor car may cause a recrudescence of its old prosperity. Picnickers come from outlying places to enjoy the excellence of its bathing facilities, lured there by its beautiful sandy beach and the splendour of its grove. But it will never rise above its present status in agriculture unless some genius devises a method of levelling the rocky hillsides and making grass grow on the unresponsive granite.

Yet on one or two of the farms great changes were apparent, show-ing that thrift and energy had reaped their reward. Comfortable-looking houses and well-kept fields indicated prosperity, and the children were as well set up and happy and intelligent as children could be. I wonder if those who enjoy such advantages cast a grateful thought backward to their progenitors who suffered and endured so much for their sakes.

Editor's Epilogue

It may be of interest to mention what eventually happened to the good Captain Harston, his wife, Mary, and the students that attended the Harston farm, as mentioned by Frederick de la Fosse.

It is necessary to look to the past and consider what was involved in farming in the backwoods of Muskoka. All aspects of life were affected by the weather. A true test was one's response to the astronomical range of the thermometer, which could rise to over 100 degrees in the summer and drop well below minus 40 degrees in the winter. Winters were long and summers short. Growing seasons were not sufficient enough to produce food for the settlers let alone grow enough feed for the livestock to survive the winters. Cattle were simply let out into the forest in the winter on their own, in hopes that they would return from the woods in the spring.

An article in *The Times* of England, August 13, 1875, was written by a James Crabtree of Ryerson Township, Muskoka, "Winter commences here in November (I mean real winter), and continues till the middle of May. There is no Spring weather; summer comes all at once, and with it every sort of venomous fly."[1]

Most of the land not occupied by lakes, swamps and streams was heavily wooded. As for the soil, there was very little and once the timbers were cut and the stumps removed, along came the rain and washed away the soil. The earth simply eroded into the creeks, rivers and lakes. It soon became evident that only a skiff of earth covered the solid bedrock.

What the pioneer did learn is that the countryside was absolutely beautiful: clean water, pristine lakes and abundant wildlife. It soon became evident that more fortunes lay in the tourist trade than in the business of farming.

The question then that has been raised, is what happened to these people? It is evident that none of students, nor the Captain, became farmers.

Charles Greville Harson (1848–1931)

Captain Charles Greville Harston sold his property, and he and his wife, Mary Regina Ellis, moved to the south to Toronto. Records collected from the Registry Office in Bracebridge, Ontario, show that he sold the last parcel of his land at Buck Lake in July of 1887. He and his wife appear to have moved to Toronto prior to this date, as his first Canadian military appointment in Toronto is recorded for December 14, 1883. On March 28, 1885, he signed on as captain of No. 4 Company, 10th Battalion of the Royal Grenadiers of Toronto.[2] Captain Harston fought with the Canadian militia forces in the Northwest Rebellion of 1885 against Riel and the Métis. He was awarded the Northwest Rebellion Medal with Clasp for his duties in this campaign.[3]

He then appears to have become involved in the insurance business in the Toronto area as an agent with the British Empire Life Ins. Co. (1887), as well as becoming Secretary Treasurer and Manager, Toronto Athletics Club (1894); Manager, Citizens Gas Control Co. Ltd. (1901); President, Greville Co. Ltd. Mining Brokers (1905).

In all, his military career spanned some 53 years, although his actual military employment would be more in the vicinity of 43 years. Charles Harston served eight years as a lieutenant with the Royal Marine Light Infantry in England before coming to Canada. During that time he passed his test for Captain (February 3, 1870) and at his own request retired with this title in 1871. He then attempted a career in the gun trade business. He acquired patent No. 2124 on August 11, 1871 for what was known as "Improvements In Breech-Loading Fire-Arms" and the patent No. 2989 on September 11, 1873 to what was also known as "Improvements In Breech-Loading Fire-Arms."[4] Some time later, now in Canada, he patented the "Harston's quick-load magazine," Patent No. 2065, on February 10, 1888.[5] The following year, on November 12, 1889, Charles Greville Harston patented his "Magazine Gun"[6] with the United States Patent Office, Patent No. 415,039, the application having been filed on March 8, 1888. The history of the rifle, however, was short-lived.

Charles Greville Harston, at about 20 years of age, poses in his
Royal Marine Light Infantry uniform. The photograph was taken
in England. *Courtesy of Mark Grantham.*

Greville Harston continued his career with the Canadian militia from
1883 to 1919. In March 1890, he became Honorary Aide-de-Camp to His
Honour, the Lieutenant Governor of Ontario.[7] While details are sketchy,
documents acquired from the Library and Archives Canada provide
details that he retired as Colonel Greville-Harston (having also acquired

a hyphenated name), at the end of the First World War.[8] He had signed on with the Canadian Overseas Expeditionary Force, with the rank of temporary brigadier-general and was added to the "General List" on June 29, 1916. He was then 67 years of age. In September of that same year, he became Chief Inspector of Arms and Munitions stationed near Brighton, England. Around December 13, 1917, Harston was accidentally shot in the left leg by the pistol of a fellow officer, while they were at the Automobile Club. From that point his health was impaired and he walked with the support of a cane for the rest of his life. Charles Harston served in the Canadian military until his retirement.

On the personal front, about 1911, he and his wife moved near the Citadel in Quebec City while he was serving in the armed forces. It was on November 7, 1912, while returning home from holidays aboard the steamer the *Royal George* that the ship went aground in the St. Lawrence River and became stranded near the shore of Isle of Orleans, about ten miles south of Quebec. Harston felt that the stress of that situation exacerbated his wife's poor health. Mary Harston died in Quebec City 32 days later, on December 9, 1912, and was buried in the Mount Hermon Cemetery. Up until 1923 Charles Greville Harston continued to live at 144 Grande Allée in Quebec City, but at some time after that he went back to England, and died at Croydon (London), on January 13, 1931. He was 82 years of age. His body was cremated and his ashes returned to Canada to be buried alongside his wife in February, 1931.

Aemilius Baldwin (1844–1925)

Aemilius Baldwin just happened to be a sibling in the then-famous Baldwin clan of Upper Canada. He was born in York (Toronto) on September 8, 1844, and died on April 3, 1925 in Bournemouth, England. Aemilius was the son of William Augustus Baldwin and Isabella Clarke Buchanan, daughter of James Buchanan (British Consul). He was the grandson of the famous Dr. William Warren Baldwin.[9] Aemilius Baldwin married Susan Cotterell and with this marriage there were three children: Alice Muriel, Eveline Gladys and Aemilius Reginald. His first wife, Susan, died October 9, 1888 in Toronto. Shortly before her death, their only son had died in August 1888. Aemilius senior then married Julia Pringle, daughter of well-known doctor, James Pringle, of Cobourg, Ontario. It appears that he conducted business around the Toronto area well into the 1920s. The letter written by Greville Harston in 1880 to the Ontario Agricultural Commission seems to suggest that Aemilius Baldwin may have been a partner in Captain Harston's agricultural scheme.

Richard Tothill (d. 1901)

Richard Hugh Tothill moved to the Barrie area, presumably before 1891, as he and his wife do not appear in the 1891 Census of the Stisted and McMurrich townships. A story, handwritten by his wife, Helen Maud Sands Tothill, records some early family history: "When my little Frank was 3 years old we moved to Barrie. Daddie had been too long on Buck Lake. He wanted a change and especially as with the exception of the Stohsbury's [Stotesbury's], we were all alone there. So we sold our animals and farm and left much to my sorrow for I loved the Beautiful Buck."[10] Richard Hugh Tothill died in Barrie, Ontario, on December 9, 1901.

William Garrett (d. 1927)

William Albin Vernon Garrett operated a sawmill in the Buck Lake area for some years. Tragically, he became caught in the saw and lost an arm. His first marriage to Ellen (last name not known) was very short as they were married in Cambridgeshire, England, in September 1883 and Ellen died in November of that year in Ilfracombe, Muskoka.[11] His second marriage was to Annie Sarah Graham Bell of Scotland, the sister of Mary Janet Graham Bell, wife of Frederick de la Fosse. Eventually the Garrett family moved back to England. There appears to have been no children in either marriage. William died at the age of 93 on May 16, 1949, and is buried in the Bournemouth East Cemetery, Dorset, England. His wife, Annie Sarah, died April 20, 1927, and is also buried at the same cemetery. It appears that William's great-grandparents were wealthy tea merchants of Scotland.[12]

Philip Graham Bell (1861–1927)

Philip Frushard Graham Bell, born December 8, 1861, in Scotland, was another individual who came to the Harston farm. His parents were Thomas Bell of Scotland and Rose Hedger formerly of Bath, England. With the death of his father and the deaths of his grandfather and mother,

Philip came under the guardianship of his uncle, Richard Bell. As his great-grandson, Gregory Graham Bell, writes, "A family story was told that Philip was a spirited youth and his Uncle Richard grew a bit tired of his exploits and arranged for him to go to Canada."[13] There he became a pupil of the Harston farm. As to his finding his way to Muskoka, there are two possibilities. One is that his uncle came across advertisements placed in British newspapers by Captain Harston, or secondly, that the relatives of de la Fosse may have known the Hedger family in Bath, England, and provided his Uncle Richard with the details.

As previously noted, Philip was the brother of Annie Sarah Graham Bell who married William Garrett and the brother of Mary Janet Graham Bell who married Frederick de la Fosse. In his text, de la Fosse notes that Philip took up land next to his on Buck Lake. Philip Frushard Graham Bell married Margaret Hodge Mackenzie in 1884. Their children were George Graham Bell (1885–1975) and Mackenzie Graham Bell (1887–1947). A daughter, Katherine Graham Bell, died in infancy. Philip's first wife, Margaret, died in 1913. During this time they had taken up residence in Toronto and summered on Lake Joseph.

Philip later married Laura Tyson McKinley (1869–1969), a widow who owned the Nepahwin-Gregory Inn on Lake Rosseau. Philip Frushard Graham Bell died in Muskoka in 1927, at the age of 66.

It is possible that Philip's brother Thomas may have made an attempt to learn farming at the Harston home on Buck Lake, but details are very sketchy. Another name, Mr. Lyall, denotes one more possible student. It is also possible that other young men came to the Harston's to learn farming. If this is so, no other details have surfaced to be included here in this new, augmented edition of *English Bloods*.[14]

Appendix A

Research evidence pertaining to *English Bloods*

───────────────
───────────────

1. Letter from C. Greville Harston to the Ontario Agricultural Commission, 1880

The following letter is taken from a copy of the original held by the Seminary of Quebec Library. The content clearly identifies the pupils to date who have come under inducement from Harston, including F.M. de la Fosse. This copy was acquired from the University of Guelph, Ontario Agricultural College on May 23, 2001, with the assistance of Sue Bennett, Manager, Development and Public Relations.

The Ontario Agricultural Commission met at four o'clock p.m. in Bracebridge, August 24, 1880. Present were the Commissioners, Wm. Brown (chairman), Edward Stock and A.H. Dymond. During the sittings of the Commissioners in the Parry Sound District, the following letter was put in and admitted as evidence:

Ilfracombe, Muskoka
Dear Sir, – I have been reading the reports of Tenant Farmers' Delegates on the Dominion of Canada as a field for settlement, and notice that this district is entirely ignored. Now, I came out to Canada in the winter of 1875–6, and know Ontario pretty well, and have farmed in East York, but in the winter of 1877–8 I moved here, and have now nearly 75 acres cleared, and I am so satisfied that for stock raising this district is far ahead of any other part of the Dominion that, besides Mr. Aemilius Baldwin, of Masquoteh, who came in with me, I have induced a

161

number of gentlemen with some capital to come from England and elsewhere to settle here, and they have all large clearings, notably H.H. Stotesbury, E.N. Stotesbury, W.A. Vernon Garratt, R.H. Tothill, F.M. De la Fosse, P.F.G. Belle, A.J.O. Sweet and F.G. Fauquier, and there are others still coming. I have a thoroughbred [sic] Durham pedigree bull and about twenty head of cattle and 20 head of sheep, and our greatest drawback is that the settlers in here are so poor that they cannot even afford to pay for the services of a good bull. If all the settlers had some means, like my friends, the country would soon become a very important part of Ontario. We have built a church and parsonage and raised $950 per annum for our clergyman, and cleared him five acres of land. I have had my house full of Toronto visitors, etc., who are astonished at what they see and could not believe the country was anything like it until they came here. If the government would only induce men of some means to come and settle here the whole Province would be largely benefited by the stock that would be raised. Surely this could be done by the Government by some push or exertion, if I alone have been the means of forming such a settlement here. As you may guess from my being able to form this settlement, I am pretty well known in England and my opinion is of some weight, so that if the Government will take some extra steps to make a push for the right class of settlers, instead of letting the district be so entirely ignored as it is in the report of the delegates, I shall be happy to give them all the assistance in my power. I trust, therefore, that you will take some action to induce the Hon. Commissioner of Crown Lands and the Minister of Agriculture to take some steps in the matter.

I am, dear sir, yours truly,
C. GREVILLE HARSTONE [SIGNED]

2. History of the Ilfracombe Mission, 1881

The following account is held at the Bibliothèque J. N. Desmarais Library, Laurentian University in Sudbury, Ontario. It has been taken from the publication *Algoma Missionary News and Shingwauk Journal* of December 1, 1883. The information was received on February 8, 1999 from Laurentian University Archivist, Martha Brown, and identifies Mr. Harston as a settler in the area.

History of the Ilfracombe Mission

Five years ago, where I am sitting in my study writing, and for many miles round here, all was dense bush, inhabited only by deer, bears, etc. Now, all has changed. There are farms and clearings to be met with in every direction, and all the land for several miles around has been taken up, and is already brought or being brought into a state of cultivation. A Mr. Smith and a Mr. White were the first settlers here. They came into the bush in the autumn of 1877, and a few months later were followed by a Mr. Harston and a Mr. Baldwin. This pioneer band had very many hardships and privations to endure. They were quickly followed, however, by others, who took up land as near Buck Lake (on which the settlement of Ilfracombe is founded) as possible. In the following autumn 1878 Mr. Harston (a retired army officer, son of the late Rev. Mr. Harston, some time rector of Sherbourne) began holding regular Sunday services at Mr. Smith's shanty, where at the first service there were only three present. Mr. Harston, like a true Churchman, adhered throughout to the prayer book, and read a sermon from some well-known divine. After a time Mr. Smith's shanty became to small for the congregation, and it was decided to adjourn to Mr. Harston's own house, a short distance off, but more commodius and more accessible from a lake. In the following winter the good and self-denying Bishop Fauquier paid the infant colony a visit, and cheered them much by his presence and sympathy. He encouraged the settlers, who were continually increasing in numbers, to try and build a church, and he promised them he would do his best to provide them with a pastor. Accordingly Mr. Harston did what he could to collect funds for a church and chiefly owing to the great kindness of Miss Barler, who inserted some of his appeals in the Net, soon he was enabled with the help of the settlers, to erect a log church with seating capacity for 60 persons. The church – after being built with much difficulty, owing to the absence of saw mills in the district – was opened for the first time on August 10th, 1879, by the Rev. Mr. Paterson, rector of Christ's Church Deer Park, near Toronto.

REV. A.S. SWEET, 1881

3. Letter from Frederick de le Fosse to Dr. Talman, dated February 17, 1937

The following letter was acquired from Frederick de la Fosse's great nephew, Gregory Bell; this letter is part of his family collection. Gregory's great-grandfather, Philip Frushard Graham Bell was the brother of Mary Jane Graham Bell who was Frederick de la Fosse's wife. While researching this document, I discovered that a copy of the same letter is contained at the Archives of Ontario, File B/DEL. At the time of the writing, F. de la Fosse was librarian and secretary-treasurer at the Peterborough Public Library.

> Feb 17th 1937
> Dear Dr. Talman
> I ought to have replied earlier to your inquiry whatso to the real name of the gentleman who figures as Captain Martin in my book – Please excuse delay which is entirely owing to stress of work –
> As I knew him in the old days he was Capt. Greville Harston, afterwards of Gen. Sam Hughes' staff in the first war, where he blossomed out as a general and went overseas to distribute medals to the Canadian troops in France.
> However, "peace to his ashes" he died a year of two ago. In England. – I am so glad you liked my book – after all the appreciation of readers is the best thing – far better then the acquisition of a few paltry dollars. – And I have had, I am glad to say many hundreds of letters and words of appreciation and not one of condemnation!
>
> Very sincerely yours
> FRED M DE LA FOSSE

4. Notes in the copy of the original *English Bloods* belonging to Mr. and Mrs. Andrew Hickling.

The book was presented to Andrew and Jessie (Howell) Hickling on October 28, 1939, by Mr. A.C. Fraser of Yearleys. The page numbers shown represent pages in the original text. The information was noted by Jessie Hickling;

> On p. 9 – leaving England for Canada; p. 20 – name Wardle – old Mr. Yearly, Teck and John's grandfather and [the community of] Yearly's

first postmaster in year 1884; p. 27 – Yearlys beside Wardle name; p. 41
– Clipping pinned, also written Trip to the old Stisted Road; p. 44 –
(re parting) The parting would be at Absalom Lamb's corner, as road
then came out at Duffield's and up by old Mrs. Purcell's near Lambs';
p. 45 – Later-the old finger-board hill at Sproats, Aspdin, where road
went through to Absolam Lamb's; p. 51 – names – Melius was Mr.
Baldwin, Barrett was Mr. Garrett, Harkins was Mr. Tothill; [a copy of
a note in Mrs. Hickling's book follows] Mr. Harkins was a Mr. Tothill,
father of the Mr. Tothill who with his son was here in summer with
there boat on top of car. Mr. Harkins [Tothill] showed me his father's
name in English Bloods and I showed him my father's name Lorenzo
Howell, mentioned only in one place in book, page 166 [handwritten
"see p. 124"]. Mr. Tothill who was here from N.S. was born at Ilfracombe. He was a rival to Mr. Jas Middleton in a foot race and jumping;
p. 56 – Mr. A. C. Fraser of Yearley [handwritten "p. 109, 147"]; p. 63 –
Alex Hamilton and Mrs. H. store. Later (Mrs. Swan), [burly dark-
bearded underlined] Mr. Swazie of Aspdin, father of Herb, Sherman
and Harry Swazie, Wesley and Harry and Mrs. Duffield; p. 65 –
[Hodags underlined] Wildcats; p. 66 – [one mulatto underlined] Mr.
Duncan; p. 67 – [Mr. Briggs underlined] Mr. & Mrs. Chas. Smith, 2
sons Jim and George; p. 68 – Jimmy White – see also page 165 and
166 [handwritten "Black"]; p. 70 [Green underlined] Holt, father of
Joe and Frank Holt, Kitty and Louie Holt; p. 75 [Tomkins underlined]
Mr. Walter Hopcraft; p. 89 – Canns Hotel Huntsville; p. 96 – Mr.
Ramey-Nicholls Schenider [handwritten "eni > ein See p 158." I believe
referenced to the spelling of the last name]; p. 97 [Wiseman and Robey
underlined] I don't know; p. 100 – [Barrett underlined] not sure [hand-
written "See p.51"]; p. 109 – Mr. A.C. Fraser [handwritten "See p. 56,
147"]; p. 112 – Sandy Hayes, I have heard Pa tell many yarns re Sandy
and his wife; p. 115 – [aphorisms underlined] a short sentence with a
great deal of meaning; p. 124 – Mr. Peters, a carpenter framed Chalmers
church on the town line in 1878. My mother and Mrs. Peters cleaned
floor of shavings for the funeral in church of Joe Warren in 1887. He
was the second burial in that cemetery, Mrs. Moore was the first. Before
the church was built Mrs. Moore was Mrs. Pace mother buried 1886.
Deed for the cemetery acre was got from Lorenzo Howell in 1886 in
spring; p. 128 – [John the Baptist underlined] Mr. Hopcraft Sr.; p. 129
– [2nd paragraph] well known ministers here. [3rd paragraph] Mr.

Manning-John McCarthy built the stone church at Ilfracombe; p. 134 – [Hanson underlined] Hanson Quinn; p. 140 – Malkins, Tippers and Manns we know; p. 141 – [Andover underlined] Dave Overhand; p. 144 – [Strauss underlined] "Strauss" The Guislers of McMurrich [handwritten "p. 205"]; p. 147 – [Fralick underlined] Fralick Fraser, Bert Fraser's dad; p. 155 – [Nate Thompson underlined] a river driver Nate Thompson; p. 158 – [Nicholls underlined] Nicholls Scheinder; old Mr. Riddel also made shingles by hand [handwritten "See p.96"]; p. 165 – [Mr. & Mrs. Black underlined] Jimmy White's baby [handwritten "See p.68"] Mr. Sweet married my father and mother in March 21 of 1881 at the home of Uncle Dick Mallough across Axe Lake. Mr. & Mrs. Lorenzo Howell to and on return from wedding drove across on the ice. A risky trip on March 21, the first day of spring; p. 166 – [Lorenzo Howell underlined] see page 205 re Bowser [handwritten "& p. 166"]; p. 168 [Samuelson underlined] Bill Johnson lived on the town line. Lamp exploded and burned Mrs. Johnson to death in bed or dress caught fire. My mother took John Johnson her baby of 6 months to keep for some time. John is now in Edmonton. Mary Middleton and mother attended the funeral; p. 177 – [Lamington underlined] Mr. Remington; p. 173 – [Mr. & Mrs. Hadmore] – Mr. & Mrs. Cudmore [Flanagan underlined] Mr. Pat OHolleran, father of Jack, George & Bob [handwritten "sp" possible directed at spelling of the name OHalleran.]; p. 187 [Whitstead underlined] Wallace Hopcraft – Ilfracombe P.O., Wm. Fraser also kept the Charlinch P.O. on old Stisted road; p. 190 – The Andersons, Mr. & Mrs., Louise, Matt, Jack & Janie. All four children now dead. Matt Anderson the last. Died in 1951 all alone in the woods, he was found dead by men who were looking for him; p. 192 – [Catesby underlined] could be old Mr. Cousin's wife [note-the book clearly says this is a bachelor]; p. 222 – Mr. & Mrs. Ed Cousins; p. 223 – Robert Fair [funeral at church]; p. 205 – re Bowser – Mrs. Bowser was a Guisler girl. [handwritten "p.144"]; p. 210 – Bedworth, name of a settler.

5. Graphic Publishers Limited of Ottawa, Ontario

Very little information was obtained regarding the relationship between Frederick M. de la Fosse and his publisher, Graphic Publishers Limited. It can be said that a gentleman by the name of Henry C. Miller, in association with commercial artist Alan B. Beddoe, had the idea to publish

Canadian authors, and produce strictly Canadian material which would be printed and bound in Canada for the Canadian reader. Henry C. Miller owned a small printing firm in Ottawa. In the inside of a long out-of-print copy of the original *English Bloods* is the line, "Produced Entirely in Canada by Graphic Publishers Press, at Ottawa, Canada." The company that began in 1924 fell victim to the vagaries of the economy and went bankrupt in 1932.

A full page advertisement on behalf of Eaton's Department Store which ran in the *Toronto Star*, page 33, on Friday, January 20, 1933, read, "Eaton's Book Department certainly made a 'coup.'" It had purchased the entire available stock of the now defunct Graphic Publishing Company. "This entirely Canadian collection by noted Canadian authors, includes cloth-bound editions, originally priced from $1.50 to $3.50 each. We offer them for .25c each. 25,000 more were available in sheet form only, so Eaton's printing department bound them with paper covers in time for this huge sale! They are priced at 2 for .25c. We firmly believe every last book will go at these phenomenal prices and suggest to librarians and other interested in quantity buying to shop early before some titles are sold out completely." Below this copy is the line: "Spotlight Sale: These titles in Paper Covers 2 for .25c." The titles included *English Bloods* by Roger Vardon. Edward St. John, in his MA thesis of 1974, notes this and iterates that the inventory was worth $29,774.43, the sale from the estate of the books was $3,000.00[1] (Supreme Court of Ontario, Bankruptcy Court, File Number 320–32).

English Bloods had been produced in two different formats. The first was in cloth hardcover with a dust jacket and the second in an olive green paper cover. As was typical of the time, the publisher produced the sheets of a book but did not necessarily provide a cover until such time as sales were made of the titles. Prior to the discovery of the Eaton's ad it was not known that soft cover copies had been produced. Had Graphic prospered and had the economy been more positive, it is likely that more copies of *English Bloods* would have been sold in cloth. The books were well-designed and solidly made.

Books by Graphic Publishers carried a logo of "the Thunder Bird," as designed by graphic artist Alan B. Beddoe. He was responsible for establishing much of the distinct style of the publishing house. The famous "Thunder Bird," the ancient and honoured mystical icon of Canadian Native People, stood for tremendous energy and the power that man felt in thunder and lightning.

When Graphic Publishers Limited went into receivership, the official reason given for insolvency was the lack of working capital. Henry Miller had left the company in 1929 and Mrs. M.H.W. Cameron took charge of financial operations. She invited Frederick Philip Grove[2] to become editor. St. John wrote, "It seemed reasonable to conclude that despite the other factors which were evident in the failure of the company, this was the basic course of the problems and it had been so since the very beginnings of the venture."[3] The whole enterprise came to an end in March of 1932. Graphic Publishers Limited went into receivership on the 28th day of April 1932. Edward St. John also wrote, "As Erick J. Spicer has stated, 'In short, I believe that the depression was the killer; mismanagement and insufficient capital had already survived for some time.'"[4]

It could be argued as to how many actual editions carried the Graphic logo. It appears that 83 books including fiction, poetry, travel, biography, history, natural history, children's books and literary criticism were produced during the lifetime of Graphic Publishers. Edward St. John sums up their accomplishment as such, "The Graphic Publishers have left an indelible mark upon the publishing scene in Canada. Their significant output will secure their position in the history of Canadian Publishing."[5]

Frederick Montague de la Fosse signed a publishing contract with Graphic on July 8, 1930, and his book was published. But in less then two years, his dream of providing readers with stories of his adventures in the Muskoka backwoods of 1878, came to an end.

6. Obituary, Frederick de la Fosse – "Librarian Passes Away At Peterboro"

Muskoka will hear with regret of the death at Peterboro recently of Mr. F.M. Delafosse, city librarian, and well known writer and commentator. Mr. Delafosse, under the pen name of "Roger Vardon," wrote "English Bloods" several years ago, a volume which dealt with the problems of early settlement in parts of northern Muskoka, and told interestingly of some of the hardships and activities of the early pioneers. He himself, was among the early arrivals in this part of Muskoka. He was cultured and refined, and came out from England to learn farming in Canada. He chose a difficult locale, when he decided to make agriculture his life interest in Muskoka. It was out of his own experiences, and his contacts with other fellow travellers, that he framed the ground work for his volume, "English Bloods." He lived in the

locality of Buck Lake. His book, now a rare volume, was popularly read by many here, and in other parts of the province.
Mr. Delafosse had reached the advanced age of 90 years.
The Huntsville Forester, (not dated)

7. Newspaper clipping – "Tragic Death at Parry Sound, 1908"

The following is copied from a newspaper clipping found on page 147 of Mrs. Andy (Jessie) Hickling's copy of *English Bloods.*

Parry Sound, Sept.17 – Two lives were lost on Wednesday in the bush fires which are now raging in the vicinity of Parry Sound. Miss Caroline Guisler and the [handwritten "p.144"] eighteen-month old child of her niece were the victims. Miss Guisler and the infant were on their way to attend the funeral of a Mrs. Cudmore, and as she [handwritten "p.173"] drove along a road by a forest, a big tree which had been burned through near the roots, fell over the buggy killing both of the occupants instantly. When found both bodies were pinned down by the burning tree, and were so badly burned as to be almost unrecognizable.

Dr. G.R.R. Richardson of Sprucedale made an examination of the remains, and decided that an inquest was unnecessary. Miss Guisler was the only daughter of her aged father who is about 90 years of age. The horse, frightened by the falling timber, broke away from the buggy and escaped. Great fears are entertained around Sprucedale as to the further spread of the fires in the Parry Sound district.

8. Excerpt from letter to Mr. John Wilson of Toronto, Ontario, from Frederick de la Fosse, dated November 24, 1944:

...I must tell you that the right name of the gentleman with whom I worked was not Martin. I had to place him and some others under false nomenclatures owing to the possibility of hurting feelings of people who would have known them as friends or relatives....[6]

Appendix B

Biographic sketch of Frederick Montague de la Fosse

FREDERICK MONTAGUE DE LA FOSSE, born at the Military Station of Roorkee in India's Bengal province on July 25, 1860, died in Peterborough, Ontario, Canada, on September 26, 1950.

When he was seven, his parents moved the family to England because of ill health. His father, Captain Charles Edward de la Fosse died in England, May 24, 1868, and his mother, Isabella Sophia (Ricketts) de la Fosse died a short time later, on June 5, 1868. Orphaned by the deaths of their parents, Frederick and his sisters, Mary Isabella and Grace Louisa made home with their mother's parents in Bath, Somerset, England. Sometime about 1870 Frederick's youngest sister, Grace Louisa, died. Around this time, Frederick came under the guardianship of his mother's brother, Colonel Montague Ricketts.

In 1873 he attended Wellington College, a school where most of the pupils were sons of army and naval officers; then transferred to Chadstock College for a year and a half. Frederick wrote, "I left school for good, having made a much better name for myself in athletics than in scholarship, and a serious problem was raised in the minds of my guardians as to what to do with me." At this point it was decided that Frederick was to go to Canada to learn farming at the homestead of Captain Harston. Frederick arrived on the Canadian shores in May of 1878. The story of his time as agricultural "pupil" at Captain Harston's Agricultural Farm was captured in the book *English Bloods*, which he wrote under the pen name of Roger Vardon. The book was published in 1930.

Following his time in Muskoka, he married Mary Janet Graham Bell of Scotland, in Toronto on March 25, 1886. This marriage produced four

The home of Frederick and Mary Janet de la Fosse, circa 1902. The home was known as "Green Gables" and later became Buck Lake Lodge. From left to right: Reginald Whitley; Frederick de la Fosse; Francis de la Fosse (standing), about 15 years of age; Mary Janet de la Fosse; young boy, not named; two young women (seated), not named. In front, seated, left to right: Phillipa de la Fosse, about 9 years old; Marjorie de la Fosse, about 11 years old. *Courtesy of Muriel (Whitley) Hopcraft.*

children: Francis Charles, born December 7, 1887; Rose Frushard, born 1888, died in infancy; Marjorie Columbine, born 1891, and Phillipa Gabrielle, born September 1893.

Frederick and his wife moved to Toronto where Frederick seemingly took on some role for Trinity College of Toronto for a brief period in the late 1800s. The family then returned to the Muskoka backwoods to a home that was known as "Green Gables" in the Stisted Township. The names of the de la Fosse children are recorded between 1896 and 1899 in the school rolls of the township. Frederick then moved his family to Lakefield, near Peterborough, Ontario where he became the copy editor for the *Peterborough Examiner* from 1907 to 1910.

On December 5, 1910, de la Fosse accepted the position of public librarian for the Peterborough Public Library. His wife Mary moved with daughter Phillipa, to California, for health reasons(a date is not known) and lived there for a time until her death on November 17, 1921. According to an announcement in *The Times* of London, England: "De La Fosse, On the 17th November, at Ontario, California, Mary Janet (nee Graham Bell), wife of Frederick Montigne De La Fosse, of Peterboro, Canada." In 1925, de la Fosse married for a second time. His wife was Amy Vernon Halliday, the daughter of a well-known Peterborough doctor.

During de la Fosse's career as public librarian he wrote the book *English Bloods,* published in 1930 by Graphic Publishers Limited of Ottawa, Canada. He next produced a manuscript known as "Western Reminiscences," which remains unpublished to this day. Among his other credits, he co-authored "A Centenary History of St. John's Church," Peterborough (1927) and privately published two books of poetry. *Verses Grave and Gray* (1937) and *A Dream and an Allegory* (1944). De la Fosse also wrote a poem on the occasion of the marriage of Princess Elizabeth

Frederick de la Fosse later in his life. *Courtesy of Trent University Archives.*

(now Elizabeth II). He was delighted with the acknowledgement received from Buckingham Palace on January 29, 1948.

Frederick de la Fosse retired from his position with the Peterborough Public Library in 1946 at the age of 86. In autumn of 1950 he suffered a fall, and ten days later, on September 26, 1950, suffering from weakness and a broken hip, Frederick Montague de la Fosse died.

Conversations with a number of people familiar with Frederick de la Fosse and his book *English Bloods* led to another discovery. It seems that, often, when asked to sign a copy of his book, he would write this poem, that follows. It was also in the preface of his "Western Reminiscences."

Go forth my little book – where'er you travel
Leave kindling hearts behind you, laughs and smiles,
Your mission still life's worries to unravel
And lead the reader on by gentle wiles
To play his part right gallantly and strongly
How shall he fail? – he cannot reason wrongly
Who breathes the spirit of the PIONEER!

NOTES

EDITOR'S INTRODUCTION

1 The name Roger Vardon is a pseudonym for Frederick Montague de la Fosse, the author of *English Bloods*, originally published in 1930 by Graphic Publishers of Ottawa.

2 As Frederick Montague de la Fosse is the author of *English Bloods*, the name "Roger" that was used originally by the author has been changed to Frederick or Fred. The identification of de la Fosse as the author was confirmed by John Frewer, grandson of Frederick de la Fosse, in his letter (dated February 5, 1992) to Dr. A. Fern Rahmel of Peterborough, Ontario. Also correspondence with Fern Rahmel produced a quote: "Grandfather always regretted having assumed a pen name (Roger Vardon). As all of the characters in *English Bloods* were real people (and a number of them still alive at the time of writing) although he used fictitious names, I believe someone per-suaded him to use a pen-name to avoid any possible repercussions!" See Trent University Archives Ref. Rahmel, Fern 94-005/1/1.

Other evidence was found in an article published in the *Muskoka Sun* on Thurs-day, September 8, 1988, where a granddaughter is talking about Frederick de la Fosse and *English Blood*s. Mrs. C.P. Keeley, Golf Club Road, Port Carling, says she is glad that her grandfather's book is still appreciated. The article notes that the name "Roger Vardon," under which her grandfather wrote the book, was not his real name, but rather Frederick de la Fosse.

Correspondence received by the editor (June 2002) from John Frewer indicated that his grandfather was unhappy with the published book and returned to Ottawa to seek out the publisher. His grandfather wanted to have the book republished with the real names but when he went to Ottawa, the company was no longer there. It seemed that they had gone out of the publishing business.

3 Captain Martin was a fictitious name given by the author to denote Captain Charles Greville Harston.

4 Buck Lake is a small lake situated on the divisional township line separating the Township of Stisted, now part of the town of Huntsville in the Muskoka District of Ontario, and the Township of McMurrich in the Parry Sound District.

5 Gravenhurst, located to the south end of Muskoka, approximately 166 km (103 miles)

north of Toronto, was originally called McCabe's Landing. The first post office there was established on August 1, 1862, with James McCabe as the first postmaster. Gravenhurst was nicknamed "The Gateway to Muskoka" by the local pioneers of the time. First incorporated as a village in 1877, it became a town in 1887. The Toronto, Simcoe & Muskoka Junction Railway reached Gravenhurst in August 1875 and, by November of that same year, this rail line had been extended to the Muskoka wharf, Gravenhurst's port on Lake Muskoka. Soon after the name of the railway became the Northern & Pacific Junction Railway. When Vernon B. Wadsworth, the surveyor of the area, reached the area in July 1860, the Muskoka Road (the Colonization Road) was a mere path in the dense forest. In the early days the economy of Gravenhurst was based on lumbering. The Gravenhurst of today is a very popular tourist destination. It is believed the name "Gravenhurst" came from a British book entitled "Gravenhurst" or "Thoughts on Good and Evil" written by William Smith, originally published in Edinburgh by Blackwood and Sons in 1862. Dr. William Dawson LaSueur, the Secretary of the Post Office Department in 1862, is thought to have been responsible for naming the post office of this community.

6 Bracebridge, also in the Muskoka District, was originally called North Falls. Its first post office was established August 1, 1864 with Alexander Bailey as first postmaster. Incorporated as a village in 1875, Bracebridge became a town in 1889. Situated on the Muskoka River and along the Muskoka Road, the town is very scenic, according to *Picturesque Canada! Season 1875, the Northern Lakes Guide to Lake Simcoe and Couchiching* (Toronto: Hunter, Rose & CO. Printers, 1875) 25. "The 'North Falls,' a cascade of sixty feet in height, is in the centre of the village; also Muskoka Falls, one hundred and fifty feet; Wilson's Falls and the High Falls are only two to three miles from the village."

The Northern & Pacific Junction Railway, also known as the Northern Railway was extended beyond from Gravenhurst, eventually reaching Bracebridge, a distance of some 18 km (11 miles) in 1885. Dr. W.D. LaSueur of the Post Office Department is also credited with assigning Bracebridge as the name to be given to the post office. Seemingly he took the name from a book titled *Bracebridge Hall* written by Washington Irving and published in both the United States and England in May, 1822. Bracebridge is approximately 181 km (112 miles) north of Toronto.

7 Utterson is located along the Muskoka Colonization Road in the Township of Stephenson, Muskoka District. The town is about 18 km (11 miles) north of Bracebridge and 16 km (10 miles) south of Huntsville. James F. Hanes was the first postmaster when the post office opened on June 6, 1864. Originally, the mail arrived by stage from Gravenhurst, and later from Bracebridge. The Northern and Pacific Junction Railway (The Northern Railway) came through Utterson at some time between 1885 and 1886.

8 Port Vernon, a small hamlet on the western shore of Lake Vernon in the Township of Stisted, is now part of Huntsville. The first post office, established June 1, 1877, under the name Port Vernon, was named after Vernon Bayley Wadsworth, a student of John Stoughton Dennis, Government Surveyor. Dennis is credited with discovering Lake Vernon and naming both the lake and the river running from it to Fairy Lake, "after his young pupil." See Florence B. Murray (ed.), *Muskoka and Haliburton, 1615–1875: A Collection of Documents*, (Toronto: The Champlain Society, University of Toronto Press, 1963) 6. It had its name changed to Hoodstown on January 1, 1879. The first postmaster was

Richard Y. Ellis. The original name was designated by Captain Charles Hood, a steamboat captain who plied the waters of Lake Ontario. During the land boom that began in 1869, Captain Hood and his wife became interested in the area around Port Vernon and filed a plan for Hoodstown (Port Vernon), even dividing the property into lots. Their hopes of the railway passing through the top end of Lake Vernon died when the Northern and Pacific Junction Railway went to Huntsville instead. The post office was renamed in his honour. As a result, both the business activity and population declined in the area. For more information, see Marjorie Demaine, Chronicles of Stisted Township, Bracebridge, ON: Herald-Gazette Press, 1976.

9 Huntsville, in the Muskoka District was named after Captain George Hunt (1830–1882). A former captain in the British infantry, he emigrated initially to Montreal, but on hearing of the free land grants being offered in Upper Canada, he moved his family to the area that would ultimately bear his name, in 1869. Hunt settled on Part Lot 14 and 15, Concession 1 of Chattey Township, now part of present-day Huntsville. He proceeded to found a settlement, building several homes and business establishments, and for a time operated a mill for the area. Captain Hunt is regarded as the founder of Huntsville. Located on the Muskoka Colonization Road, the settlement was situated on the banks of the Vernon or Muskoka River, and midway between Vernon and Fairy lakes. The first post office established January 1, 1870 had Captain George Hunt as postmaster. Huntsville was incorporated as a village in 1886, and became a town in 1900. The Northern and Pacific Junction Railway (Northern Railway) reached northward from Gravenhurst through Bracebridge, reaching Huntsville in 1886. Huntsville is about 34 km (21 miles) north of Bracebridge, and approximately 214 km (133 miles) north of Toronto.

10 There are many variants on the spelling of the surname of Frederick de la Fosse including: DelaFosse, Dela Fosse and Delafosse. The decision was made to use "de la Fosse," the spelling used by members of the family contacted by the editor.

11 Colonel Montague Ricketts was the brother of Isabella Sophie (Ricketts) de la Fosse, Frederick de la Fosse's mother. The source for this information is contained in a letter written by Mrs. Mary McAskill, granddaughter of Frederick de la Fosse, dated March 10, 1992, The letter is in the Trent University Archives, Rahmel, Fern, 94-005/1/1.

12 In this new edition, the name of the real person operating the training farm, Captain Charles Greville Harston, replaces the fictitious name of "Captain Martin" used by de la Fosse in the original printing of *English Bloods*. The names Captain Martin and Mrs. Martin have been changed to read Captain Harston and Mrs. Harston. This corrected information was confirmed by Gail Stupka in 1995, a local genealogist and historian living in the Township of Stisted.

Also from the *Chronicles of Stisted Township* by Marjorie Demaine, is the following quote, found on pages 137–38:

> "Ilfracombe, on the south end of Buck Lake in the northern part of Stisted was newly settled in the 1870s. The residents were gentlemen of good position and means from England. Captain Harston who lived on lot 23, concession 14, taught them "farming." They made large clearings in the bush and planned to build an Anglican Church to be endowed with funds procured from England. Some of

these early gentlemen were John Easton, Tom and Phil Bell, Aemilius Baldwin, Fred de la Fosse, Vernon Garrett, two Stotesbury brothers, one living at each end of the lake, the Price family at the Narrows and others who all received their apprenticeship to the 'Farming' Profession."

Other evidence was taken from *A Track Through Time, A History of The Township of McMurrich* by Janice R. Madill and published by the Township of McMurrich in 1994, 107: "One of Harston's boarders was a writer, and he told the story of the first three years spent between 1880 and 1883 [the dates should have been 1878 to 1881] in Ilfracombe, in his book, *English Bloods*." Frederick M. de la Fosse is the "writer" being identified.

13 *Official Telephone Directory, City of Toronto and Suburbs, October 1899.* Bell Canada Archives, Ref. 10875. On Reel #6 Ontario East 1906 in the Huntsville Public Library.

INTRODUCTION BY FREDERICK DE LA FOSSE

1 In the original 1930 publication there was no introduction included with the text. This introduction, attributed to Frederick Montague de la Fosse, the original author of *English Bloods*, was taken from an annotated typescript that is now part of a collection in the Trent University Archives, Fonds Level Description, Rahmel, Fern 94-005. The material was donated to the Trent University Archives by John Frewer of Toronto, a grandson of Frederick de la Fosse. "A Literary discovery: the 'western reminiscences' of F.M. de la Fosse, Peterborough's first librarian" by Fern A. Rahmel, can be found in *Occasional Paper* number 15, published by the Peterborough Historical Society, November 1994. Copies can be obtained from the Publications Committee Chairman, Peterborough Historical Society, 270 Brock Street, Peterborough, Ontario K9H 2P9.

2 Frederick M. de la Fosse was born in 1860 and *English Bloods* was published in 1930. He was in his late sixties when he began to write this book. The "grand climeratic" is his description of what some might call the "prime" of his life.

3 The actual date for this "Introduction" is unknown but one would assume it was written before 1930.

I VOYAGE TO THE CANADIAN BACKWOODS

1 A brief background on Frederick de la Fosse's childhood history helps set the scene for his story. In his unpublished manuscript "Western Reminiscences," Frederick de la Fosse writes, "Shortly after our arrival at Bath my father and mother, who never recovered their health in England, died with in two weeks of each other...."

Captain Charles Edward de la Fosse and his wife Isabella Sophie (Ricketts) de la Fosse returned to a place in Bath, Somerset, England in about 1867. Charles had been employed with the East India Company in Bengal, India. He and Isabella returned with their three children, daughter Grace, daughter Mary and son Frederick. Grace died in infancy. Frederick's father and mother both died shortly after their return to Bath because of fever. See Rahmel, Fern; Trent University Archives. Ref. 94-005/1/1. According to a letter dated March 10, 1992 from Mary McAskill, Frederick de la Fosse's granddaughter, to Dr. Fern Rahmel at Trent University,

"Both of his parents died of fever and he was sent with his sister Mary back to England, Bath. I believe they were brought up by his Mother's family. His Mother's brother Col. Montague Ricketts was his guardian – he one who shipped him off to Canada. Dad said it was because while Granddad was at Military College in England he was more interested in Cricket (he was a star) & other sports & his uncle thought he wouldn't pass the exams and disgrace the family. Can you imagine Granddad disgracing anyone!" (Trent University Archives Ref# 94-005/1/1.)

Captain Charles Edward de la Fosse died on May 24, 1868, and his wife Isabella Sophie de la Fosse died on June 5 of that year. Isabella's brother, Colonel Montagu Poyntz Ricketts became the children's guardian, according to Mary McAskill's letter.

As this story begins, we find that just months before Frederick's eighteenth birthday, his uncle, Colonel Ricketts, had decided that Frederick needed a more responsible education. The Colonel had been corresponding with an army friend; the friend just happened to be Captain Charles Greville Harston. Consequently, the Colonel had purchased a ticket for Frederick, for passage from Liverpool, England, to Canada aboard the sailing steamship, the *Scandinavian*, owned by the Allan Steamship Company. Frederick boarded the vessel on May 16, 1878, and arrived at the port of Quebec City on May 27, 1878. This information is from three sources: 1) correspondence with Hugh Casement of Germany (his ancestral home is in Northern Ireland) a family researcher of the de la Fosse surname; 2) correspondence with Dave Ricketts of Dundas, Ontario, a family researcher of the Ricketts surname, and 3) the sailing dates of the *Scandinavian* taken from the Library and Archives Canada, microfilm shiplists C-4529.

2   The East India Company consisted of a group of merchants in the City of London, England. The Company, granted a Royal Charter on December 31, 1600, by Queen Elizabeth I, was formed for the purpose of business trade with India and the East Indies, and lasted nearly 260 years. A revolt known as "The Indian Rebellion," lasting from 1857 to 1859, put an end to the company. Following the rebellion, the British Government took control of India and the East India Company.

3   According to *More Secret Remedies* published by the British Medical Association in 1912, Cockles Antibilious Pills were prepared by the late James Cockle, Surgeon and Apothecary. "A box, price 1s. 1 1/2d., was found to containing 16 pills. The directions vary from 'One Pill to be taken an hour before dinner' to 'Two or three at any time.' Chemical and microscopical examination indicated the presence of aloes (Socotrine), a little soap, powdered colocynth, powdered jalap, and another vegetable tissue." The medical description suggests that the pill was a remedy for indigestion and several varieties of bilious and liver complaints. There is a possibility that this remedy might have prevented the effects of seasickness.

4   The *Scandinavian* embarked from the port at Liverpool on May 16, 1878, and arrived

eleven days later at the Quebec port on May 27, 1878. The *Scandinavian* was a sailing steamship, propelled by a steam screw, with a speed of 11 knots. It had four decks and three masts. On this voyage the ship carried 308 passengers across the Atlantic Ocean to Canada. Information from the Library and Archives Canada, shiplists 4529.

5   Oldfield – this name is not changed from the original. The name was found as passenger on the *Scandinavian*, and designated as "Gentleman of England." LAC, shiplists C4529.

6   Levinsky – this name is not changed from the original. The handwritten name found on the shiplist would appear to be Levinsky, although the last three letters are difficult to decipher, LAC shiplists C4529.

7   Point Levis, the town and river port of Quebec, was on the south side of the St. Lawrence River. Today it is called Levis City. The original settlement was founded in 1647, and chiefly railway yards and wharves occupied the riverbank. According to *Britannica, The New Encyclopedia, Vol. 7, 1994:* "From the heights above the town, the British general James Wolfe bombarded and destroyed part of Quebec city in 1759. In 1861 the community's name changed to honour Francois Gaston de Lévis, who commanded the French forces in Canada after the death of the Marquis de Montcalm during Wolfe's siege. Now an industrial centre, Levis has dry docks equipped to accommodate the largest ships. Major manufactures are foundry and machine shop products, lumber, tobacco, and furniture. The city's lowland, between high cliffs and the river, is occupied primarily by railway yards and wharves; while its Hightown area, atop a steep incline, is largely residential."

8   Chichester Skeffington – this name is not changed from the original. The name, found on the LAC shiplists C4529, would appear to be C.A. Shiffington. Because these names are handwritten, it is difficult to tell if the surname is Shiffington or Skeffington.

9   The Wolfe/Montcalm Monument was erected in Quebec City in 1827 in recognition of James Wolfe (1727–1759), the British General, and Louis Joseph Montcalm (1712–1759), the French General. The French soldiers under the command of General Montcalm and the British soldiers under the command of General Wolfe met on the Plains of Abraham on September 13, 1759. The Plains of Abraham was a fairly level field adjoining the upper part of the City of Quebec. The battle lasted less then 15 minutes. Three bullets struck Wolfe and he died a few hours after the battle. Wolfe's successful campaign won Canada for the British Empire. Wolfe died on September 13, 1759. Montcalm, also wounded in the battle, died the following day, September 14, 1759.

10 *The Canadian Oxford Dictionary* (1998) defines "cicerone" as a guide who gives information about antiquities, places of interest, etc. to sightseers. The source of the word can be traced as a reference to eloquent, classical language, in the style of Cicero.

II FROM THE CANADIAN SHORES

1   The chapter heading for Chapter II is missing in the original publication. This could possibly be a printing error or an oversight not caught by the original publisher. The chapter heading that has been included in this version was taken from an annotated typescript (written in Frederick M. de la Fosse's own handwriting) acquired from the Trent University Archives, Reference #92-1007.

2   During the Franco-Prussian War of 1870–71, fought between France (under Napoleon III) and Prussia, Prussian troops advanced into France and decisively defeated the French troops in January 1871. The French defeat marked the end of the Second Empire, while the Prussian victory led to the creation of the New German Empire. Otto Edvard Leopold von Bismarck became the first chancellor of the German Empire (1870–91).

3   The Rossin House Hotel was situated on the southeast corner of King and York streets in Toronto. Built in 1835, but destroyed by fire 1862, it was rebuilt and eventually became known as the Prince George Hotel. It was considered one of the grander hotels of the time. Information from *The Canadian Guide Book* by Charles G.D. Roberts, (New York: D. Appleton And Company, 1891), under the subheading of "Toronto," 24. "Toronto of the Present," is the line, "Rooms rented for $3 to $4 a night." The building was torn down in the 1960s.

4   In the original text, the name Wardle was used. This has been changed to Yearley to represent George Samuel Yearley. This name (Yearley) and many other corrected names have been identified from a two-page document transcribed by Mrs. Muriel (Whitley) Hopcraft (See Appendix A. 4). Muriel was married to Lorne Hopcraft, grandson of John Hopcraft (Sr.), the first census taker of the area. The information is from a telephone interview with Fred Hopcraft, on February 13, 2002. He is Muriel (Whitley) Hopcraft's brother-in-law.

The two pages from Muriel Hopcraft were taken from a copy of *English Bloods* that had been presented to Andrew and Jessie (Howell) Hickling on October 28, 1939, by A.C. Fraser of Yearleys (or Yearly). This settlement is in the Township of Stisted, in the Muskoka District. (The name of the community is clearly written as Yearleys with the 's,' in Muriel Hopcraft's notes.) Mrs. Hickling had written many personal notes and collected photographs of the settlers of the Stisted/McMurrich area over a period of many years. Her personal notes contain names of the settlers that Frederick de la Fosse had written about in his book *English Bloods*.

Many names of the settlers can be easily located on the maps of Stisted and McMurrich townships as found in *The Guide Book & Atlas of Muskoka and Parry Sound 1879*, published by H.R. Page in 1879. Also, many of the names in the text have now been corrected back to original names, are contained in the 1881 Census of Stisted and McMurrich Townships. Archives of Ontario (AO) C-13244.

The Hickling and Hopcraft families were among some of the earliest settlers in the Stisted Township area. Mr. Alexander Hickling Sr. located land there through the "Free Grants and Homestead Act" of October 1877. John Hopcraft Sr. is the grandfather of Fred (Hopcraft) Lorne (Hopcraft) and Elsie (Hopcraft) Bennett. He came into the area about 1875 and by 1881 was the census taker for the townships of Stisted and McMurrich. John Hopcraft began taking the 1881 Census on April 26, 1881, and completed the enumeration on June 6, 1881. AO Film C-13244.

In an interview with the editor in November 2001 (handwritten notes recorded the interview), Norm Yearley identified himself as the great-grandson of George Samuel Yearley. He confirmed the information regarding his great-grandfather from a copy of *English Bloods* given to him by his father, Rupert Leslie Yearley. The settlement in the Township of Stisted that was named after Yearley received its first post office on August 1, 1884. The first postmaster was George S. Yearley. See *Chronicles of Stisted Township*, by Marjorie Demaine, page 148: "In 1884, a post office was established. George S. Yearley was the first postmaster and it was named after him." This is the George S. Yearley of *English Bloods*. Today, the community of Yearley lies within present-day Huntsville.

5 Scientific Name – *Osmunda regalis*; Common Name – The Royal Fern. This very large and beautiful fern is found in moist woodlands, marshes, swamps, and sometimes on wet cliffs. The whole leaf can grow to a length of about three metres (nine feet) long. The plant tends to favour soils or water that are slightly acidic, and can be found from Newfoundland to Saskatchewan and south to Louisiana and Florida. Its fiddleheads can be prepared for eating, somewhat like asparagus.

6 Scientific Name – *Sagittaria latifolia*; Common Name – The Common Arrowhead. Found along the shores of lakes, as well as the edges of rivers and swampy areas, this plant grows in shallow water and is know for its showy white flowers. Also known as the Duck Potato, the plant grows about 60 cm (two feet) tall, with a leaf shaped like an arrowhead. The outer end of the root is called a "corms," and the small tubers that grow on this root are about five centimetres (two inches) in diameter. Native Peoples harvested the corms for food. They are quite bitter when raw, but tasty after cooking.

7 The British Lion Hotel is located in Bracebridge, Ontario. In 1870, William F. Burden built the hotel on the northwest corner of Ontario and Dominion streets. The hotel is long gone and today, the Bracebridge Registry sits on the site. The name Burden was originally spelled Burdon in de la Fosse's original text of 1930. Burden is the correct spelling of the name, according to the Archives of Ontario, 1871 Census C-10023, Township of Macaulay. For more information, see: Robert J. Boyer, *Bracebridge Around* 1930, Bracebridge, ON: Oxbow Press, 2001.

III MY TRIP INTO THE INTERIOR

1 The Muskoka Falls is part of the South Muskoka River, just a short distance from Bracebridge, about five kilometres (three miles) to the south. The falls are comprised of a series of cascades totalling a height of approximately 50 metres (150 feet).

2 Brobdingnagian refers to something being gigantic or colossal. The name is taken from Jonathan Swift's *Gulliver's Travels* where "Broddingnap" is a land where everything exists on a massive scale.

3 Johnny, named as one of the sons of George Samuel Yearley, can not be specifically identified. He may be Henry, Robert or Frederick Yearley, one of the Yearly sons as listed in the AO 1881 Census C-13243, Township of Macaulay and Village of Bracebridge.

4 Bill, named as son of George S. Yearley, was identified as Thomas Yearly by Norm Yearley, in the November 2001 interview. Rupert Leslie Yearley died in 1974. The information that "Bill," Thomas Yearley (1861–1903), was his grandfather, was given to him by his father, Rupert, when Norm was a young man.

5 The Gilliloo bird was possibly a local name for an owl or hawk. Norm Yearley

suggested that it was the noise that two branches make when rubbing together in the wind. Then again George Yearley may have been playing a prank on Frederick, the newcomer.

6 Hodag was identified as a term referring to bobcat or lynx, or, as Jessie Hickling indicated, "wildcats."

7 The 1981 edition of *The Oxford English Dictionary* Vol. 1 A-O, (published in the United States), defines handspike as a wooden bar or pole, used as a lever or crowbar.

8 This is a game played with a small ball, somewhat like racquetball or squash. Using the ceiling, the floor, the side walls and the front wall (thus providing five walls – or five court). The court is open at the back. The players wear a glove on their hand and using the force of the hand, hit the ball forward against the front wall, trying to strategically outwit their opponent and cause the returning shot to be missed.

IV THE GOVERNMENT ROAD

1. The "Government Road" would have been the Muskoka Colonization Road, begun in the late 1850s. See Florence B. Murray ed., *Muskoka and Haliburton*, 1615–1875. (The Champlain Society for the Government of Ontario,) 64. "The Muskoka, perhaps more than any other colonization road in time fulfilled the dream of those who planned it. The route chosen for it determined the location of villages and the flow of men and supplies for generations to come. When the government decided to open Muskoka for settlement it issued instructions on October 11, 1856, and April 17, 1857, to Charlie Unwin to survey trail lines to the Great Falls on the Muskoka River…both proved to be too costly and David Gibson surveyed a third line…." And on page 70 see "The first grant for the Muskoka Road was made in 1857, and the Minister of Agriculture, in his annual report for that year, announced plans for a road 'to run from the head of navigation of Lake Couchiching at a point called Washago Mills to the grand falls at Muskoka…David Gibson gave out contracts for a bridge over the Severn River and the first part of the road…. From the termination of the navigation on Lake Couchiching where a wharf has been erected, to the Great Falls of Muskoka – a distance of 21 miles – all streams have been substantially bridged and the road has been opened and the country along it is being rapidly settled." The announcement, however, may have been a little premature: "In 1861 the bridge over the North Branch of the Muskoka River at Bracebridge was partially constructed, and by the end of 1863 the road was 24 miles beyond the falls, in the vicinity of Vernon and Fairy lakes where Huntsville now stands, but the bridge over the Vernon, or Muskoka River was not completed until 1870."

2 Stisted Road travelled north from the colonization route (Muskoka Road) through Utterson, and at this point headed northwest, running up through the middle of the Township of Stisted. There, the Stisted Road continued through small communities such as Lancelot, Ashworth and Aspdin, eventually crossing the Boundary Line into the McMurrich Township of the District of Parry Sound. The portion of this road that extended from Lancelot to Aspdin no longer exists. For more information see Marjorie Demaine, *Chronicles of Stisted Township*, published 1976 by Herald-Gazette Press, Bracebridge, Ontario.

3 Xenophon (c.435–354 B.C.) was a Greek historian, writer and military leader of significance.

V THE HARSTON HOMESTEAD

1 The original name given was "Melius." According to Jessie Hickling's two-page document, this individual was Mr. Baldwin. Muriel (Whitely) Hopcraft was able to supply the first name of Aemilius, see Appendix A. 4.

2 "Barrett," the individual, as identified by Jessie Hickling, was Mr. Garrett. The 1881 Census of Stisted and McMurrich townships lists a William Garrett; an early map of McMurrich Township identifies a William Albin Vernon Garrett on Con. 1, Lots 7, 89. W.A.V. Garrett married one of Philip Bell's sisters, Annie Sarah Graham Bell, while Frederick de la Fosse married the other sister, Mary Jane Graham Bell. The two men who were "pupils" at the Harston's school became brothers-in-law. It is recorded in the 1881 Census of Stisted Township that Philip's brother, Thomas Bell, was also living with the Harstons.

3 The name, originally written as "Harkins," is identified by Jessie Hickling as Mr. Tothill. Correspondence with Martha (Tothill) Woody in 2002 (Martha is Richard Hugh Tothill's great-granddaughter), confirmed this identification and added the given names of her grandfather as Richard Hugh Tothill.

4. De la Fosse refers to his being a product of the Public School System in England. The British Public School System catered primarily to the sons of wealthy parents whose children were sent to these expensive schools. The school curriculum, at that time, was dominated by Greek and Latin and teaching methods that were very traditional.

VI HARSTON'S AGRICULTURAL FARMING SCHOOL

1 As with chapter II, the heading was missing in the original publication.

2 Samuel Smiles, *Self-Help*, London: John Murray, 1882 (2nd ed.). The book was first published in 1859, publisher not known.

3 Online research produced some background on patents for stump pullers being taken up in 1840. It is not clear as to when a stump puller was first used in the Muskoka area. Muskoka of the late 1870s seemed to have been twenty or so years behind the general adoptions of new inventions. It is important to remember that the area was just being settled and the roads were but roughed-out trails with logs that acted as bridges.

4. *Tyro* is from the medieval Latin, and in this instance, refers to a beginner or novice.

5. It was a common practice in pioneer days to invite neighbours to come together to work on a special communal task that required many hands. Food and drink would be provided so the event was also a social gathering. Among the most common were bees held for barn raising and quilting. In this instance, the bee is a logging bee.

6 Tincture of arnica refers to a medicine prepared from a plant bearing yellow, daisy-like flower heads (genus *Arnica*) that was used for treating bruises, etc.

7 In the original text, the name appeared as "Hamilton." According to Jessie Hickling, this person was Alexander Hamilton.

VII THE SETTLERS

1 The heading was missing in the original text.
2 In the original text, this name was written as "Briggs." According to Jessie Hickling, this settler was a Mr. Smith.
3 Lamb's quarters, a tall weed related to beets and spinach, is also known as pigweed or goosefoot. The plant grows anywhere from 30 cm to 3 m (1–9 ft) tall, and the leaves can be cooked and eaten. A quote from the *World Book Millennium 2000* states that "American Indians ate leaves to treat stomach aches and prevent scurvy. Cold tea used for diarrhea; leaf poultice used for burns." Information is from Stephen Foster and James A. Duke, *Medical Plants and Herbs*, (Boston: Houghton Mifflin Company, 2000) 245.
4 This is Mr. White, according to Jessie Hickling. The name in the original text was written as "Black."
5 This "elderly being" was Mr. Holt, according to Jessie Hickling. The name in the original text was written as "Green."
6 "Delectation" is a literary term derived from Old French, meaning pleasure or enjoyment.
7 As noted in Chapter V, this individual is believed to be Aemilius Baldwin, who may have held an interest in Harston's enterprise. He was born in 1894, the year his grandfather, William Warren Baldwin, died. See more information in the Epilogue.
8 Fustian is defined as thick twilled cotton cloth with a short nap, usually dyed in dark colours.
9 The name was originally written as "Tompkins," but, according to Jessie Hickling, this "shy young man" was Walter Hopcraft.
10 Lucerne is the name used in Europe for the plant that is called "alfalfa" in North America. Used as feed for cattle, alfalfa belongs to the pea family, *Fabaceae* or *Leguminosae*. The scientific name is *Medicago sativa*. A perennial, it grows from year to year without replanting, attaining a height of about one metre (three feet). Flowers grow on the stems in clusters and are usually purple, but some can be green, white, yellow or multi-coloured. Taken from *The World Book Millenium 2000*, page 514 and also discussed in *The New Standard Encyclopaedia and World Atlas*, Odhams Press Limited, London, 1932.

VIII COMMUNITIES OF THE DISTRICT

1 Lake Vernon is the largest lake in Stisted Township, Muskoka.
2 Fox Lake is a small lake in Stisted Township, situated between Buck Lake and Lake Vernon.
3 Captain Charles Hood, as noted earlier, acquired land around Port Vernon and set up the potential of a town site there, on the speculation that the Northern and Pacific Railway would extend that way. It did not.

4 According to Jessie Hickling, the names Bright, Jock Henderson, Hilditch, Mr. and Mrs. Piper and Mr. and Mrs. Meade, were not changed in the original.

5 Cann's Hotel, in Huntsville, was owned by Mr. William Cann. The hotel, set on the corner of Brunel Road and Main Street, was one of the first to be built in Huntsville.

6 A bail is one of the smaller sticks placed on top of a wicket. In the sport of cricket, a wicket is a set of three stumps and two bails at the end of the pitch. The wicket is guarded by a batsman who, with his bat, attempts to prevent the ball from hitting the wicket.

7 Bernard Phillips, this name has not been changed from the original. His name is recorded in the 1881 Census of Township of Chaffey, AO film C-13243.

IX PREPARATION OF THE LOG SHANTY

1 The name in the original was William Ramey. It is believed that this name was not changed except that correct spelling for the surname should have been Rhamey. See Janice Madill, *A Track Through Time, A History of The Township of McMurrich*, 1994. His name is also listed in the 1881 Census of Stisted and McMurrich Township, OA C-13244 and on page 90 of *The Guide Book and Atlas of Muskoka Parry Sound*, published in 1879 by H.R. Page.

2 In the original, the name was shown as Nicholls, but, according to Jessie Hickling, this individual is Nicholas Schneider.

3 This name was correct in the original, according to Jessie Hickling.

4 It was not possible to locate any reference to a Mr. Robey.

5 This surname was originally written as "Pell." Correspondence between the author and Gregory Bell in 2002 revealed that the individual was Philip F.G. Bell. Gregory Bell is the grandson of Philip Frushard Graham Bell, born in Edinburgh in 1861. In 1884, he married Margaret Hodge Mackenzie (1857–1913), daughter of William Innes Mackenzie (1857–1913) (the founder and developer of the Parkdale District of Toronto), and Euphemia Marshal Grieve (1836–1907). He died in Muskoka in 1927 at the age of 66.

6 Another example of de la Fosse's erudite style, "whilom," is an archaic form from the Old English word *hwilum*, meaning former or erstwhile.

7 A hunter takes a stand in the woods and sits for hours, staying as still and quiet as possible, waiting for deer or moose to come along in the forest or field. In this instance, they would paddle quietly about the lake in a canoe. Of interest is the "Wildlife Chronicle, A History of Ontario's Wildlife Legacy," published for *Hunting Heritage, Hunting Future*, August 2000: "1821…Upper Canada's first game regulation was instituted in 'An Act for the Preservation of Deer within the Province.' Deer were not to be taken or killed between January 10 and July 1, but outside of this protected season, there was no limit on take. Violators could be fined forty shillings for a first offence. There were no government agents to enforce this law, however. Enforcement was dependent on informers who were rewarded with half of the fine money. The other half of the fine went to the Receiver General for the province. Indians were exempt from this legislation. [In] 1839…The first general game law for Upper Canada was passed, establishing protected seasons for all classes of game. Deer or fawns were

NOTES

not to be hunted between February 1 and August 1.... This law also contained the first ban on Sunday hunting and shooting.... [In] 1856...'An Act to alter and amend the Game Laws of Upper Canada' was assented to. Deer, moose, elk, reindeer or caribou were not to be hunted, taken or killed between February 1 and August 1.... [In] 1868...The first game legislation for the Province of Ontario was established through a re-enactment of the game laws of 1856. The open seasons for game were shortened, but no provision was made for more effective enforcement of this legislation. The open season for big game became September 1 to December 1.... [In] 1871.... The open season for game was amended once again with the big game season being extended (September 1 to December 19).... [In] 1880.... an amendment to the Act protecting game animals and furbearers, provision was made for the Councils of any county, city, town, township or incorporated village to appoint a game inspector who would be responsible for enforcing the provisions of the Act."

X LOCAL DENTISTRY

1   The Seidlitz powder, in this situation, had been prescribed for a sprained ankle. Sedilitz powder is a medical concoction derived from drinking a mixture of effervescing salts with water. The powder was generally used as a mild cathartic, meaning purgative, for purifying (a laxative). From *Webster's Third Dictionary*, Vol. iii, S-Z, G&C. Merriam Co., 1981, 2057.
2   This name was originally written as "Sandy Fayes." According to Jessie Hickling, this individual was Sandy Hayes.

XI PURCHASING CATTLE AND SHEEP

1   It was not possible to identify the name "Issachar."
2   According to Jessie Hickling, this name, a Mr. Peters, had not been changed.
3   *Webster's Deluxe Dictionary, Tenth Collegiate Edition*, 1998, indicates that "caudle" is from the Middle English term "caudel," derived from the Old North French term "caut," meaning warm. It would seem that Mrs. Peters gave Mr. Peters a very hot or heated lecture.
4   The name of Rev. William Crompton has not been changed, according to Jessie Hickling, nor have the names of the clergy listed in the same paragraph: Rev. Lawrence Sinclair, Rev. William Chowne, Archdeacon Gilmour and Canon Llwyd, nor the names of the clergy in the remainder of this chapter. Most of them were part of the See of Algoma, created in 1872, the result of the severing off of the northern portion of the Diocese of Toronto (established in 1839). This boundary for the new diocese was at the Severn River, about 145 kilometres (90 miles) north of Toronto. It extended north and west to the height of land beyond Lakes Huron and Superior.
    The first bishop for this new diocese was Bishop Frederick Dawson Fauquier (1873–1881). See Edward Francis Wilson, E. & T.B. Young, *Missionary Work Among the Ojibway Indians* (London: New York: Society for Promoting Christian Knowledge, 1886) 125.

186

NOTES

Fauquier, of English background, was born in Malta in 1817, where his father may have been attached to the garrison as part of the civil administration (Britain has assumed control of that island in 1798). He emigrated to Upper Canada in 1836. As bishop he was charged with expanding the church's ministry among the settlers and the Native Peoples, and finding funds to keep the diocese functioning.

Following his death, the position was taken by Edward Sullivan (1881–1896). He had emigrated from Ireland in 1852. Along with raising money and recruiting clergy, he travelled extensively across the diocese. In his first year alone, he is recorded as having travelled several hundred kilometres by land and water. By 1893, when failing health compelled him to take a necessary rest, he had 26 new churches built, 10 others rebuilt and 68 churches were debt free. He retired in 1896. From Henry James Morgan's *The Canadian Men and Women of the Time, a Handbook of Canadian Biography*. Toronto: W. Briggs, 1898.

The bishops, particularly Sullivan, made extensive use of lay readers. Many of these men, such as William Crompton and Thomas Llywd were subsequently ordained and played leading roles in the history of the diocese. Sullivan died in January 1899. The third bishop was George Thorneloe (1897–1927). Born in Coventry, England, in 1848, he came to Canada with his parents when he was ten years of age. He became bishop of the See of Algoma in 1897. He declined other opportunities to serve other dioceses in order to remain with his people in Algoma. See H. J. Morgan, 1898. As mentioned, Rev. William Crompton had been appointed by Bishop Fauquier as a travelling missionary. He had been one of the first settlers of Aspdin in Stisted Township. At the time, there being no church nearby, he read prayers for the families in his own log house. Instrumental not only in helping build the first church in Aspdin but also in helping found 22 churches in the surrounding country, he was ordained deacon in 1875. This information is taken from "An Account of St. Mary's Church, Aspdin, Muskoka, Ontario," published by the Diocese of Algoma.

The other lay reader mentioned, Thomas Llywd, was born in 1837 and came to Canada in 1864. He settled in the Gravenhurst area where he remained for eight years. He ultimately became the first rector of All Saints Church in Huntsville. He was appointed Archdeacon by Bishop Edward Sullivan.

Another that should be mentioned is Reverend Lawrence Sinclair, born in Edinburgh in 1847. He responded to Bishop Sullivan's recruitment of clergy, and was ordained at Rosseau in 1880. Initially he was in charge of the appointments of Ravenscliffe, Hoodstown, Novar, Axe Lake and, of interest to this book, Christ Church of Ilfracombe (geographically speaking it is the most northerly church in Muskoka). Upon his retirement in 1918, he was asked by Bishop Thornloe to continue his duties. He did so for another eighteen years. It was he who walked the one-hundred-mile circuit every weekend (leaving Friday and returning Monday) to hold church services in the northern Muskoka area. In 1923 he and his wife moved to Huntsville.

Another minister was Gowan Gillmor (de la Fosse spelled the name as Gilmour) who came in 1891 as the new rector of the Church of the Redeemer in Rousseau. He remained there until 1907, during which time he took religious services to the construction men building the Canadian Pacific Railway. His experiences are recorded in "Gillmor of Algoma, Archdeacon and Tramp" written by E. Newton-White.

21

Also of note is the Rev. A.W.H. Chowne who began his ministry at six stations, including Rousseau, in 1880. His story is told in "A History of the Church of the Redeemer," Rosseau, Ontario, compiled by Evelyn Parker, Isabel Matthews Swanson and Audrey Tournay.

XII THE FIRST WINTER

1 An ewer is defined as a large pitcher or water jug with a wide mouth.
2 In the original, the name was presented as Hanson. According to Jessie Hickling, this individual is Hanson Quinn.

XIII WINTER WOODSMAN

1 Dr. Emile Coue was a physician, born in Troyes, France, on February 26, 1857. He had a reputation for healing the sick in a miraculous way. He devoted much time to studying how to cure illnesses by suggestion, his fundamental idea being that, if the patient believes himself to be getting better from an illness, he has taken an important step to that end. It was not a religion, and did not claim to be so. One would repeat, "Every day in every way, I am getting better and better." And they did. Dr. Coue died July 2, 1926. See *The New Standard Encyclopaedia and World Atlas*, (London: Odhams Press Limited, 1932) 54.
2 As noted earlier, Hoodstown, in the Port Vernon area, and named after Captain Charles Hood, competed for the extension of the Northern and Pacific Junction Railway heading north from Gravenhurst. Ultimately, it was determined that the best route would be for the railway to go through Huntsville instead. As a result, both business activity and population of the Port Vernon area declined.
3 The name Malkin had not been changed, according to Jessie Hickling.
4 Neither the name Tipper, nor the name Mann had been changed in the original, according to Jessie Hickling.
5 This name was originally written as "Andover," but according to Jessie Hickling, the correct name is Overhand.
6 "Days of the Maypole," refers to the first day of May. In England, the day was the celebration of the opening of spring, and took the form of dancing and singing around the Maypole on the village green and crowning a girl as Queen of May.
7 This name was originally written as "Strauss." According to Jessie Hickling, the original name would have been Guisler.
8 To cut the Gordian Knot is to solve a problem by force or by evasion. Here, the solution was force. The term "Gordian" is based on a story about Gordius, King of Phrygia, who, according to legend, tied an intricate knot that remained tied until cut by Alexander the Great. From *The Canadian Oxford Dictionary*, (Oxford University Press 1998), 604.
9 This was Fralick Fraser. According to Jessie Hickling, this name was originally written as "Fralick."
10 Sarsaparill was a local name for "Wild Sarsaparilla" or "Hairy Sarsaparilla." This wild

perennial grows about one metre (three feet) tall with ill-scented, oval shaped leaves, and bears small greenish-white flowers. The plant is found in moist woods. The root bark was made into a tea and used as a "blood purifier" by Native Peoples. The leaf tea was used to induce sweating. From *A Field Guide to Medicinal Plants* by Steven Foster and James A. Duke, Boston: Houghton Mifflin Company, 1999.

XIV THE SECOND YEAR

1 SPCK is the Society for Promoting Christian Knowledge. Founded in 1698, it is the oldest Anglican mission agency. Its mission is to work with Christians of all denominations to help people grow in the Christian faith, especially through the ministry of Christian education and literature. On March 8, 1698, a group of five friends met at Lincoln's Inn in London, U.K., to prepare for the departure of one of their number for America. Thomas Bray, an Anglican priest, was to visit the colony of Maryland on behalf of the Bishop of London. Not knowing how long he would be away, the friends resolved to form a society to ensure that the many good works with which he was involved could continue in his absence. The primary concern of the society's founders was to "counteract the growth of vice and immorality," which they ascribed to "gross ignorance of the principles of the Christian religion." Bray only stayed in Maryland for a few months, but the Society for Promoting Christian Knowledge which was formed that day is still active almost three hundred years later. Information is from www.spck.org.uk.

2 Alexander Begg – this name has not been changed according to information from Janice Madill, *A Track Through Time, A History of the Township of McMurrich*, 27–30, 31–51. Mr. Begg tried to form a Temperance Society in this area but he later found that the settlers liked to take a drink. Mr. Begg was a writer for the *Northern Advocate* during his time in the area. After his idea for a Temperance Society failed, he moved to New York City.

3 Beggsborough, a small hamlet in McMurrich Township, was named after Alexander Begg. A post office, established there on February 1, 1876, with the first postmaster being Magnus Begg, was the first to open in McMurrich Township, and was the first to be closed March 1, 1892. There is no doubt that the loss of the post office in 1891, coupled with the railway passing through Sprucedale in 1892, lead to the demise of the small settlement that once sat on the water's edge of the Beggsboro Creek. Today the area is part of the Sprucedale settlement. Information on the post office from LAC. ArchivaNet: On-line Research Tool, under "Post Offices" and "Postmasters."

4 Today Sprucedale is a small hamlet in McMurrich Township, a short distance northwest of the original Beggsborough. The first post office was established, January 1, 1901, with John Boys appointed as the first postmaster, Ibid, LAC.

5 Nate Thompson – this name has not been changed, and is correct according to Jessie Hickling.

6 Menominee Island is an island in Vernon Lake in Stisted Township. The name in the original text had been changed to Gallagher's Island. It is now called Gallagher's Island.

7 Michipicten is a community in Northern Ontario near the former Port Arthur (now Thunder Bay). This portion of Frederick de la Fosse's story refers to a point in his life after he left the Muskoka area sometime between 1883 and 1884. He travelled west and later returned to Ontario where he found employment in Port Arthur with a Mr. Furlong, a land surveyor, who was interested in surveying mining locations. One of Frederick's tasks was to carry samples of copper quartz to an essay office in Port Arthur for his employer of that time. Information taken from the Thunder Bay Historical Society, *Eighteenth and Nineteenth Annual Report, Paper of 1926–27 and of 1927–28*, "Reminiscences of a Vagabond by Fred M. de la Fosse."

8 Port Arthur is now part of the City of Thunder Bay, in northwestern Ontario.

9 A drawknife is a knife with a handle at each end, at right angles to the blade. The drawknife would be pulled towards the user to remove wood from a surface.

10 Mr. Sweet – this name has not been changed, according to Jessie Hickling.

11 Bowser – this name has not been changed.

XV EMIGRANTS IN THE COLONY

1 In the original, this name was written as "Samuelson." According to Jessie Hickling, this is Bill Johnson.

2 Mr. Remington was originally presented as "Lamington." The correct name is Mr. Remington, according to Jessie Hickling.

3 Mr. and Mrs. Cudmore originally appeared as "Hadmore." The correct name is Mr. And Mrs. Cudmore, according to Jessie Hickling.

4 Mrs. O'Halleran was originally shown as "Mrs. Flanagan." The correct name is O' Halleran, according to Jessie Hickling.

XVI WILD LIFE IN THE WOODS

1 De la Fosse is likely referring to the passenger pigeon. According to Edwin C. Guillet, *The Pioneer Farmer and Backwoodsman* (Toronto: T.H. Best, 1963) 70–71, "Wild pigeons disappeared about the same time [reference is to wild turkeys becoming extinct in the 1890s] and none of the species are [sic] are known to exist anywhere, but stuffed specimens may be seen in the Royal Ontario Museum." For a full description and history, see Margaret Mitchell, *The Passenger Pigeon in Ontario*. Toronto: University of Toronto Press, 1935.

2 Today, these birds are extinct.

XVII A PERMANENT SETTLEMENT

1 Wallace Hopcraft is correct, according to Jessie Hickling. This name in the original text was written as "Whitstead." According to Fred Hopcraft, Wallace Hopcraft was his great uncle.

2 A Christadelphian is a member of religious belief that rejects the doctrine of the

Trinity and expects a second coming of Christ. The religion was founded in the United States by Dr. Thomas in 1833. Members were also called Thomasites. Taken from *The Compact Edition of the Oxford English Dictionary*, Volume 1 A-O, 388, and from *The Canadian Oxford Dictionary*, 1998, 264.

3 Goitre is a condition in which the thyroid gland becomes enlarged, generally believed related to a lack of iodine in diet in early days. Today, the use of iodized salt has largely eliminated this condition. Possibly at the time, the ingestion of "snow-water" was believed to be the cause.

4 It was not possible to determine any information about the name Catesby. Since *The Great Gatsby* by F. Scott Fitzgerald was published in 1925 and, as de la Fosse was a literary man, he may have taken some literary licence, modelling Catesby after the mannerisms of Gatsby.

XIX TRIALS AND TRIBULATIONS

1 Jessie Hickling identified the surname Bedworth as the "name of a settler." This name has not been changed.

2 The name Tyrall could not be identified. Possibly this is another student who came to Captain Harston's Agricultural School, and who was named Mr. Lyall. An article in *The Muskoka Sun*, September 8, 1988, reads: "Granddaughter tells of Frederick de la Fosse. He was joined over the three years by two other young Englishmen, who had also read the ad in the English paper. One was a Mr. Lyle and the other was Philip Graham Bell, whom I grew up with in Muskoka knowing him as Uncle Phil. His sister came from Scotland to visit Philip Graham Bell at one time, or soon after he had done his three-year stint with the 'Farmer,' and she married my grandfather." The granddaughter referred to here is Mrs. C. P. Keeley.

XX OUR THIRD YEAR

1 This refers to the tool and style of cutting grain manually prior to the invention of a reaper. Cradling involved using a scythe-like knife with a cradle-like framework attached to the long handle. Cryus Hall McCormick (1809–1884) was an American inventor (of Irish descent) who developed a mechanical reaper. His new machine combined with many of the steps involved in harvesting crops, greatly increased crop yields, decreased the number of field hands for the harvest, lowered costs, and revolutionized farming. It has been said that it was his father's genius as a simple inventor that may have been the true source of the reaper. In 1831, his father, Robert H. McCormick, produced what became known as the reaper. It is said that Robert gave the invention to his son, Cyrus, as a gift, which Cyrus patented in 1834. It wasn't until his father's death, July 4, 1846, that Cyrus began to advertise himself as the inventor of the mechanical reaper. Reverend Patrick Bell, born the son of a farmer in Forfarshire, Scotland in 1801, is recognized as having invented a horse-pushed reaper in 1827–28. He spent four years in the Fergus, Ontario, area, acting as the tutor to the family of the Honourable

Adam Fergusson, and is known to have brought a scale model of his invention to Canada with him in 1822. "As Bell did not patent his invention, it was copied by various people in Britain and in the United States"; from E. Guillet, "The Evolution of Farm Machinery" in *The Pioneer Farmer and Backwoodsman*.

Having adopted the concept of mechanical scissors as the basis for shaping a cutting blade, rather than using the principle of rotating sickles, he, by 1828, had manufactured a full-sized machine. By 1832, a dozen of his reapers were in operation in Scotland, and examples had been sent to Poland, America and Australia. From "Patrick Bell," unpublished manuscript by Pat Mestern of Fergus, Ontario.

2 In Roman mythology, Ceres is the goddess of agriculture.

3 The term "snath" refers to the wooden shaft or handle of a scythe.

XXI MOVING ON TO OUR LOTS

1 This chapter was taken from a second transcript titled "Western Reminiscences" an unpublished manuscript written by Frederick M. de la Fosse, which was turned over to the DelaFosse Branch of the Public Library in Peterborough, Trent University Archives Ref. 92-1007. This manuscript, which is noted in "A Literary Discovery" by Fern A. Rahmel, 1994, unveils an autobiographical account of Frederick M. de la Fosse when he left the Muskoka region to see the country and seek employment with a survey crew that travelled across Western Canada. In this new chapter (shown here as XXI), de la Fosse describes his life "after his three years tutelage under the supervision of Captain Harston." It is to be noted that this XXI and the two chapters that follow, are included as new materials, an extension to the original text. Although this new work was written several years after the release of *English Bloods*, these three chapters complement the conclusion of the original story. They shed light on the lives of de la Fosse and the other students as they acquired land and built their homes. As stated earlier, de la Fosse left the Muskoka District about 1883 and returned sometime in 1884. When he departed the area, he entrusted his home and land to a family by the name of Price. Shortly after returning to the Muskoka area, Frederick's house burnt to the ground. De la Fosse had also planned to marry Mary Jane Graham Bell who had moved from Scotland to live with her brother, Philip Bell. However, this setback meant that their marriage had to be postponed. OA microfilm MS 932 (1869–1920).

2 In the original text, the name was written as Handy. Mr. Handey is documented as being the Crown Land Agent in the 1881 Census of Perry/Proudfoot Townships. AO, C-13243, 20.

3 Emsdale is a small community in Almaguin, about nine kilometres (14 miles) north of Huntsville.

4 Parry Sound District is in the geographical district of Northern Ontario, northwest of Muskoka District. Georgian Bay borders the Parry Sound district to the west, Sudbury and Nipissing District on the north and Muskoka to the south and east. Originally this territory was occupied by First Nations people. Once the Europeans made their way into the area, it became known for the tall white pines that covered the land and ultimately attracted many lumber companies. The district was opened

for settlement under "The Free Grants and Homestead Act of 1868," by the Department of Crown Lands, Toronto, April 18, 1868. The Town of Parry Sound was incorporated in April 1887.

5 The reference here is to Charles Dickens' *Pickwick Papers*. The book was originally serialized under the title *The Posthumous Papers of the Pickwick Club*.

6 Myrmidon is a noun defined as "an unquestioning follower," the example given being the warlike Thessalian who went with Achilles to Troy. From *The Canadian Oxford Dictionary*, 1998, 960.

XXII SEEKING EMPLOYMENT IN WESTERN CANADA

1 As discussed in the first note in the preceding section, this chapter is original material from de la Fosse's unpublished manuscript, "Western Reminiscences."

2 Thomas' English Chop House was located at 30 King Street West. The proprietor was M.A. Thomas. Toronto Reference Library, Digital Collection, Toronto City Directories, Call No. 910.7135 T59, *Toronto Directory for 1878*, 131.

3 A couple by the name of Peter and Mary Price who had a child in 1888, lived in the Ilfracombe area. This may have been the Price that Frederick de la Fosse had looking after his property while he went out west.

XXIII RETURNING TO THE BUSH

1 As with Chapters 21 and 22, this chapter is from an original unpublished manuscript.

2 At the conclusion of Chapter 22, Frederick de la Fosse leaves his Muskoka home in the care of a man named Price and strikes out to seek employment in the Canadian West. In the "Papers of 1926–27 and of 1927–28," *The Thunder Bay Historical Society, Eighteenth and Nineteenth Annual Reports*, 62, a story appears entitled "Reminiscences of a Vagabond" by Frederick Dela Fosse, written during 1883–84. Frederick writes: "I am not a vagabond, although for a space of a year and a half I deliberately cut loose from the hum-drum existence of a life in the woods in order to see something of the world outside…I determined to hire out with a surveying party to survey townships in the Province of Alberta."

After a summer's work he found himself back in Winnipeg as his employer had departed without paying him for his work. The Canadian West was full of young remittance men such as himself and he outlined the harshness of his existence. His later travels took him to Fort William (now part of Thunder Bay, Ontario), where he spent much of his time cutting wood for various people and camps. His paper is a collection of detailed experiences, humourous and otherwise. De la Fosse concludes his story with:

"The day came when I found I had my fill of adventure and hardship. It had proved a very useful experience. I had gone out to see the world in the rough and found it rougher even than I had expected, but it cured me of the accursed vice of the Englishman. I had started in with an overweening pride of my nationality and in the belief that an Englishman was the superior of any other creature on earth. I had discovered that within decent bounds such a pride was right and fitting but that it didn't make the Englishman, per se, any better than anyone else and that even in the outer ranges of civilization, there was being reared a race of men who could hold their own in the company of Englishmen or anyone else. I returned home a chastened individual."

3 Ilfracombe is a hamlet on the northerly most edge of Stisted Township, on the southern shore of Buck Lake. Wallace Hopcraft was the first postmaster when the post office was established on January 1, 1878. The post office name was changed to Charlinch on May 5, 1883, but renamed Ilfracombe on June 1, 1883. It closed on June 10, 1907 and reopened July 1, 1911, and remained in operation until October 4, 1950. See also Florence Ellen Carter, *Place Names of Ontario* (London: ON, Phelps Publishing Company, 1984) 561–62: "Ilfracombe, dispersed rural community, Stisted Township, Muskoka District. Located about 13 kilometres (8 miles) west of Novar station on Grand Trunk Railway and about 50 kilometres (34 miles) north of Bracebridge. Population 130 in 1892 and 26 in 1972."

4 Buck River flows out of Buck Lake into Fox Lake in Stisted Township of Muskoka, Ontario.

5 Haldane Hill was in the Township of McMurrich in the Parry Sound District, Ontario. This post office was established on September 1, 1878. the first postmaster was John McIntyre Murray, LAC.

6 The map of McMurrich Township shows the property of Charles Smith, immediately south of de la Fosse's land.

7 Coign of vantage is defined as a favourable position for observation or action.

8 This famous line, "far from the madding crowd's ignoble strife" was taken from the poem "Elegy Written in a Country Churchyard." The poem was written by the famous British poet Thomas Gray (1716–71).

9 This may have been John Cooper of Lots 23–24, Concession 1. However another Cooper, who died in 1900, lived in the Ilfracombe area and was buried in the local cemetery.

10 On March 25, 1886, Frederick M. de la Fosse married Mary Jane Graham Bell, sister of Philip F.G. Bell.

EDITOR'S EPILOGUE

1 James Crabtree, "Emigration To Canada" in *The Times* of England, August 13, 1875, 4.

2 From the Library and Archives Canada: "Headquarters, Ottawa, 10 April 1885. General orders. Active militia No.4 Tenth Battalion, Royal Grenadiers. To be Captain, from 27th February 1885: Lieutenant Charles Greville Harston, formerly Lieutenant in the Royal Marine Light Infantry," 199.

3 Captain C.G. Harston is mentioned in Major Charles A. Boulton, (Heather Robertson ed.) *I Fought Riel, A Military Memoir* (Toronto: Lorimer, 1985) 152.

4 Information regarding these two patents is from The Patent Office, Concept House, Cardiff Road, Newport, S. Wales, England.

5 Information on "Harston's quick-load magazine" is from the Royal Armouries, Armouries Drive, Leeds, Yorkshire, England.

6 The patent history of Harston's "Magazine Gun" is as follows: Patented in England, Oct. 27, 1887, No. 14, 650; in Belgium, Feb. 24, 1888, No. 80, 759; in Victoria [Australia], March 26, 1888, No. 5, 725; in New South Wales, March 28, 1888, No. 578; in Queensland, April 3 and Nov. 2, 1888, No. 503; and in India, April 30 and May 17, 1888, No. 64/595. Information from the Patent and Trademark Office, Washington, D.C.

7 Library and Archives Canada, Headquarters, Ottawa, 18th April, 1890, 224.

8 "The Militia List of the Archives of Canada," 1885, 1886, 1887, 1897," RG 150, accession 92–93/166, box 3820, and extracts from the *Canada Gazette*, 1918, 2.

9 William Warren Baldwin (1775–1844), Canadian politician and lawyer, was the first to propose the principles of responsible government. His son Robert's development of the idea influenced Lord Durham's report of 1839.

10 Family history anecdotes, handwritten by Helen Maud Sands Tothill, not dated. A copy of this letter was sent to the editor (Nov. 18, 2002) by Martha Preston (Tothill) Woody, great-granddaughter of R.H. Tothill. Her branch of the Tothill family live in Texas, USA.

11 Obituary of Ellen Garrett in *The Times* (England).

12 Information on William Albin Vernon Garrett from Vernon Green of Bournemouth, England.

13 From an unpublished family history, "Biography of Philip Bell," written by Gregory Graham Bell, grandson of Philip Graham Bell.

14 In conclusion, I can only note that I have tried to be faithful to Frederick de la Fosse's story, while filling in the many gaps in information. Regrettably, despite contact with multiple sources, I do not believe that I was able to acquire all of the facts. To those readers of the book who have an interest and possibly a connection to early pioneer history in Muskoka, I issue this invitation; Should you have information to share, please do contact me through my publisher.

APPENDIX A

1 Information on the value of the books from the Supreme Court of Canada, Bankruptcy Court, File Number 320-32. See also Edward Stuart St. John, MA thesis, *The Graphic Publishers Limited 1925–32*, Carleton University, Ottawa. Appendix D (p. 118) of the thesis contains information acquired from the files of the Canadian Authors Association, Volume One, held at that time in the Public Archives of Canada, now the Library and Archives Canada.

2 E.S. St. John, 1974.

3 Frederich Philip Grove (1879–1948) was born in Germany and emigrated to Canada in 1909. Author, teacher and translator, his works largely achieved more fame after his death. His fictionalized biography, *In Search of Myself* (1946), was written well after his experience with Graphic Publishers. The book won a Governor General's Award.

4 Ibid.

5 Ibid.

6 Letter to Mr. J. Wilson is part of the private collection of Allan Trussler.

SELECTED BIBLIOGRAPHY

BOOKS

Barlow, Shirley *et al.*, *Gravenhurst: An Album of Memories and Mysteries*. Gravenhurst, Ontario: Gravenhurst Book Committee, 1993.

Belton, John, A., *Canadian Gunsmiths From 1608: A Checklist of Tradesmen*, with an Introduction by S. James Gooding. Historical Arms Series No. 29. Alexandria Bay, NY & Bloomfield, Ontario: Museum Restoration Service, 1992.

Boulton, Major Charles A., *I Fought Riel: A Military Memoir*. Edited by Heather Robertson. Toronto: Lorimer, 1985.

Boyer, George W., *Early Days in Muskoka: A Story About the Settlement of Communities in the Free Grant Lands and of Pioneer Life in Muskoka*. Bracebridge, Ontario: Herald-Gazette Press, 1970.

Boyer, Robert J., *A Good Town Grew Here: The Story of Bracebridge, Ontario, From 1860 to Municipal Incorporation, 1875, and from 1875 to 1914*. Bracebridge, Ontario: Herald-Gazette Press, 1975.

_____, *Bracebridge Around 1930: Youthful Memories of Muskoka's District Town*. Bracebridge, Ontario: Oxbow Press, 2001.

Carter, Floreen Ellen, *Place Names of Ontario*. London, Ontario: Phelps Publishing Company, 1984.

Chadwick, Edward Marion, *Ontarian Families: Genealogies of United Empire Loyalists and Other Pioneer Families of Upper Canada*. Lambertville, New Jersey: Hunterdon House, 1970.

Champion, Thomas Edward, *History of the 10th Royals and of the Royal Grenadiers From the Formation of the Regiment Until 1896*. Toronto: Hunter, Rose Co., 1896.

Cookson, Joe, *Tattle Tales of Muskoka*. Bracebridge, Ontario: Herald-Gazette Press, 1976.

Demaine, Marjorie, *Chronicles of Stisted Township*. Bracebridge, Ontario: Herald-Gazette Press, 1976.

Demaine, W.H., *Stories of Early Muskoka Days: Memoirs of W. H. Demaine*. Edited by Marjorie Demaine. Bracebridge, Ontario: Herald-Gazette Press, 1971.

Denniss, Gary, *A Brief History of the Schools in Muskoka*. Bracebridge, Ontario: Herald-Gazette Press, 1972.

Foster, Steven and James A. Duke, *A Field Guide to Medicinal Plants Eastern and Central North America.* Boston: Houghton Mifflin, 1990.

_____, *A Field Guide to Medicinal Plants and Herbs of Eastern and Central North America.* Second Edition. Boston: Houghton Mifflin, 2000.

Gooding, James, S., "The Gunsmiths of Canada." With "Update '81." Historical Arms Series No. 14. Ottawa: Museum Restoration Service, 1974.

Gravenhurst Historical Committee, *The Light of Other Days.* Cobourg, Ontario: Hayes Printing Co. 1967.

Guillet, Edwin, C., *The Pioneer Farmer and Backwoodsman.* 2 vols. Toronto: Ontario Publishing Co., 1963.

Higginson, T.B., *The Sportsman's Paradise: Historical Notes on the Burks Falls District 1835–1890 and the Village of Burks Falls, 1890–1965.* Burks Falls, Ontario: Old Rectory Press, 1965.

Hutcheson George, F., *Head and Tales: Memoirs of George F. Hutcheson.* Bracebridge, Ontario: Herald-Gazette Press, 1972.

Jones, Robert Leslie, *History of Agriculture in Ontario, 1613–1880.* Toronto: University of Toronto Press, 1946.

Lundell, Liz, *The Estates of Old Toronto.* Erin, Ontario: Boston Mills Press, 1997.

Madill, Janice Roslyn, *A Track Through Time: A History of The Township of McMurrich, Parry Sound District, Ontario: A Celebration of 100 Years Since Incorporation, 1891 to 1991.* Sprucedale, Ontario: Township of McMurrich, 1994.

Mitchell, Margaret H., *The Passenger Pigeon in Ontario.* Toronto: University of Toronto Press, 1935.

Morgan, James Henry, ed., *The Canadian Men and Women of the Time: A Hand-book of Canadian Biography.* Toronto: W. Briggs, 1898.

Murray, Florence, *Muskoka and Haliburton, 1615–1875: A Collection of Documents.* Toronto: Champlain Society for the Government of Ontario, 1963.

Northern Railway Company of Canada, *The Northern Lakes Guide to Lakes Simcoe and Couchiching; the Lakes of Muskoka, and Lake Superior, via The Northern Railway of Canada: giving a description of the lake and river scenery, with the best spots for water-side summer resorts, hotels, camping outfits, fishing and shooting, distances and cost and travel: also a map of the Muskoka district.* Toronto: Hunter, Rose, 1875.

Parker, Evelyn and Isabel Matthews Swainson and Aubrey Tournay, *A History of the Church of the Redeemer, Rosseau, Ontario, 1871–1983,* not dated.

Petry, Bob, *Bracebridge: An Early Settlement in Muskoka.* Toronto: Lynx Images, 1999.

Pryke, Susan, *Huntsville With Spirit and Resolve.* A Project of Heritage Huntsville. Huntsville, Ontario: Fox Meadow Creations, 2000.

Reaman, George Elmore, *A History of Agriculture in Ontario.* Don Mills, Ontario: Saunders of Toronto, 1970.

Roberts, Charles G.D., *The Canadian Guide-book (Part 1: The Tourist's and Sportsman's Guide to Eastern Canada and Newfoundland).* New York: D. Appleton, 1891–92.

Rose, George Maclean, ed. *A Cyclopaedia of Canadian Biography: Being Chiefly Men of the Time: A Collection of Persons Distinguished in Professional and Political Life, Leaders in the Commerce and Industry of Canada, and Successful Pioneers.* 2 vols. Toronto: Rose Publishing Company, 1886–88.

Thompson, Nancy R., ed. *A Good Town Continues: Bracebridge 1915 to 1999*. Bracebridge, Ontario: 125th Anniversary Committee, 1999.

Wilson, Edward F., *Missionary Work Among the Ojebway Indians*. London: Society for Promoting Christian Knowledge; New York: E. & J.B. Young & Co., 1886.

MAPS

Hamilton, William Edwin, *Guide Book and Atlas of Muskoka and Parry Sound Districts*. Maps by Jno Rogers; sketches by S. Penson. Toronto: H.R. Page and Co., 1879.

NEWSPAPERS

Exeter Flying Post, Devon, England
Peterborough Examiner, Peterborough, Ontario
The Huntsville Forester, Huntsville, Ontario
The Gazette, Montreal, Quebec
The Globe, Toronto, Ontario
The Muskoka Sun, Bracebridge, Ontario
The Quebec City Chronicle, Quebec City, Quebec
The Times, London, England
The Toronto Star, Toronto, Ontario

PAPERS, PAMPHLETS AND ARTICLES

A History of Christ Church. Ilfracombe: Muskoka, Ontario. Hunstville. Self published, first written by Allan Trussler. (This history was first written in 1963 by Allan Trussler and then revised for the church's centennial in 1986)

"A History of Ontario's Wildlife Legacy," in *Hunting Heritage, Hunting Future*, 2000.

Algoma Missionary News and Shingwauk Journal

All Saints' Church, Huntsville: our parish history, 1871–1968. Self-published, 1968.

An Account of St. Mary's Church, Aspdin, Muskoka, Ontario, Diocese of Algoma. Bracebridge, Ontario: Society of St. John the Evangelist, copied from The Aspdin Church News, November 1893. Proof Copy: Please notify any errors or omissions to the Rev'd L.E.C. Frith, S.S.J.E., Bracebridge, Ontario, 1936.

Brown, Enid, *Stephenson Township: Its Founders and Early Church Life, 1868–1957*. Utterson, Ontario: Printed by the Woman's Association of Utterson United Church, 1958.

Brown, Wm., Edward Stock and A.H. Dymond, "Ontario Agricultural Commission, Appendix R 2, Evidence Taken In The Electoral District of Muskoka and Parry Sound." Toronto: Printed by C. Blackett Robinson, 1881.

De la Fosse, Frederick, M., "Reminiscences of a Vagabond," The Thunder Bay Historical Society, Eighteenth and Nineteenth Annual Report, Paper of 1926–27 and of 1927–28.

SELECTED BIBLIOGRAPHY

Jocque, Violet, "The Pioneer and Late Comers, Little Lake Joseph, Joseph River and Peninsula 1865–1979," not dated.

Rahmel, Fern, "A Literary Discovery: The 'Western Reminiscences' of F.M. de la Fosse, Peterborough's First Librarian." Occasional Paper 15 published by the Peterborough Historical Society. Peterborough, Ontario: Pronto-Print Inc. 1994.

St. John, Edward Stuart, "The Graphic Publishers Limited 1925–32." A thesis submitted to the Faculty of Graduate Studies in partial fulfilment of the requirements for the degree of Master of Arts in Canadian Studies, Carleton University, Ottawa, Ontario, January 1974. (Published by the Historical Society of Ottawa, 1992.)

Scovell, Beatrice, "The Muskoka Story," not dated.

OTHER SOURCES

Library and Archives Canada
  http://www.collectionscanada.ca
  Post Offices and Postmasters
  Soldiers of the First World War
  Art and Photography, Canadian Illustrated News
Toronto Public Library, Digital Collections
  http://digit.tpl.toronto.on.ca
London, England, *The Times* 1785–1985 Digital Archives
  http://infotrac.galegroup.com/itweb/free4_tda
The Archives of Ontario
  http://www.archives.gov.on.ca
Early Canadiana Online, Canadian Institute for Historical Microreproductions
  http://www.canadiana.org
The Toronto Star, Pages of the Past
  http://thestar.pagesofthepast.ca
Stupka, Gail, ed., *Pioneer Families of Stisted Township*. Self-published, 1986.
Johnstone, Catherine L., *Winter and summer excursions in Canada* [microfilm]. London: Digby, Long, 1894.
Huntsville Public Library, The Muskoka Room, The Local History Files.

INDEX

Algoma Missionary News and Whing-wauk Journals, 162
Allan Steamship Line, 6, 7, 178
All Saints Church (Huntsville), 187
Amiens (France), 9
Anglican(s), Anglican Church, 81, 176
Ashworth (ON), 182
Aspidin (ON), 82, 116, 165, 182, 187
Axe Lake, 187

Bailey, Alexander, 175
Baldwin:
    Aemilius, 34–36, 41, 42, 48, 52, 57, 59,
      60, 81, 89, 94, 97–100, 117, 118, 120,
      133, 134, 142, 151, 152, 158, 159, 161,
      163, 165, 177, 183, 184
    Aemilius Reginald, 158
    Alice, 158
    Eveline Gladys, 158
    Isabella Clarke (Buchanan), 158
    Julia (Pringle) (2nd Mrs. Aemilius), 159
    Muriel, 158
    Robert, 195
    Susan (Cottrell) (1st Mrs. Aemilius),
      158
    William Augustus, 158
    William Warren (Dr.), 158, 184, 195
Barler, ___ (Miss), 163
Barrie (ON), 115, 159
Bath (England), 4, 159, 160, 270, 277
Beddoe, Alan B., 166, 167

Bedworth, ___ (Mr.), 127, 128, 166, 191
Begg, Alexander (Mr.), 95, 189
Begg, Magnus, 189
Beggsborough (now Sprucedale), 95, 189
Bell:
    Annie Sarah Graham, see Annie
      Sarah Garrett
    George Graham, 160
    Gregory Graham, 160, 164, 185, 195
    Katherine Graham, 160
    Laura Tyson (McKinley), 160
    Mackenzie Graham, 160
    Margaret Hodge (MacKenzie), 160
    Mary Janet Graham, see Mary Janet
      de la Fosse
    Philip Frushard Graham, 64, 77–80,
      118, 119, 121, 124, 127, 128, 134, 137,
      147, 148, 159, 160, 164, 176, 183, 185,
      191, 192, 194, 195
    Richard, 160
    Rose (Hedger), 159
    Thomas, 159
    Thomas Jr., 160, 177, 183
Bell, Patrick (Rev.), 191
Bennett, Elsie (Hopcraft), 133, 180
Bennett, Sue, 161
Boulogne (France), 9
Bournemouth (England), 158
Bowser, ___ (Mr.), 125, 166
Bowser, ___ (Mrs.), 103, 166
Boys, John, 189

Bracebridge (ON), xi, 12–14, 16, 24, 68, 75, 95, 105, 156, 161, 175, 181, 194
Bracebridge from the North Falls, 17
Bright, ___ (hotel keeper), 58, 185
British Empire Lite Ins. Co., 156
British Lion Hotel (Bracebridge), 14
Brown, Martha, 162
Brown, William, 161
Buchanan, Isabella Clarke, see Isabella Buchanan
Buchanan, James, 158
Buck Lake, x, xi, 28, 29, 52, 114, 117, 128, 140, 156, 159, 160, 169, 174, 176, 184, 194
Buck Lake Lodge, 171
Buck River, 142, 194
Burden, ___ (Mrs.), 14
Burden, William F., 14, 181

Cambridgeshire (England), 159
Cameron, ___ (Mrs. M.H.W.), 168
Canadian Illustrated News, 6, 35, 41, 49, 66, 69, 99, 31, 139
Canadian Overseas Expeditionary Force, 158
Canadian Pacific Railway, 140, 187
Cann, William, 185
Cann's Hotel (Huntsville), 58, 165, 185
Casement, Hugh, 178
Catesby[?], ___ (Mr.), 118, 119
"Centenary History of St. John's Church," 172
Ceylon (now Sri Lanka), 137
Chatterly, Township of, 176, 185
Chop House (Toronto), 137, 193
Chowne, William (Rev.), 82, 186, 188
Christ Church Deer Park (Toronto), 163
Christ Church (Ilfracombe), 81, 187
Christadelphian, 116, 190
Chronicles of Stisted Township, 176, 181, 182
Church of the Redeemer (Rousseau), 187
Citizens Gas Co. Ltd., 156
Cobourg (ON), 158
Cockle's Antibilious Pills, 6, 178
Cooper, John[?] (Mr.), 144, 145, 194
Coue, ___ (Dr.), 87, 188

Cousins, Mr. & Mrs. Ed., 166
Crabtree, James, 155
Crompton, William (Rev.), 82, 186, 187
Croydon (England), 158
Cudmore, ___ (Mr.), 107, 166, 190
Cudmore, ___ (Mrs.), 107–109, 169, 190

Dana, W.J., 30
Deer Hunting in Muskoka, Last Day of the Season, 66
De la Fosse:
  Amy Vernon (Halliday), 172
  Charles Edward (Capt.), 170, 177, 178
  Francis Charles, 170, 171
  Freda, xii
  Frederick Montague, xii, xiii, 3, 5, 23, 29, 33, 44, 68, 80, 100, 114, 128, 155, 159, 160, 161, 162, 164, 166–174, 176, 177, 179, 180, 182, 183, 185, 190–195
  Grace Louisa, 170, 178
  Isabella Sophia (Ricketts), 170, 176, 177
  Marjorie Columbine, 171
  Mary Janet Graham (Bell), 159, 160, 164, 170, 171, 183, 192, 194
  Mary Isabella, 170, 178
  Phillipa Bagrielle, 171
  Rose Frushard, 170
DelaFosse Branch (Peterborough Public Library), 192
Demaine, Marjory, 176, 181, 182
Dennis, John Stoughton, 175
Diocese of Toronto, 186
Dodge, Bernadine, xii
Dream and an Allegory, A, 172
Dymond, A.H., 161

East India Company, 5, 177, 178
East York (now part of Toronto), 161
Easton, John, 177
Eaton's Department Store, 167
Ellis, Richard Y., 176
Emsdale (ON), 132, 192
England, x, 4–6, 9, 14, 18, 34, 45, 47, 50, 82, 90, 116, 129, 134, 140, 142, 156–159, 162, 164, 168, 170, 195

English, x, 4–6, 9, 14, 18, 34, 45, 47, 50
English Bloods, x–xiii, 114, 160, 164, 167, 168, 170, 173, 174, 176–178, 180, 181, 187, 188, 192
English Channel, 9

Fairy Lake, 175, 182
Fauquier, Frederick Dawson (Bishop of Algoma), 82, 137, 163, 186
Fauquier, F.G., 162
First World War, 158
Forest Clearing, 35
Forest Clearing II, View of the Clearance, 3rd Year, 131
Forest Pathway, A., 30
Fox Lake, 58, 89, 184, 194
Franco-Prussian War, 180
Fraser, A.C. (Mr.), 164, 180
Fraser, Fralick (Mr.), 92
Frewer, John, 174, 177
Furlong, ___ (Mr.), 190

Garrett:
    Annie, Sarah Graham (Bell) (2nd Mrs. William), 159, 160, 183
    Ellen (1st Mrs. William), 159, 195
    William Albin Vernon, 29, 34, 35, 37, 50, 65, 67, 72, 75, 76, 85, 89, 94, 118, 120–122, 134, 137, 138, 159–160, 162, 165, 176, 183
Garrison Club (Quebec City), 8
Geisler, ___ (Mr.), 91
Geisler, ___ (Mrs.), 91, 92, 188
Gibson, David, 182, 187
Gillmore (Gilmour), ___ (Venerble Archdeacon), 82, 186
Government Road, 26, 42, 182
Grantham, Mark, 33, 157
Graphic Publishers Ltd., x, 166–168, 172, 174, 195
Gravenhurst (ON), xi, 10, 13, 14, 17, 41, 104, 174, 175, 187, 188
Green Gables (later Buck Lake Lodge), 171
Green, Vernon, 195

Greville Co. Ltd. Mining Brokers, 156
Grieve, Euphemia Marshal, see Euphemia Mackenzie
Grove, Frederick Philip, 168, 195
Guide Book and Atlas of Muskoka and Parry Sound, The, 28, 29, 185
Guisler, Carol (Miss), 92, 169
Guisler, ___ (Mrs.), 91, 92, 188

H.R. Page (Publishers), 28
Haberer, Eugene, 7, 139
Haldane Hill (ON), 142, 194
Halliday, Amy Vernon, see Amy de la Fosse
Hamilton, Alexander (Mr.), 42, 43
Hamilton, ___ (Mrs.), 43, 165
Handey, ___ (Mrs.), 132, 192
Hanes, James F., 175
Harston, Anna Dew, 33
Harston, Mary Regina (Ellis) (Mrs.), 32, 34, 35, 41, 45, 55, 62, 70, 74–76, 91, 118, 124, 125, 133, 155, 156, 158, 176
Harston, Charles Greville, (Capt.), xi, 14, 31, 33–42, 47–49, 52, 54, 55–57, 60, 62, 68–70, 74, 75, 77, 78, 85–87, 94, 97–102, 113–115, 118, 121, 123, 125–127, 129, 130, 132, 133, 149, 153, 155, 156–164, 170, 174, 176–178, 183, 192, 194, 195
Harston, ___ (Rev. Mr.), 163
Hartson Agricultural School, xiii, 170
Hayes, Maggie, 74
Hayes, Sandy, 73, 74, 165, 186
Hedger family, 160
Henderson, Jock, 58, 185
High Road to Gravenhurst, Township of Morrison, 12
Hickling, Alexander Sr., 180
Hickling, Andrew (Mr.), 164, 180
Hickling, Jessie (Howell) (Mrs. Andrew), 164, 169, 180, 182–186, 188–190
Hilditch, ___ (postmaster), 58, 185
Hogan, J., 13, 88
Holt, ___ (Mr.), 47, 50, 184
Hood, Charles (Capt.), 58, 176, 184, 188

Hoodstown (Port Vernon), 58, 89, 175, 176, 187, 188
Hopcraft:
    Fred, 40, 52, 96, 114, 128, 180, 190
    John Sr., 180
    Lorne, 180
    Muriel (Whiteley) (Mrs.), 180, 183, 192, 194, 195
    Wallace, 116, 120, 166, 190, 194
    Walter, 50, 165, 184
Howell, Lorenzo, 113, 165, 166
Hughes, Sam (Gen.), 164
Hunt, George (Capt.), 176
Huntsville (ON), xi, 12, 57, 58, 62, 72, 77, 82, 94, 95, 98, 115, 118, 142, 145, 176, 181, 182, 185, 187, 188
Huntsville Cricketers, 56
Huntsville Forester, The, 169
Huntsville, Muskoka, 59
Huntsville Public Library, xi

India, 4, 9, 141, 170, 177
Interior of a Settler's Shanty, 47
Ilfracombe (ON), 28, 81, 117, 142, 159, 161, 163, 166, 176, 177, 187, 194
Issachar, ____, 77

Johnson, Bill (Mr.), 104–106, 166, 190
Johnson, John, 166
Johnson, ____ (Mrs.), 105, 166

Keeley, Mrs,. C.P., 174, 191

Lake Joseph, 160
Lake Muskoka, 175
Lake Ontario, 176
Lake Rousseau, 160
Lake Vernon, 57, 58, 89, 175, 182, 184
Lakefield (ON), 171
Lancelot (ON), 182
LaSueur, William Dawson (Dr.), 175
Laurentian, University, 162
Levinsky, ____ (Mr.), 7, 179
Library and Archives Canada, 157
Lincoln, Abraham, 39

Liverpool (England), 6, 9, 178
Llwyd, Thomas (Mr.) (Rev.) (Canon), 82, 107, 186, 187
Log House near Huntsville, 63
Log Shanty near Gravenhust, 20
Log Shanty near Huntsville, 105
Logging, 39, 41
Logging bee, 40, 42, 46, 47, 135, 138, 147
Logging Bee in Muskoka, 49
Logging Bee in Muskoka, 49
Lumbering in the Backwoods, 41
Lumbermen's Camp, 88
Lyall, ____ (Mr.), 160

Mackenzie, Euphemia Marshal (Grieve), 185
Mackenzie, Margaret Hodge, see Margaret Bell
Mackenzie, William Innes, 185
Madill, Janice R., 177, 185, 189
"Magazine Gun," 156
Making Maple Sugar in Canada, 139
Malkin, Mr. & Mrs., 89, 188
Manitoba, 6, 8, 140
Mann, ____, 89, 188
Manning Arcade (Toronto), 137
Martin, Capt., see Captain Greville Harston
McAskill, Mary (Mrs.), 176, 178
McCabe, James, 175
McCabe's Landing (Gravenhurst), 175
McCormickm, Cyrus Hall, 191
Meade, Mr. & Mrs., 58, 185
Medicine Hat (AB), 140
Menomiee Lake, 96, 189
Métis, 156
McMurrich, Township of, x, 29, 133, 159, 166, 174, 177, 180, 183, 189, 194
Michipicoten, 98, 189
Miller, Henry C., 166–168
Montreal (QC), 7, 9, 176
Mormon, 116
Mount Hermon Cemetery, 158
Murray, John McIntyre, 194

Muskoka, District of, x, xi, xiii, 6, 9,
    12–14, 45, 54, 72, 83, 85, 87, 96, 133, 141,
    145, 149, 155, 159–161, 168, 170, 171,
    174–176, 180, 182, 185, 187, 190–194
Muskoka Falls, 16, 175, 181
Muskoka Lake, 13
Muskoka Lake, 13
Muskoka River, 16, 175, 181, 182
Muskoka Colonization Road, see also
    Government Road, x, 175, 182
Muskoka Sun, 174, 191

Nepahwin-Gregory Inn, 160
Newton-White, E., 187
Nipissing (steamship), 11
North Falls (Bracebridge), 175
Northern Advocate, 189
*Northern Railway of Canada: direct route
    to the highlands & lake district*, 22
Northern & Pacific Junction Railway
    (formerly Toronto, Simcoe &
    Muskoka Junction Railway), 175, 176,
    184, 188
Northwest Rebellion (1885), 156
Northwest Rebellion medal, 156
North-West Territories, 140
Notman and Sandham, 41
Novar (ON), 187, 194

O'Halleran, Pat (Mr.), 107, 166
O'Halleran, ___ (Mrs.), 108, 109, 190
Oldfield, ___, 7, 179
Ontario Agricultural Commission, 159, 161
Ottawa (ON), x, 167, 174
Overhand, Dave (Mr.), 89, 166, 188

Parker, Evelyn, 188
Parry Sound, District of, x, 133, 161, 174,
    192
Parry Sound (ON), 133, 169, 193
Patterson, ___ (Rev. Mr.), 163
Peterborough (ON), xiii
Peterborough Examiner, 171
Peterborough Public Library, 164, 171,
    173, 192

Peters, John (Mr.), 78, 79, 165, 186
Peters, ___ (Mrs.), 79, 92, 186
Phillips, Bernard, 61, 185
Picturesque Canada, 30, 175
Piper, Mr. & Mrs., 58, 185
Point Levis (QC), 8, 179
Port Arthur (ON), 98, 190
Port Vernon (ON), xi, 58, 77, 175, 176,
    184, 188
Preston, James Esson, 11
Preparing to Burn Timber, 99
Price, Peter[?] (Mr.), 140–144, 177, 192, 193
Pringle, James (Dr.), 158
Pringle, Julia, see Julia Baldwin

Quebec, City of, 5, 8, 9, 158, 178, 179
Quinn, Hanson, 84, 166, 188

Rahmel, Fern A. (Dr.), xii, 174, 177, 178,
    192
Raising bee, 68, 134, 135, 138
Raising the Shanty, 69
Ravenscliffe (ON), 187
Rhamey, William 62–65
Remington, ___ (Mr.), 106, 107, 166, 190
Richardson, G.R.R. (Dr.), 169
Ricketts, Dave, 178
Ricketts, Montague Poyntz (Col.), xi, 4,
    5, 170, 178
Robey[?], ___, 63, 64
Rogers, John, 28
Roman Catholics, 81
Rosseau (ON), 82, 187, 188
Rossin House (Toronto), 9, 18, 180
Royal George (steamship), 158
Royal Grenadiers of Toronto, 10th Bat-
    talion, 156
Royal Marine Light Infantry, 156, 157, 194
Ryerson, Township of, 155

SPCK (Society for Promoting Christian
    Knowledge), 94, 189
Samuelson, ___, 166
Scandinavian (steamship), 6, 178, 179
Schell, F.B., 13, 88

Schneider, Nicholas, 62, 63, 100, 166, 185
Scotland, 134, 159, 170, 191
See of Algoma (Anglican), 82, 186, 187
Self-Help, 39, 183
Sherbrooke (QC), 7
Sinclair, Lawrence (Rev.), 82, 186, 187
Skeffington (Shiffington), Chichester, 8, 179
Smith, Charles (Mr.), 45, 103, 142, 143, 163, 165, 184, 194
Smith, ___ (Mrs.), 45, 70, 165
Smith, F. Hopkinson, 30
Spicer, Erick J., 168
Sprucedale (ON), 95, 169, 189
Starnes, ___ (Mr.), 8
Stisted Road, 30, 42, 135, 182
Stisted, Township of, x, 28, 159, 171, 174, 176, 180, 182–184, 187, 189, 194
St. John, Edward Stuart, 167, 168, 195
St. Lawrence River, 8, 158
Stock, Edward, 161
Stotsebury, E.N., 162, 177
Stotesbury, H.H., 162, 177
Straits of Belle Isle, 8
Stumping, 146
Smiles, Samuel, 39, 183
Stephenson, Township of, 175
Stupka, Gail, 176
Sullivan, Edward (Bishop), 82, 107, 187
Swanson, Isbel Matthews, 188
Sweet, A.S. (Mr.) (Rev.), 103, 163
Sweet, A.J.O., 162

Talman, ___ (Dr.), 164
Temperance Society, 189
Thomas, M.A. "Gus," 137, 193
Thompson, Nate, 96–98, 166, 189
Thorneloe, George (Archbishop), 82, 187
Times, The (London, England), 155, 171, 194
Tipper, ___, 89
Toronto (ON), 6, 9–11, 14, 28, 56, 60, 64, 76, 92, 104, 105, 113, 118, 137, 145, 156, 158, 162, 169, 170, 171, 175, 176, 180, 186
Toronto Athletics Club, 156

Toronto Daily Star, 137, 167
Toronto, Simcoe and Muskoka Junction Railway, 175
Tothill, Frank, 159
Tothill, Helen Maud (Sands), 146, 159, 195
Tothill, Richard Hugh, 29, 34–37, 42–44, 48, 53, 59, 60, 69, 72, 87, 90, 91, 94, 95, 97, 100, 114, 115, 117, 122, 125, 126, 132, 133, 135, 138, 146, 159, 162, 165, 183
Tournay, Audrey, 188
Track Through Time, A History of the Township of McMurrich, A, 177, 185, 189
Trent University, 178
Trussler, Allan, 195
Tryall[?], ___ (Mr.) [Mr. Lyall?], 128, 191

United States, 113, 137, 191
United States Patent Office, 156
University of Guelph, 161
Unwin, Charlie, 182
Upper Canada, 158, 176, 185, 187
Utterson, Muskoka, 23
Utterson (ON), xi, 23, 175, 182

Vardon, Roger, see Frederick de la Fosse
Vernon Lake, 189
Veron River, Entrance to Fairy Lake, 57
Verses Grave and Gray, 172
View of Quebec, from Levis, 6

Wadsworth, Vernon B., 175
"Western Reminiscences," xii, 172, 177, 192, 193
Weston, James, 49, 66
White, George Harlow, 12, 17, 20, 23, 47, 57, 59, 63, 105
White, Jimmy (Mr.), 45, 103, 163, 165, 166
White, ___ (Mrs.), 103, 184
Wiesbaden (Germany), 140
Wilson, John (Mr.), 169, 195
Wiseman, Humble, 63–65
Woody, Martha Preston (Tothill), 117, 183, 195

Yearley, Thomas Bill, 17, 20, 26, 27, 46, 181
Yearley, Johnny[?], 19, 181
Yearley, George Samuel (Mr.), 11, 13,
    16–19, 24–27, 39, 42, 43, 46, 48, 74, 164,
    180–182

Yearley, Norm, 180, 181
Yearley, ___ (Mrs.), 17–20
Yearley, Rupert Leslie, 180, 181
Yearley (Yearly) (ON), 164, 180, 181
York (later Toronto), 158

ABOUT THE EDITOR

PHOTOGRAPH BY JON SNELSON.

SCOTT D. SHIPMAN WAS BORN IN Weston, Ontario, and discovered his passion for writing as a young boy growing up in Bolton, Ontario. Eventually he moved with his family to Huntsville in the Muskoka District.

Since that day Scott has loved the great serenity of the area. In the early 1980s, Scott married his lifetime companion, Peggy. They have two children, son Collin and daughter Carly.

It was when Scott's father asked him to research historical background on the former Bigwin Inn, the fabled resort in the Lake of Bays area, that Scott stumbled upon *English Bloods*. His passion for writing combined with his keenness to know more about early Muskoka pioneers combined to produce this new edition.